To
Grandpa Atterbury
1868

Jacob Knapp

AUTOBIOGRAPHY

OF

ELDER JACOB KNAPP.

WITH AN INTRODUCTORY ESSAY

By R. JEFFERY.

New York:
SHELDON AND COMPANY.
BOSTON: GOULD AND LINCOLN.
1868.

Stereotyped at the Boston Stereotype Foundry,
No. 19 Spring Lane.

PREFACE.

After Elder Jacob Knapp had concluded to go to California, and spend the winter in holding protracted meetings in that distant State, he engaged me to revise and prepare his manuscripts for publication. In the mean time he was called away from home, and I have been unable to consult him, even by letter. This fact has enhanced the delicacy and responsibility of my undertaking. It was not intended that I should prepare an original work, but simply edit the papers which the Elder might place in my hands.

I have, therefore, aimed to restrict myself to this service. I have not sought to express my views, to use my illustrations, to present my style, but his. Knowing that his long-continued and widely-extended ministry had given him an established reputation for originality in thought and expression, I have endeavored to allow him to state his own views in his own way. Especially have I refrained from making serious modifications of his sermons, because in them the reader will look for illustrations of those characteristics of power which, under God, have made his pulpit efforts so effectual in attracting and fixing the attention of the throngs that have waited on his ministry.

It is possible that in the mention of dates, and the spelling of proper names, the work will contain some mistakes, as in these particulars I have followed the manuscripts before me, except in those cases where my own knowledge of the references has enabled me to act independently. For the statements of occurrences and the views of doctrine I do not hold myself responsible.

I regret that the limited time allotted me has not permitted me to execute my task more satisfactorily; but I bring my labors to a close with the conviction that the services of Elder Knapp deserve an elaborate presentation, and with the prayer that the perusal of this book may make him a blessing to those who have never seen his face or heard his voice.

R. JEFFERY.

CHICAGO, ILLINOIS, *December*, 1867.

INTRODUCTORY ESSAY.

ELDER KNAPP AND HIS MINISTRY.

Evangelism, in the strict sense of the word, means the preaching of the gospel to the destitute — in regions where its ordinary ministrations are not enjoyed.

But, in modern times, the term has acquired a modified application. It is now generally used to designate those efforts in connection with, or in excess of, the ordinary services, by which a church puts forth extraordinary exertions for the salvation of men, in its own immediate vicinity. These extraordinary services consist, for the most part, of continuous exercises of preaching and prayer for several successive weeks, during which time the members of the church are urged to unusual exertions, in order to awaken the interest of the unconverted around them to the concerns of their everlasting well-being; while the public ministrations are intended to bring men, by every consideration and motive which the gospel can present, to an immediate surrender of their hearts to the authority of Christ as Lawgiver and Savior.

Experience has enabled the people of God to correct many abuses which the excitement incident to such continuous appeals to their religious sensibility might naturally produce; but the practicability and desirableness of such an order of appointments is no longer an experiment. Its consistency with the established doctrines of grace is no longer a problem. Events have proven that God has wonderfully honored this instrumentality; and now the system of "*protracted meetings*" is a recognized agency in the kingdom of God.

Prior to the institution of this peculiar system of measures, there had prevailed throughout the Southern States the custom of holding "*meetings of days*." These, however, consisted, more especially, of a convocation of the brethren from a distance of several miles, for the purpose of enjoying a season of spiritual refreshing in connection with a series of doctrinal, denominational, and emotional sermons. They were not primarily intended as a means of religious awakening among the impenitent.

Forty years ago the institution of protracted meetings was comparatively unknown. It took its rise amid the suspicions and denunciations of men who conscientiously believed the innovation to be a presumptuous inconsistency with the divinely appointed methods of promoting the spread of the gospel. The tendency of such measures was deplored as disastrous to the true interests of the churches, and the grounds on which they were advocated were repudiated as positively antagonistic to the standards of doctrinal orthodoxy. Many of our fathers passed away sighing out their lamentations over the departing glories of Israel.

The opposition which was then manifested to protracted meetings, was not based on those excesses in the methods of conducting them which experience could correct, nor on usages the propriety of which time would determine, but on the high ground of the utter inconsistency of special human exertions for the conversion of men with the sovereignty of God in the purposes of redemption. Regeneration being a divine work, it was concluded that the conjunction of human agency in promoting it was a needless and arrogant presumption. The salvation of each sinner being an act of electing grace, therefore it could not be affected by human efforts. The gathering in of God's elect being according to his purpose and will, it was thought that his purpose and will would be accomplished independently of means and measures. God was able to achieve his own intentions without our agency; he knew who would be saved, and who would not be saved, and how to secure the salvation of those who were ordained unto eternal life; and in his own time he would bring his purposes to pass. The strength of God's people was to "lie still" in regard to all questions concerning the dissemination of the knowledge of Christ; and the chief concern of each disciple was, by processes of introspection, metaphysical analyses, and spiritual experiences, to settle, if possible, the great question of his own ordination unto salvation.

Such was the system of theology — itself a perversion and abuse of the doctrines of grace — which prevailed throughout the Baptist denomination half a century ago. As a matter of course, it wrought out its logical results in producing a state of conscientious apathy concerning the spiritual condition of the great mass of mankind. No wonder that there were no Sunday schools in connection with churches, the theology of whose members forbade them to pray even for the conversion of their own children; and who studiously avoided giving any suggestions or instructions to them, lest the workings of the Spirit should be interfered with and grieved, and thereby the sovereign and elective purpose of God should be defeated! No wonder that missionary enterprises in behalf of the heathen world were disapproved of, by Christians whose theological views taught them the needlessness of using any means for the conversion of their nearest neighbors! No wonder that institutions for the training of young men for the ministry were scouted at as "minister-making machines," by a people who deemed it a chief evidence of a man's call to preach, if he could step from the workshop or the plough into the pulpit, and descant for an hour on some religious topic, especially a doctrine of grace, without previous discipline or special preparation! No wonder that measures looking to a successive and persistent pressure of the claims of salvation on the attention of men were repudiated, as an outrage on the order of the gospel, by men who denied the right of a minister to call on sinners to repent! In that day it was more than a minister's position in a church was worth, to presume on a course of urgency in behalf of the salvation of the unconverted; and even they, whose zeal for souls could not be restrained by their Procrustean theories, ventured to reach the doctrine of "works" by the slow and guarded approaches of qualifying explanations and repeated asseverations of their soundness on the cardinal doctrines of grace. And finding at length that the strongholds of their cherished dogmas were being assailed, their advocates found themselves unconsciously roused to a state of activity, in their zeal to denounce those who would not let them be "at ease in Zion."

But while, as might be supposed, these doctrinal perversions of great truths bore their legitimate fruits, in repressing the ardor of Christian sympathy and effort, in inducing an indifference to the spread of the gospel and the salvation of men, and in drying up all the springs of benevolent action, yet there were some who proclaimed their inconsistency by violating the logic of their creeds, and who braved the suspicions and denunciations of their brethren by their earnest and laborious endeavors for the conversion of the impenitent. Holcombe, in Philadelphia, amid a storm of abuse which scrupled at no outrage, persisted in preaching a free salvation, and in urging men to repent. Benedict, in the city of New York, ceased not for many years to warn sinners day and night with tears; but he was called to encounter the silent reprobation or the open protest of brethren who prided themselves on their soundness in the faith.

When, however, in the lapse of years, it became a demonstrated fact that sinners could be "soundly" converted, as the result of special efforts; when the churches which were composed of these "man-made converts" became numerous and influential, while the churches which maintained their opposition to new measures began to die out; when from the ranks of those converted in protracted meetings there went forth a new order of ministers in full sympathy with such instrumentalities, — it was easy to predict that the stone which the builders rejected would soon become the head of the corner; that the very measures which at first were repudiated as God-dishonoring presumptions, would come to be recognized as an important and almost indispensable agency in promoting the glory of God.

Instances are now rare in the Baptist denomination, in this country, of a church specially committed against seasons of protracted effort. On the contrary, they have come to be regarded as among the established means of grace; and in numerous instances the conducting of them is considered among the regular services of the pastor, and his own acceptability, in great measure, is determined by his success in carrying them on. The great proportion of our present membership has been brought into the church in connection with some form of protracted effort; and despite the many instances of falling away, it may be confidently asserted, that the proportion of apostates is not greater than formerly; while nearly all those who are prominent and reliable, on whom the responsibilities of church affairs now devolve, were converted in connection with these special instrumentalities.

Nor is this all. The marked difference which distinguishes the type of modern piety from that of a former generation, may be confidently ascribed to the influence of this system of measures. Formerly, the proofs of piety were drawn from subjective experiences; now the value of these experiences is very greatly determined by the fruits which they objectively produce. It is now not so much a question, What does a man feel for Christ? as, What does he do for him? It is now more thoroughly understood that the love of Christ in the heart will constrain the life, not merely to acts of sobriety, temperance, and godliness, but to a self-sacrificing zeal in good works. Men are now generally converted in the atmosphere of prayers, anxieties, and labors in their behalf; and thus their first impressions of consecration to Christ are associated with the idea of active and self-sacrificing endeavors for the salvation of their fellows. They know that they owe their own conversion to the blessing of God on the efforts of others for them; and they very naturally conclude, either that their hopes are vain, or that similar exertions for others may result in bringing them to the enjoyment of the same glorious hopes. So that this has come to be an age of Christian activities.

The several agencies for the dissemination of the gospel, which are at present sustained by Baptists in this country, have only quite recently begun to enter upon an era in their development which indicates their permanent hold on the convictions of the churches, and which gives an assured earnest of the mighty influences they are destined to exert. Heretofore they have been compelled to fight their way into a positive existence, against the hinderances of false views of the laws of the kingdom of Christ, inveterate prejudices, and the absence of well-conceived and fairly-tried methods of organization. But these obstacles are now removed. The churches give a ready response to the various appeals that are made upon their sympathies, efforts, and contributions. The great necessity is no longer to convince Christians of the consistency of human efforts with divine purposes, but to carry them forward to that measure of endeavor which is demanded by the logic of their present convictions of the relation that God has established between his purpose and our use of means for their accomplishment.

We do not say that this marvellous change in the spirit of our denomination is due solely to the influence of protracted meetings, because it is well known that missionary endeavors, Sunday school instruction, and ministerial education found their advocates long before the era of "special efforts." Many of the earliest and most distinguished friends of these institutions did not look with favor on protracted meetings. But it is also true that these several movements of Christian benevolence were stoutly resisted as unwarrantable innovations on the methods of grace; and until the time when the system of protracted meetings came to be fairly recognized, they were able to maintain only a feeble existence, and found but little favor with the people among whom they were introduced. But in proportion as the churches came to recognize the desirableness of protracted meetings, and to be composed of persons converted in such meetings, the opposition to such institutions began to disappear, and their friends and supporters began to increase; so that now facts may be adduced in sufficient numbers to justify the assertion, that the warmest supporters of missions, of Sunday schools, of institutions for the education of young men for the ministry, are men who have been led to appreciate the importance of protracted meetings, who cordially coöperate in carrying them on, and who, in many instances, were themselves brought to Christ through their influence. And it is a matter of common observation, that never is it so easy to induce a church to make large contributions for a benevolent object, never so easy to pay off a debt, to improve a Sunday school, to contribute to missions, to furnish support for indigent students, to endow colleges, or to do any other work of active and sacrificing service for the cause of Christ, as when it is in the full tide of a religious revival; and none are so willing to respond to these appeals as those who are most deeply interested in the progress of such a special work of grace.

Now, among the agents whom God has employed for the bringing about of this marked and blessed change in the spirit of our churches, *Jacob Knapp* occupies a place of indisputable prominence.

It is too soon to write a just estimate of the value of his services among the churches. He is still living; his work is not yet done; the estimate of his contemporaries is necessarily affected by their familiarity with the details of his history; and he has not altogether outlived the prejudices which the assaults of a former generation of enemies created against him. The time will come, however, when these things will be forgotten, or be mentioned as matters of curious comment. Posterity will speak of Elder Knapp as the pioneer and champion of modern evangelism. At the present day few know of the reproaches that were heaped on the heads of Wesley, of Whitefield, of Howard, or of Payson; but all men recognize them as leaders in the Zion of our God, whose services and names will be held in everlasting remembrance.

There are several facts in the history of Elder Knapp which conspire to give him a place of enduring reputation in relation to the system of modern evangelism, especially among Baptists. He was perhaps the first man, at least in the Northern States, who devoted himself exclusively to the work of conducting protracted meetings. He ventured on the providence of God in making the experiment at a time when the results were problematical. He continued in his course despite the accumulations of every form of persecution. His labors were crowned with wonderful success in the conversion of thousands to Christ. He has outlived many other evangelists who began after him, and still continues in the work, — "his eye undimmed, and his natural force unabated." He is permitted to witness the triumph of the system which he has done so much to inaugurate; to rejoice that even churches which might not wish to secure his individual services, rely, nevertheless, upon his methods for their increase in power and usefulness; and to know that when the memory of his assailants will be forgotten, or remembered chiefly because of their opposition to him, the system with which his name and life are associated will continue to operate as a potent agency in hastening on the latter-day glories of the Lamb. His declining years are cheered by the retrospect of a useful life; and the hardships he has endured, are made to appear as "light afflictions" in view of the anticipated rapture of receiving the plaudit of his Savior, and of recognizing at the judgment-day thousands on thousands of souls, who, redeemed through his instrumentality, will constitute the jewels in the crown of his everlasting rejoicing.

It is quite probable that, in the present day, a man of Elder Knapp's abilities, attainments, and style, starting forth as an evangelist, would not acquire any marked distinction, nor achieve any wonderful success. The characteristics of John the Baptist, and his manner of preaching, were eminently adapted to fit him for his peculiar position as the herald of the coming Messiah; but he might not have been so well suited for a later age in the development of the kingdom of God. Men of different qualifications were needed to meet the exigencies that were presented by the advancing demands of the mission of Christ.

Luther was specially raised up and qualified for the work unto which God had called him in inaugurating the era of the Protestant reformation. Calvin was better adapted to analyze and adjust the grand doctrinal formulas which were to constitute the confession of faith of succeeding generations of the church; while Wesley could do a work which neither Luther nor Calvin could have performed, in awakening Christendom to the necessities of organized forms of spiritual activity.

And, in like manner, the accomplished facts of history show that Providence called Elder Knapp to a peculiar service, and a knowledge of his traits proves his personal adaptation to the mission unto which he was called.

The work to which, about the year 1832, he felt himself constrained to consecrate his life, was one involving peculiar trials. He was about to enter on an experiment. He was about to challenge the conscientious scruples of nearly all the leaders in that portion of the American Zion to which he belonged. He was about to excite the opposition of inveterate prejudices. He was about to cut loose from all stated sources of support, and rely on the voluntary contributions of people who, at the best, were accustomed to do but little for the support of ministers, and whose opposition to his undertaking would prompt them to contribute less to him. He expected to present views of doctrine which he knew many Christians would deem subversive of the gospel of Christ, and which would arouse the intensest hatred of the great mass of the unconverted. And when at length his labors should come into demand, he was destined to undergo exhaustive draughts on his powers of physical and mental endurance.

A man with the prospects of such a life needed to possess, in an eminent degree, the force of strong convictions, an unyielding purpose, patient forbearance, great boldness, clear perceptions, versatile genius, simple tastes, economical habits, imperturbable self-possession, ready wit,* a good knowledge of human nature,

* As an instance of Elder Knapp's quickness in *repartee*, it is related that, while holding a meeting in the Mulberry Street church, in the city

an adaptation to persons of different tastes, an iron constitution, a humble spirit, and a firm reliance on the sustaining grace of God.

All these characteristics Elder Knapp has exhibited to a remarkable degree. Perhaps there is no minister of the gospel living who has toiled harder, has been opposed more, has complained less, and has accomplished so much.

True to the spirit of his mission, he has seemed to regard himself the subject of God's special providence. He has endeavored to follow its indications, and has accepted its allotments. His pastorates were with a rural population, and he began his work as an evangelist in a sparsely settled community, and was glad to devote his services to churches which were too poor to sustain a stated pastorate, and withal had very crude notions of the duty of doing much for the support of ministers. Now, the fact that such was the condition of the churches with which Elder Knapp's earliest labors were associated, furnished a favorable opportunity of testing the strength of his own faith in the willingness of God to provide for the support of his family, and to give success to his labors for the salvation of men. Churches that were unable to support pastors were glad to avail themselves of his temporary aid, even though they might doubt the advisability of his method. Churches that had pastors were unprepared to appreciate the importance of his labors, and the pastors themselves were either opposed to his mission, or unwilling to encounter the opposition which a proposition to invite his aid would provoke.

But soon it became a matter of observation, that the churches which had secured the services of Elder Knapp were beginning to enjoy a degree of prosperity which suggested the desirableness of invoking his labors with churches which had hitherto stood aloof from him. At length the ministry of Elder Knapp became the theme of general comment. Despite the early

of New York, a young man rose in the presence of a vast congregation, and requested prayers for the *devil.* Elder Knapp quietly remarked, "Brethren, this young man has asked you to pray for his father."

prejudices that prevailed against this order of measures, despite the criticisms which his plain and somewhat eccentric style awakened, it became evident that God was with him, and through him was doing wonders. His services ere long came into general demand, and churches distinguished for their wealth, influence, and refinement, called him to labor among them. In these new and more trying positions the ministry of Elder Knapp was attended with still greater success than elsewhere or before. During the few weeks of his presence in any of the principal cities of the Union, the community was convulsed. Crowds on crowds thronged to hear this plain, outspoken man of God; churches were roused to new and unthought-of measures of action; and thousands of impenitent men and women, from all classes of society, were converted to God.

About the years 1841 and '42 his ministry appears to have culminated. God permitted a cloud to come over him; but while this trying dispensation of Providence seemed to divert the consideration of the churches from the workman, it did not impede the progress of the work. Protracted meetings, as a system of measures, had acquired a permanent place in the agencies to be henceforth employed by the people of God.

Nor was Elder Knapp himself to be set aside. But in other regions he was destined to continue his labors. During the last twenty years he has devoted the greater part of his time among the feeble churches of the growing West, many of which he has lived to see assume positions of great promise for the spread of the gospel in this wonderful portion of our vast republic.

Another element in the ministry of Elder Knapp — and one, too, which qualified him to be a leader of the people during the last forty years — was his earnest sympathy with the spirit of philanthropy. It is impossible to say what would have been the measure of his influence, if he had stood aloof from all the enterprises of modern reform, or lent to them his opposition; but, as a matter of fact, he has stood in the front rank of every movement which contemplated the elevation of humanity, and has rejoiced in every undertaking that proposed to give the gospel to the world. Many men in his circumstances would have thought that, in order to success in one peculiar mission, they must keep silence on every other topic which divided the sentiments of community; but he shunned not "to declare the whole counsel of God," and has provoked storms of opposition, which would not have arisen, if he had not lashed the waves of popular passion into fury by his fearless denunciations of all manner of sin, and his earnest advocacy of every measure of right.

He was among the pioneers in the temperance movement. He acted as an officer in several such organizations, demanded of those converted in his meetings abstinence from everything that could intoxicate, and was permitted, in the providence of God, to start that mighty wave of temperance reform known as the Washingtonian movement, which nearly thirty years ago swept through the land.

He was known as an avowed anti-slavery man, at a time when the utterance of such sentiments invoked reproach and persecution, and dared to lift up his voice in behalf of the slave in the very citadel of the slave power, and in a church whose congregations could hear the cries of the victims of the slave mart mingling with their own songs of devotion.

He has always been the consistent friend of missionary enterprises and ministerial education. Many indigent students at Hamilton are indebted to his sympathizing aid for the means of carrying on their studies; and on one single afternoon, during the progress of a meeting in Albany, he raised seven thousand dollars for Madison University.

Though disapproving at one time of some measures adopted by the Board of Foreign Missions, he did not allow his opposition to their policy to weaken the ardor of his devotion to the cause itself; but during the three years in which he was most open in the expression of his disapprobation, he paid to the society out of his scanty income the sum of eight hundred dollars.

Withal he has maintained an inflexible devotion to his conscientious convictions of denominational truth. Being a Baptist from a firm persuasion that the cardinal views held by this people were taught in the Word of God, no amount of persecution could alienate him from coöperation with his brethren in the faith, and no measure of inducements could allure him to cast his lot with the people of another name. At one time a lady of great wealth, in Syracuse, connected with the Episcopal church, offered to provide for the support of his family during his lifetime, in order that he might the more fully devote himself to his calling; but considerations of delicacy, and a desire to remain entirely free to utter his convictions, prompted him to decline the generous proposal.

It is hardly to be supposed that any man could enter upon a career of such marked antagonism to the prejudices of his contemporaries, could undertake to do battle against the conscientious convictions of good men, and to denounce the hypocrisies and flagrancies of bad men, without provoking decided opposition and creating for himself malignant enemies. And it is a still greater marvel that he should be able to hold on to such a policy throughout the long period of nearly forty years. Yet such is the fact in regard to the history of Jacob Knapp. Despite the fearful forms of opposition which he has been called to encounter, the perils he has been compelled to meet, not the least of which have been "perils among false brethren," he has held on to the even tenor of his way. To-day he preaches the same gospel that he preached forty years ago; to-day he is the same plain, fearless, quaint, and pungent expounder of the truths of God as he was when he first began. Flattery has not cajoled him, abuse has not intimidated him, ingratitude has not embittered him, misrepresentation has not angered him, and, at nearly the age of threescore years and ten, in the review of these trials, he is able to exclaim with Paul, "None of these things moved me; neither counted I my life dear unto myself, so that I might finish my course with joy, and the ministry which I have received of the Lord Jesus." Though keenly appreciative of the confidence and sympathy of his brethren, though deeming the disfavor of any an affliction, yet regarding himself called to this peculiar work, he has not dared to be disobedient to the heavenly vision, and his sustaining consolation has been the conviction that the Lord was with him, "working mightily."

Doubtless this persistency of purpose, this undaunted courage, this patient endurance, are among the elements of his history, which explain his power. But in addition to these, much is to be ascribed to the strength of his thoughts, the plainness, simplicity, and quaintness of his style, and, when before a congregation, the eloquence of his earnestness, the aptness of his illustrations, the directness of his appeals, and the freshness of his utterances.

Undoubtedly, to many minds, some of Elder Knapp's expressions have been distasteful, and, brought to the standard of a cultured criticism, are open to censure; but to this it may be said that these eccentricities in Elder Knapp's preaching have always borne the air of naturalness. They have not seemed oddities in his mind, but the words of truth and soberness. They have fittingly expressed the shades of his thought, and have conveyed to the minds of his hearers clear and forcible presentations of the truth. Besides, his singularity of style has given distinctness and reputation to his ministry. Thousands, perchance, have been attracted to hear him preach from motives of curiosity, whom a tamely correct and an exquisitely fine preacher could never have interested, and to whom these peculiarities of utterance have proved arrows shot at a venture; while hundreds of others, in the exercise of a noble charity and a wise discretion, have overlooked what they regarded as minor defects, because they clearly recognized the great amount of good the Lord was pleased to accomplish through him, because of the great amount of truth he was preaching, and because of the evident sincerity of the motives which inspired him.

But the real secret of Elder Knapp's power with men has

been his power with God. It is an ungracious task to say fulsome things about the piety of any living man. Elder Knapp has his faults; he has made mistakes; but that he is a man of God, those only can doubt who do not know him, or whose inveterate prejudices should awaken suspicions of their own want of the grace of charity. If it had been possible to fasten reproach upon the personal integrity and Christian consistency of Jacob Knapp, it would certainly have been done. The effort to blast his reputation, to destroy his influence, to drive him from the ministry, to make his name a byword and a reproach, has been formally, persistently, and perhaps conscientiously made. But at every point the undertaking has failed.

Being so conspicuously before the public for so many years, compelled to sojourn in so many different families, called to come in contact with such a countless variety of characters, his conduct has necessarily been exposed to the closest scrutiny. And if there had been furnished the occasion, there have been bad men who with hawk-like avidity were waiting to seize upon his slightest defects; and there have been good men who have watched him with painful expectations of making the sad discovery.

But through these many years, amid so many vicissitudes, God has mercifully preserved him. In purity of deportment, in gentleness of spirit, in quietness of behavior under fearful provocations, in magnanimity towards enemies, in constant habits of communion with God, the hundreds of families with which he has sojourned bear unanimous testimony. And when at one time the attempt was formally undertaken to investigate his conduct, the verdict in these particulars, his enemies being judges, was emphatic in his behalf.

It is, perhaps, too soon, or too late, at the present, to enter upon a detailed account of the investigation to which we allude — too soon, because something is due to participants in it who are still living, or are only recently dead; too late, because what ought to be said should have been said at the time. Yet the fact that nothing was said then is a reason why something should be said now.

It is not proper for us, neither is it our purpose, to attempt a partisan defence of Elder Knapp. Nor is it necessary. The investigation was conducted by men of tried integrity and clear judgment — men who enjoyed and commanded the confidence of the denomination. To their verdict Elder Knapp was willing to submit his case, and by their verdict he has ever since been content to abide. But unfortunately, for reasons beyond his control, that verdict was never published to the world; and Elder Knapp has been compelled, for the last twenty years, to suffer, in silence, the disadvantages which their silence occasioned, and to meet the suspicions and hinderances which the busy and untrammelled action of his enemies created against him.

Shortly after the season of his marvellous successes in New England, a reaction set in on several of the churches with which he had labored. This reaction was partly natural, partly produced by the mismanagement of the churches themselves, and partly by the anxiety of the enemies of revivals to prove them failures and disasters. The result was, that a wide-spread impression was created, not only that the measures of Elder Knapp were unfortunate, but that his motives were sinister. Rumors became rife that the course he pursued, especially in Boston, was designedly calculated to create the impression that he was very poor, in order to induce the people to dispense contributions of unwonted liberality. Reports of these rumors reached Hamilton, where Elder Knapp resided, and a vigorous correspondence was maintained between certain parties with regard to the actual state of his finances and the measures he had taken to increase them.

On returning from holding a protracted meeting, Elder Knapp came home, on one occasion, to find the community agitated with conflicting rumors; and finding that these rumors were likely to spread and hinder his usefulness as an evangelist, he called at once for an investigation. The matter by mutual consent was at first referred to a private committee. This committee, in an enlarged form, finally met in the month of June, 1844. It was composed of brethren, the mention of whose names is a guaranty of the justice of the decision they would be likely to reach, to wit, Dr. Nathaniel Kendrick, Dr. G. W. Eaton, Deacons S. B. Burchard, William Cobb, and A. Pierce, to whom were added, prior to the June meeting, Rev. B. N. Leach, Pastor of the Baptist Church at Hamilton; Professor S. W. Taylor, Clerk; Deacon William Colgate, of New York City; and Deacons Sage and Barton, of Rochester, N. Y.

"The brethren of the committee,* having thoroughly examined the whole matter, united (we believe no one dissented) in the deliberate opinion that there was '*nothing in the case which ought to interrupt Elder Knapp's connection with the church, or his labors as a minister of the gospel.*' THIS WAS A DECISION UPON THE MERITS OF THE CASE; *not an important particular was left out of the case.*

"After this main result was attained, the next inquiry was, 'What particulars are there concerning which suggestions can be made, with probable advantage to the brethren?' Every such particular was carefully selected, and one of the committee was appointed to speak to parties touching these particulars, and to announce to them the committee's general conclusion. This he did with a clearness, a pathos, a faithfulness, and an effect which cannot be adequately described. Elder Knapp, interrupted with irrepressible emotion, expressed his thanks to the brethren for their kindness, their patience, and their faithfulness. [The other party to the trial] expressed himself in a most feeling and appropriate manner to the individual members of the committee, and expressed his happiness in what had been accomplished.

"The closing scene can never be effaced from the memory of the brethren present. Every heart was warm and tender.

---

* I quote from an explicit and detailed account of the trial, prepared at the time by Professor Taylor, and certified to by several witnesses.
R. J.

It was a scene of Christian embraces and tears of joy; the brethren all rejoiced in what they fondly regarded as the end of a matter of most painful and intense interest, likely, if long agitated and mismanaged, to jeopard the interests of the Hamilton Literary and Theological Institute, the peace and prosperity of the Hamilton church, and of Zion still more extensively; and especially the good name and usefulness of the two brethren whose difficulties had been removed. The brethren reckoned the great and good work accomplished. Nothing remained except to prepare such an *account* of the *adjustment* as the parties, together with the members of the committee, would be willing to subscribe, and such a one, likewise, as might serve to allay public excitement, and satisfy the candid Christian public.

" This was thought to be the work of a few minutes. It was only to give a short and general account of the settlement; and this was immediately attempted: but the form not proving entirely satisfactory, and Elder Knapp and Deacons Colgate, Sage, and Barton being obliged to leave town immediately, the committee, having directed four of their number to prepare for the public eye the requisite account of the settlement, adjourned *sine die*."

The want of the few additional minutes needed to frame the account of that settlement, has been fraught with results of momentous import to the kingdom of Christ. Many of these results, we believe, have proved and are destined to prove great blessings to the church and the world; but to Elder Knapp personally the results have been an entail of intense mortification and severe discipline.

Shortly after the adjournment of the committee, side issues arose, outside influences obtruded themselves, much time was lost by correspondence with the different members of the committee, and finally, when, after the lapse of months, the form of the report was agreed upon, one of the principal parties to the trial refused to subscribe his name. This party was not Elder Knapp.

In this way Elder Knapp was deprived of all the benefit

which he had hoped to derive from the publication of the verdict; nay, more, the withholding of the report from the public was being construed to his injury, and he was finding his access to the churches hedged up by the suspicions, surmises, and scandals which these uncontradicted rumors had produced.

Finding at length that he should not be able to derive any benefit from the verdict of the committee, Elder Knapp resolved to appeal to the Baptist Church at Hamilton, of which he was a member. Of this church he asked a formal and thorough investigation of all the rumors affecting his reputation.

With this request, after some discussion as to the necessity of it, — seeing that no formal charge had been preferred against Elder Knapp, — the church complied; and a large committee was appointed to investigate all matters, and report the evidence and their conclusions to the church.

In due time this committee made a full and exhaustive report, and presented their conclusions, which were adopted by the church. This report covered some matters of investigation which were incidental to the main charge, and had arisen since the adjournment of the committee. Without going into these details, it will suffice to give here the verdict of the church regarding the great question at issue. There were five resolutions adopted. The second, and third, and fourth pertain to these incidental affairs, and exonerate him in regard to them; the other two read as follows: "I. *Resolved*, That it is the opinion of this church that Elder Knapp's language or form of expression in regard to his property was not so definite as might be desirable, and that we can conceive that it might be easy for individuals to receive from it an erroneous impression; but still we do not think we have evidence that he intended that it should have such an effect."

The last resolution is, "Finally, in view of the whole matter, this church is prepared to state its opinion, that there is in the case, as it now stands, nothing which ought to interrupt Elder Knapp's connection with the church, or interfere with his labors as a gospel minister."

In the charges that were preferred against him, it was not alleged that he had ever asked the churches for a cent of compensation, or, except in one or two private conversations, had made any allusions to his finances. But his appearance before Boston audiences in plain and somewhat rural attire created the impression that he must be very poor, and prompted some kind-hearted people to contribute money and presents to him, under that supposition. The sufficient answer to such a charge is, that matters of dress are matters of taste. What may seem extravagance to one may not appear to be such to another, and what one would regard good enough may seem uncomely to another. Elder Knapp, from early life, was economical in his habits, and very plain in his tastes; and he avers that the prospect of going to Boston tempted him to indulge in unusual expenses, in order to appear before a Boston audience in becoming attire.

It was in no instance shown that he had made direct representations of poverty; but the investigation proved that he had given in an over-estimate of his property. It was shown that he had accumulated some property, but not from his income as an evangelist, but that his income from that source had been inadequate for the support of his large family; and several members of the committee expressed their unwillingness to purchase his property at four fifths of the price at which he had estimated it to be worth.

The decision reached by the church was not altogether satisfactory. The resolutions had evidently been prepared in the spirit of compromise. Many thought that justice to Elder Knapp demanded a more unequivocal expression of sympathy and approval; a few thought that a more explicit tone of censure ought to have been expressed. The community had been agitated for months, opinions had become divided, friends had become alienated, issues had been made, and pride had been roused.

The consequences followed. Professor Taylor was induced to remove to Lewisburgh, Penn., and there lay the foundations of that noble institution now known as Lewisburgh University. Professor Maginnis lent himself vigorously to the attempt to remove the Madison University from Hamilton to Rochester. The agitation of this question ensued; and finally two institutions of learning were secured to the Baptist denomination, — one in Hamilton and one in Rochester, — each well endowed, manned by an able corps of teachers, and filled with students. Elder Knapp removed to Illinois, and in this western world continued his work as an evangelist, in communities where the churches were too poor to give him much compensation, and in communities in which there were no churches at all, and where the only remuneration he could receive was the satisfaction of doing good, without reward from men.

In the review of this whole matter, it seems to be just and proper to say, good men differed. "The contention between them was so sharp, that," as in the case of two good men centuries ago, "they departed asunder, the one from the other;" and that the contention in this case, as in that, has turned out to the furtherance of the gospel. In these results let all rejoice, even those who have personally suffered the most.

At the same time, the retrospect of this unfortunate affair cannot fail to bring great consolation to Elder Knapp. He has learned many valuable lessons and gained much rich experience, the realization of which must fill his heart with humble gratitude to God. A scrutiny into his life-long conduct, invigorated as it was by personal animosities, was able to fix upon no greater fault than a foible, and was able to make no sufficient ground of complaint even on such a point. The brethren whc were participants in the investigation, and unanimously attested his integrity, were men whose eminent and widely-known reputation for probity and sagacity challenges the confidence of the public. God has graciously kept him from sinking under the trial, and retiring from the ministry. By reason of his removal to the West, the sphere of his influence has been enlarged. He is still enabled, at an advanced age of life, to labor for the salvation of souls, and finds his declining years cheered with numerous expressions of the cordial sympathy and confidence of his brethren. He is comforted by the reasonable expectation that his name will be cherished in the hearts of coming generations. He is nerved to still greater efforts in honor of the Savior, by the hope that when he shall rest from his labors, his works will follow him, in the adoption of his measures as permanent instrumentalities for promoting the cause of Christ. And the few years yet remaining to him on earth are cheered by the joyous anticipation of meeting, in the final gathering, multitudes who will forever ascribe their position in the blood-washed throng to the blessing of God on the preaching and prayers of JACOB KNAPP.

CONTENTS.

AUTOBIOGRAPHY.

CHAPTER I.

CHAPTER II.

CHAPTER VII.

CHAPTER VIII.

CHAPTER IX.

CHAPTER X.

CHAPTER XI.

CHAPTER XII.

CHAPTER XIII.

CHAPTER XIV.

CHAPTER XV.

CHAPTER XVI.

CHAPTER XVII.

CHAPTER XVIII.

CHAPTER XIX.

CHAPTER XX.

CHAPTER XXI.

VIEWS ON VARIOUS SUBJECTS.

SERMONS.

APPENDIX.

INTRODUCTION.

In the early part of my ministry as an Evangelist, I had no intention of publishing anything myself concerning my labors, nor of leaving anything for others to publish after I was dead. Consequently I kept no journal, and wrote nothing with that end in view.

As time rolled on, and important events continually multiplied, I was advised by friend after friend to be preparing something which might be useful after my decease. I began to write somewhat, but was heartless about it, and finally destroyed all I had written, lest it might minister to an unholy ambition, and come in conflict with my determination to "crucify the flesh, with the affections and lusts."

At length many persons urged the subject of my publishing, as a matter of duty. They assured me that a history of my labors would be of great benefit to those who would come after me. This view had great weight with me. I therefore began to write again, but only occasionally; not thinking that what I might prepare would be made public while I was in the land of the living. In the year 1866 I consulted many eminent brethren, in whose judgments I had more confidence than in my own. They advised me to prepare a history of my ministry for publication at once. They assured me that my hesitation to do so arose from the dictates of false delicacy, that the rising ministry and the present age ought not to be denied the benefits of my long experience.

On reflection I could see that I was outliving my generation, and that another had already risen, which knew not *Jacob*. I realized that soon those who would be most interested in this work, by reason of their personal relations to my ministry, would be gone, while many who could bear witness to the truth of the marvellous things I might relate, would be where their testimony could not be had.

In view of these considerations I went to writing an account of the different meetings, and of the remarkable incidents which occurred in them, as best I could from recollection. There will be, doubtless, some mistakes in the accounts given, as many years have elapsed since several of the occurrences related took place; but I am confident that they are substantially correct, and not overdrawn. If I had kept a strict account of all the incidents of my life as they transpired, the work would have been far more comprehensive and interesting; but the details of many events have faded from my memory, while of others I think it well to say nothing, because, at this distance of time, their verity could not be easily corroborated.

The peculiar nature of my ministry, covering, as it does, a period in which I was called to encounter the opposition of deep-seated prejudices, has necessarily brought me in conflict with many, who, more or less conscientiously, have set themselves to hinder the success of my labors and disparage my influence. Many of these are now dead; a few are still living; but in reference to none do I wish to perpetuate unkind memories, and therefore have purposely avoided mentioning such by name, except wherever fidelity to truth and an intelligible statement have compelled me to do so. In the language of the lamented Lincoln, I do sincerely say that "with malice towards none, and charity for all," I submit my book to the prayerful and candid consideration of the Christian public.

JACOB KNAPP.

AUTOBIOGRAPHY

OF

ELDER JACOB KNAPP.

CHAPTER I.

Birth, Parentage, and early Religious Instructions.—Experience of Conviction and Conversion.—Backsliding.—Removal West.—Attending School in the East.—Ball-room and Prayer-meeting.—Re-consecration.—Baptism.

I WAS born in Otsego County, in the State of New York, on the 7th day of December, 1799. My father was in moderate circumstances. I lived with my parents during most of the period of my minority.

My parents and grand-parents on my father's side were Episcopalians; consequently I was brought up to attend the church, and was taught the Creed and Catechism from my infancy. My mind was early, and at times deeply, impressed with divine truth. From the first of my remembrance I had seasons of secret prayer, and of deep anxiety about the future welfare of my soul; but I was not led to hope in Christ as my Savior until the summer of my seventeenth year, when it pleased God to take from me my dear mother.

This sad bereavement led me, more than ever before, to feel my need of a Comforter and Friend which this world could not afford, and to see the emptiness and vanity of all terrestrial enjoyments. I separated myself for a time from rude company, and betook myself to the Bible, hymn-book, prayer, and the house of God. My health declined in consequence of my distress of mind; so much so, that I remember that, coming one day from the woods where I had been to pray, my father remarked, that as my health was so poor, he should have to put me to a trade. I thought to myself, "Little does my father guess my disease, or the kind of treatment which the nature of my case demands." I often repaired to the barn or the grove in the silent hours of the night, and poured out my soul in prayer to God.

At length, one Lord's day morning, I took my Bible and hymn-book, and repaired to the woods, with a determination never to return without relief to my soul. I went some distance from human sight or hearing, laid myself down on a grassy knoll, and prayed and read, and read and prayed. All the promises seemed beautiful, and of more value than all the world besides; the hymns appeared glorious; but, "Ah," thought I, "I can never sing them in heaven; this happiness is for another." I felt my vileness; all my sins rose before me like mountains. I thought I had prayed, read the Bible, attended meetings, and done all that was in my power to do; and yet I seemed to grow worse and worse, more and more despicable in the sight of God. Not as yet understanding the way of salvation, but trusting to my own righteousness, and now discovering that to be worthless and an offence to a holy God, I felt myself sinking down into despair. I saw clearly the righteousness of God in sending me to the lowest hell. At this moment the earth seemed to open beneath me, and hell appeared to be yawning for my reception. I closed my eyes, fully expecting to open them no more until I opened them in hell, and lifted them up with the rich man in torment.

But, to the joy and rapture of my soul, after a short space of time passed in this condition, my load of guilt was gone. I rose up quickly, turned my eyes towards heaven, and thought I saw Jesus descending with his arms extended for my reception. My soul leaped within me, and I broke forth into singing praises to the blessed Savior. The sweet melodies of the birds seemed to make harmony with my songs, and, as I looked around me, the sun shone with a lustre not his own, the majestic trees, swaying to the gentle breeze, appeared to bow in sweet submission to the will of Heaven. All nature smiled, and everything, animate and inanimate, praised God with a voice (though unheard before) too loud and too plain to be misunderstood. At this moment I lost all concern about heaven or hell; my soul was wholly absorbed in loving and praising Him whom angels adore and all nature magnifies. I then knew the peace there was in believing in Jesus, and I saw that he had borne the guilt of my sins, and "become the end of the law for righteousness to every one that believeth."

Soon after this I was led to examine the word of God, to know what he would have me to do. I found very shortly that God commanded me to repent and be baptized. Nor was I at a loss to find out what baptism was. Though but a youth, and always taught that sprinkling was baptism, and that infants were proper subjects, yet I saw that in the days of the apostles the candidates were required to bring forth fruits meet for repentance, to believe with all the heart, and that when they had repented and believed they went down into the water and came up out of the water, being buried. This procedure I could not think necessary in order merely to sprinkle a person.

About this time, in Masonville, Delaware County, near which place my father then resided, there was a revival among the Baptists. I attended the preaching, and saw some converts baptized. The scene produced a powerful impression on me. "This," thought I, "is the way in which John the Baptist, Philip, and all the apostles baptized;" and the more I read the more I was confirmed in my convictions that my having been sprinkled in infancy would not answer the commands of God, to believe and be baptized. Nor could I find food for my hungry soul in the forms and ceremonies of the Episcopal church, though heretofore I had ever held her in such high veneration as the Holy Catholic Church.

For a long time I felt it both a duty and a privilege to be "buried with Christ in baptism," but inasmuch as I was under age, and my father and grand-parents were very much unreconciled to my joining the Baptist church, and I could in conscience join no other, I remained out of any, designing when of age to arise and follow my Lord. I continued to enjoy the presence of Jesus for some length of time, say ten or twelve months. But beginning about then to enter into the ranks of young company, and joining heartily in many of their amusements, I found myself yielding to the temptations that surrounded me, and experienced a serious decline in spirituality: like Peter, I began to follow Jesus "afar off."

The summer of 1817 I spent in Cayuga County, N. Y., during which time I lived far from God. I became so exceedingly rude that I often delivered orations and made speeches concerning religion for sport. One day, I remember, I was sent for by a wild set of young men to preach the funeral sermon of a horse. This request shocked me, and served to open my eyes as to my condition. During all this period of criminal wildness I frequently had seasons of secret prayer and of weeping and bitterness over my course of living, and as often resolved to reform. I never could, even in my most distant wanderings, hear religion ridiculed, or the name of Christ profaned, or his people reproached, without great pain. Such allusions would pierce my heart like a dagger, and become the occasions of great compunction.

About this time, I removed with my father, into a new country, on the head waters of the Ohio River. There I was cut off from all religious privileges. During the first year of my residence I did not hear a single sermon. There were no religious meetings whatever in the neighborhood. At first the sense of these deprivations served to quicken within me an appreciation of those opportunities and blessings which I had so sadly neglected and abused, and I formed a determination to lead a new life. For a while I succeeded in carrying out my resolution, but very soon I found my need of the appointed means of grace, and again I wandered far from God.

In December, 1818, assisted by my father, I returned to Delaware County, N. Y., for the purpose of attending school.

I was overjoyed to see my young companions again; and, after being urged somewhat, I consented to attend with them a New Year's ball, for which they were then busily making preparations. I yielded, however, to their importunities with reluctance, excusing myself on the ground of my long absence, and resolving that this should be the last in which I would engage. Shortly before the time fixed upon, I learned that the Baptist church had appointed a prayer-meeting for the same night in the school-house across the way from the ball-room. This coincidence disturbed me very much. I thought of the language of Christ, "He that is not for me is against me." I repented of my engagement, but thought I could not go back. I prayed and wept in secret places and in the silent hours of the night. The Spirit seemed to say to me, "Here are two meetings; one in which to worship God, and for what is the other?" The answer was forced from my lips, "To serve the devil. It is against Christ." Then I exclaimed, with tears streaming down my cheeks, "Hast thou done so much for me, O thou blessed Jesus, and am I against thee? Am I scattering abroad?" And straightway I resolved that instead of attending the ball, I would go to the prayer-meeting; that I would desert the devil, and serve him no longer. I found him to be a cruel master, and Jesus to be full of kindness and tender mercy.

God, in his infinite goodness, had impressed the minds of some other of my companions in a similar manner; and two or three of them, who had designed to attend the ball, went with me to the meeting. While this band of praying disciples was engaged in songs and supplications, we could hear the music of the fiddle, and the company of dancers could at the same time catch the sound of voices in prayer and songs of praise. The exercises of the meeting discovered no unusual amount of religious interest; but my own feelings were deeply moved, and I covered my face in order to conceal them. With difficulty did I withhold an expression, and my heart almost burst within me. At length the meeting was brought to a close; and as the brethren rose up to depart, I opened my mouth, and gave vent to the burden of my heart. This done, the devil was vanquished. All fell on their knees, and I attempted to pray in public for the first time; others followed me. From that moment a revival commenced, which resulted in the conversion of sixty young people, who were added to the church that winter. Of this number, nine were convicted on that same evening, while in the ball-room, under the voice of prayer which they heard from across the street.

At this time I began to be strongly impressed with the conviction that it was my duty to be baptized and unite with the church. The command, "Arise and be baptized," kept ringing in my ears night and day. But I was under age, more than two hundred miles from home, and well knew the unwillingness of my father to my joining a Baptist church. I hesitated to take this important step without informing him of my wishes and obtaining his consent. After much prayer and many tears, I sat down and wrote him a letter, telling him all my heart, and begging his permission to do what I felt God in his word required of me. Week after week did I wait for an answer; but none came. As the time drew near when I was to return to my home in the west, knowing that there was no church within many miles of it, I made up my mind to confer no longer "with flesh and blood," but to obey God rather than man.

Accordingly, I told my experience to the Baptist church at Masonville, and was received as a candidate for baptism. This was in the month of February, 1819. On the next Lord's day the great desire of my heart was gratified: I was buried with Christ in baptism. My soul experienced an ecstasy of delight. I had suffered so much in consequence of neglected duties, and had overcome so many obstructions in the path of duty, that the consciousness that I was permitted to follow the example of my precious Savior seemed to make this day the happiest of my life. I wondered how I could have neglected this beautiful ordinance so long. For some time after this I never came near the spot without thinking, what a pleasure it would be to be buried again in the same symbolic grave.

CHAPTER II.

Return Home. — Neighborhood Efforts. — Choice of a Calling. — Return East to obtain an Education. — School at Masonville. — Visit to Columbia County, and Journey back. — Academy at Gilbertsville. — Economy. — A Revival. — School-teaching in New Lisbon. — Conflicts as to Duty. — Hamilton Institution. — Licensed to preach. — Marriage and Pastorate at Springfield. — Second Pastorate at Watertown, N. Y. — Reflections on ministerial Worldliness.

I WAS now nineteen years of age. It being the custom of my father to give his sons their time when they were twenty years old, I returned to my father's house, and remained subject to him during the appointed time. All this while I was thirsting for knowledge and better qualifications for usefulness. My mind was greatly impressed with the duty and the desire of preaching the gospel. But how to obtain a suitable education I did not know. I was poor, had no friends who could or would help me, and was not aware of the existence of any ministerial education society. I labored, as God gave me opportunity, according to my ability. Realizing the great religious destitution of the country where my father resided, I appointed prayer-meetings in the neighborhood, gathered together the few scattered sheep in this portion of the western wilderness, and was encouraged to continue in these efforts, and strengthened in my convictions concerning preaching the gospel, because it pleased God to crown these humble efforts with success in the conversion of several souls.

When the time came in which I was to choose my path in life, my father offered to assist me quite liberally, considering his means, in buying a farm and clearing up land. My brothers were doing so with flattering prospects. But farms and earthly possessions were nothing to me. A nobler ambition urged me on; and yet, pressed down with a sense of my own insufficiency, I knew not how to achieve it. Still I felt my sufficiency to be of God; in him I put my trust, and resolved to go forward. I believed that God called me to the work of the ministry, and had full confidence that he would provide a way in which I should be the better fitted to enter upon it.

In this simple faith I went forth, like Abraham of old, not knowing whither I was going, or how I should be able to reach the end of my journey. I merely felt that in case I could get back into Delaware County, some way would be opened in which I could prosecute my desire for an education. In this spirit I shouldered my pack, took leave of my friends, and set my face towards the east. As I passed a new clearing of my elder brother, I sat down on a log and lifted up my heart to God in prayer that, during my absence, my own mind might undergo as great an improvement as his farm promised to present. Having but few clothes beyond those I had on my back, only five dollars in money, and a journey of two hundred and ten miles to perform, I resolved to save every penny possible, and yet pay for everything I received. When hungry and fatigued, I would seek out a spring of water, and, sitting down by its side, would refresh myself with provisions from my knapsack. In this manner I accomplished my journey at a cost of only fifty cents, having saved four dollars and fifty cents with which to commence my education for the ministry.

When I reached Masonville I found a place at once, where I could obtain board and lodging by doing the chores of the family. Here I continued, pursuing my studies, for a short time; when one of my uncles, residing in Columbia County, invited me to go home with him and attend school there. I did so, and remained with him till about the breaking up of winter. By this time I was at a loss to know what to do, for I was nearly out of clothing, and had no means wherewith to buy more. I concluded to return to Delaware County, and engage in the work of rafting lumber, until I could earn sufficient for the renewal of my wardrobe and the expenses of another winter's tuition.

I started on my journey of one hundred and twenty miles on foot, with but twenty-five cents in my pocket. It rained severely all day ; but I trudged on, till I reached the Hudson River. Here I paid one half of my twenty-five cents for ferriage across. With one half of the remainder I paid for my night's lodging. Throughout the next day I continued on through a drenching rain, for I could not afford to wait over. Towards night I fell in with a man in a wagon who asked me to ride. But this apparent relief turned out to my greater disadvantage ; for while we were stopping to feed the horse, a dog stole the bundle containing my few clothes and provisions. Here, then, I was, tired and hungry, among strangers, with no money, and no one to befriend me. I inquired for a chance for labor, but could learn of none. I went on my way until ten o'clock at night. I then called for lodgings, for which I paid my last sixpence, going to bed hungry and getting up hungry. On the next day I pursued my journey till about twelve o'clock, when I reached the house of a friend, by whom my necessities were relieved. During all these distresses my confidence in God remained unshaken, and I counted them as nothing if I could only accomplish my purpose.

I then hired myself out to a man, with whom I was to raft and run lumber to Philadelphia. The water fell and left us on the way. He failed, and I lost the principal part of my wages.

Shortly after my return from this adventure, I heard of an academy at Gilbertsville, Otsego County ; and trusting in God to direct my steps and help me on, I arrived at this place near the end of April, 1821, with but few clothes for the summer, and about money enough to pay for one quarter's tuition. I called on Mr. Collins, the principal of the Institution, and made known to him my situation and my wishes. He seemed to take an interest in my case, and recommended me to several families, who, he thought, might be willing to let me do work about the house for my board. But after making several fruitless applications, Mr. Collins told me that I might board with him, do what few chores he needed to have done, and pay him in full whenever I was able to do so. I felt extremely grateful for his kindness, but yet I could hardly endure the thought of running in debt. However, I concluded to accept the offer, and accordingly commenced my studies.

Not being accustomed to study closely, my mind being altogether undisciplined, I made only slow progress in acquiring knowledge. I was often reminded of the remark of my father, as I was leaving home, — that he feared, if I went off among the Baptists with a notion of preaching, I would spend two or three years making out nothing, and would come back poor and disgusted. Daily did I repair to the grove north of the academy, and pour out my soul in prayer to God to strengthen my memory, discipline my mind, and aid me in my studies. In this grove I shed many tears and enjoyed many seasons of communion with God. I applied myself to study with diligence, and practised a rigid economy, going in my shirt sleeves in order to save my coat for the winter.

At the close of the first quarter I went to work through harvest season, by which means I was able to provide for the expenses of the ensuing term, and as the evenings lengthened I chopped wood by moonlight to obtain articles I could not do without.

During the second term I attended the Baptist meeting on the hill; and as they had no minister, I was called upon to take charge of the meetings. It pleased the Lord to pour out his Spirit gloriously. When I first went there, there was but one youth in the place who professed religion, and within about two months nearly all the young people in the place were converted to God. Towards the close of this quarter I began to feel more than ever straitened as to what course to pursue. I was not able to earn enough during vacations to meet the necessary expenses of term time, nor did I feel myself competent to teach school in that vicinity. While I was thinking and praying about it, the Lord inclined the hearts of the good sisters of the place to prepare me a suit of clothes for the winter; besides, I had several invitations from brethren, both Baptist and Presbyterian, to board a few weeks in their families. In this manner, I was enabled to pursue my studies until some time in January, when I received and accepted a request to take charge of a school in New Lisbon, Otsego County. Here the Lord was pleased to bless my efforts for the conversion of the children connected with my school. In particular do I remember one instance in which a son of a Romanist professed his faith in Christ, even though taken from school because prayer and religious instruction were maintained there. During this winter I spent my evenings in holding meetings in different neighborhoods (though I did not pretend to preach), and God was with me, and many souls were converted.

But as the winter began to wear away, I felt it to be necessary for me to decide whether I should preach the gospel, or abandon the thought of it altogether. A sense of my insufficiency was ever bearing upon my spirits, and, yielding to the impression which it produced, at length I concluded to give up the idea, and turn my attention to some other pursuit. But no sooner had I reached this decision, than trouble rolled in upon me like a flood. I was well nigh driven to despair. One night, especially, I remained concealed behind the seats of the schoolroom, while being occupied for purposes of worship, lest I should be called on to take part in the exercises, and so continued unobserved till the meeting was dispersed. I staid all night in the school-house, and all the next morning till the hour for school arrived. My mind was in no fit condition for the proper discharge of the duties of my station, and I could not refrain from tears in the presence of my scholars. I dismissed the school with a determination to remain in the building all the next night, although thirty-six hours had then elapsed since I had tasted food. But about dark one of the brethren came after me, concluding, from a statement of one of the children, that something was the matter with me. I dared not, however, open my mind to any one respecting my impressions, so that I could gain but little relief from the sympathies of friends.

But "man's extremity is God's opportunity." On the next day, on going to the post-office, I found a letter, which proved to be from Hamilton, Madison County, inviting me to visit the Institution,* which had been recently established there for the purpose of educating young men desirous of entering the Baptist ministry, and encouraging me to attempt a regular course of study. I then saw that God, in his providence, was opening the way for me, and that all I had to do was to trust him and move forward.

I also felt greatly rebuked for my past distrust and unbelief. I wept and prayed; "thanked God and took courage." Yet there was one thing that still troubled me. Before I could be admitted into the Institution at Hamilton, it was needful that I obtain from the church of which I was a member a formal license to preach. To proceed in this matter myself seemed a formidable undertaking. In those days the prevailing opinion among Baptists was, that if a young man was truly called of God to preach,

---

* In the year 1812, Rev. Daniel Hascall, pastor of the Baptist church at Hamilton, and Rev. Nathaniel Kendrick, pastor of the church at Eaton, in mutual conference, conceived the idea of an Education Society, in aid of indigent young men desirous of studying for the ministry. The Society was organized in 1817, and chartered in 1819 under the name and style of the Baptist Education Society of the State of New York. Under the auspices of this Society, Hamilton Literary and Theological Institution was founded in 1820. Hascall was appointed the classical and Kendrick the theological instructor. Hascall continued sixteen years, and resigned; Kendrick, twenty-eight years, and died. The Baptist denomination will hold the names of these venerable men of God in everlasting remembrance.

For a considerable period the course of instruction comprised four years, afterwards six, and finally eight. About 1846, the Institution was chartered as Madison University. In addition to sending out multitudes of young men into the Christian ministry, this noble Institution is identified with the founding of Rochester University, New York, and of Lewisburg University, Pennsylvania, besides being the grand pioneer in the culture of that zeal for ministerial education which now constitutes one of the glories of the Baptist denomination.

Madison University still maintains her educational prestige, and her hold on the gratitude and confidence of the denomination, whose present greatness is owing, under God, so much to agencies which have made her name illustrious.

he would be unable to restrain the expression of his convictions. It was deemed a sort of interference with the work of the Spirit for any of the brethren to introduce the subject, and afford any encouragement. But my views of my own insufficiency were so oppressive, and my dread of being rejected so intense, that it was with the greatest difficulty that I could bring my mind to broach the matter, and ask the church to grant me a license.

At length, however, I concluded to do so. Accordingly I closed my school, and, going to Masonville, opened my mind to one of the deacons. He named it to others of the brethren, and the church invited me to preach before them. And in complying with this invitation, I made my first formal attempt at sermonizing. This was in the spring of 1822. The church, after hearing me once, gave me a license, and recommended me to the Institution at Hamilton, informing me (to my surprise) that it had long been the opinion of the brethren that I ought to devote myself to the work of the ministry. Immediately, I started on foot for Hamilton, a distance of about fifty miles.

Shortly after my entrance into the Institution, Professor Hascall requested me to preach in a neighboring school-house. Overwhelmed with a sense of my inability, I took the stand and announced my text. But no sooner had the words passed from my lips, than my eye fell on the form of my venerable instructor. His presence entirely unmanned me. I managed, amid much confusion of thought, to get through the discourse, fully expecting that he would advise me to give up the thought of preaching, and leave the Institution. After waiting some time, and hearing nothing from him, I ventured to call upon him, and unburden my heart of its apprehensions and misgivings. Instead, however, of discouraging me, he bade me go on. Shortly after this I was sent to preach, on the Sabbath, to the church in Morrisville, the county seat. This was the first instance in which I had been asked to preach in a meeting-house. The thought of doing so filled me with fear and trembling. But the Lord strengthened me, and gave me liberty.

As I had not been accustomed to study in early life, I found it very difficult for a time to keep up with some of my classmates in the lessons. Yet I applied myself with diligence, and as I was blessed with a good constitution, and maintained vigorous exercise, I was enabled to go through the course without impairing my health. In the month of June, 1825, I received my diploma, and accepted a call from the Baptist church in Springfield, Otsego County, N. Y. On the first day of the September following I was married to Electa Payne, of Hamilton. One week previous to my marriage I was ordained.

During my studies at the Institution my spirituality declined, and I entered quite deeply into the spirit of a man-pleasing policy. I fancied that the gospel might be so preached as not to give offence. It seemed to me that it might be made attractive to men by means of its external appointments. I imagined that fine meeting-houses, tall steeples, good bells, and smooth sermons were calculated to make the religion of Christ popular. Alas! I did not then realize that the prophets and apostles, John the Baptist, and Jesus Christ himself, were not able to preach the truth without causing many to be offended. Nor did I understand that in every age in which the church had striven to make herself acceptable to the world, to the same degree had she been deprived of her beauty and her power. O! when will ministers and Christians learn that the "carnal mind is enmity against God," and a true presentation of the gospel consists not in flattering the natural taste of the unsanctified heart, but by "manifestation of the truth, commending it to every man's conscience in the sight of God"?

During the first year of my pastorate, I devoted my time wholly to my work; nor were my labors entirely devoid of God's blessing. The numerous difficulties which had long existed in the church were settled, and the number of members and attendants increased. After a while, however, under the advice of my brethren in the church, and influenced by the example of other ministers, I was induced to purchase a small farm, supposing that I could carry on the work of farming without detracting from the efficiency of my services as a pastor. Nor did I really find out my mistake during my stay with this people. Though there was no general breaking forth of God's power, yet there was a prevailing state of harmony, and about sixty conversions. These results I tried to accept as grounds of encouragement, and evidences that I was in the path of duty.

After serving this church five years, I accepted a call from the Baptist church in Watertown, Jefferson County, N. Y., and entered upon my labors there in the month of September, 1830. My family being at that time small, I did not for the first year keep house, and was, therefore, free from household cares, and enabled to devote myself exclusively to my pastoral work. The Lord was with me. A revival of religion marked the very beginning of my labors, and continued for about one year. The church being small and poor, they failed to give me enough for the current support of my family. And it will be a matter of life-long regret that I did not trust more implicitly in God for my sustenance, and concern myself only about my Master's business. Had I done so, I have no doubt but that my family would have suffered no lack, and my ministerial work would have been attended with much greater success. Instead of doing this, I again bought a farm near the village, thinking that I could superintend it without any serious disparagement of my usefulness. But the experiment proved to be a great hinderance, alike to my own piety and the growth of the church. Though, during a ministry of three years with this people, I baptized into the fellowship of the church about two hundred converts, yet towards the end of that time I began to feel that I was unfaithful to my trust, that I was entangling myself with the affairs of this life, and that God was displeased with my course.

CHAPTER III.

Protracted Meetings a Novelty. — Resolution to become an Evangelist. — Counting the Cost. — Resignation of Pastorate. — Results of the Labors of eighteen Months among the Churches. — Trials. — Opposition. — Pecuniary Losses. — Application to the State Convention. — Application rejected. — Mortification of Feelings. — Fasting and Prayer. — God's Presence and Direction. — Blessed Results. — Trust in God for Support. — Method of preparing Sermons. — Re-conversions needful.

ABOUT this time, 1833, the practice of holding protracted meetings began to enter in amongst the Baptist churches. These were of rare occurrence, and generally looked upon with distrust and opposition. There prevailed among Baptists, views of the sovereignty of the Holy Spirit in the conversion of men, which led to a practical denial of the necessity of all human agency in bringing sinners to consider the claims of the gospel. The theology of that day was, that God evinced his sovereignty independently of means, rather than through them; that human agencies were interferences with the divine purposes, and that all experiences that might result from the use of means were to be rejected as "man-made" conversions.

As might be expected, such teachings worked out their results in the spiritual apathy of professors of religion, in the absence of any great concern for the salvation of men, and in the paucity of the numbers that were being added to the churches. But as the news of the outpouring of God's Spirit in connection with these "protracted" efforts, reached me, my own soul was set on fire with zeal for the spread of the kingdom of Christ. I looked upon the past eight years of my ministry as comparatively wasted. I felt that I had turned aside for "filthy lucre." My motives seemed to have been impure. I thought I would have given worlds for the lost opportunities which I had failed to improve. And regarding the care of my farm as a burden and a hinderance, I embraced the first opportunity of selling it, in the following spring, at great pecuniary sacrifice. Thus I broke from all worldly concerns, and consecrated myself anew to the service of God. I viewed the unconverted as toppling on the brink of hell, and many of the churches, and ministers too, as sleeping at their post. I felt a special moving of soul that God called me to devote the remainder of my life to the direct work of an evangelist among the churches; striving to awaken them to the necessity of a higher standard of active piety in laboring directly for the immediate conversion of men. This conviction became the necessity of my nature, and I could not resist it. I saw no alternative. God clearly bade me go forth into fields already white for the harvest, and I was not disobedient to the heavenly vision.

Yet it is proper to state, that I did not reach this conclusion without counting the cost. I saw that I should be cutting myself loose from any certain and regular source of support. Many of the churches were so feeble as to find it a matter of great difficulty to raise the meagre salaries they had promised to their pastors; and, at the best, very few had even approximate conceptions of the duty and blessedness of liberality in supporting the gospel; and, withal, I knew I must meet with great opposition from many in the churches, who would denounce my endeavors as "new-fangled measures;" and much ridicule from ungodly men, who would make common cause with these Sanballat sort of Christians in hindering the work of God. But "none of these things moved me." I resolved to forsake houses and lands, wife and children, and go forth, trusting in God for the support of my family, and relying on his promises of grace to help in every time of need.

On the first Sabbath in September, 1833, I preached my farewell sermon to the dear people of my charge, and found it no small trial to tear myself away from their endearments, aud especially from the precious lambs which had been brought to hope in Christ through my labors. Leaving my family in Watertown, I spent the following eighteen months in visiting the churches of Jefferson and Lewis Counties, and laboring with them in protracted meetings. God was with me, and converts were multiplied. His Spirit was poured out plenteously in nearly every place in which I labored. My services were not confined to Baptist churches, but in Presbyterian and Methodist churches I preached repentance and faith as God gave me opportunity. It was thought by some, who were counted reliable judges, that not less than two thousand souls were converted during these eighteen months. As near as I can now remember, I baptized over four hundred converts into the fellowship of churches which were at the time destitute of pastors.

But notwithstanding all these powerful attestations of God's approval, I was called on to encounter great opposition, alike from professed Christians and the avowed enemies of Christ; ay, even from ministers of the gospel. My motives were impugned; my sermons were dissected, and detached sentences were taken from their connection and set forth in distorted forms; and the religious journals were closed to any accounts of the "wonderful works of God." About this time, also, I met with several severe losses in pecuniary matters, so as to render my reliance for support still more precarious. Altogether the occasions of my rejoicing in view of my successes in laboring for the conversion of sinners, was challenged by a series of conflicts and trials which hitherto I had not dreamed of, and which I found to be exceedingly distressing. It seemed as though all the devils in hell were let loose upon me, until I could almost say with Dr. Payson, "The Lord has taken from me one thing after another, until there remains no more to be taken, and disappointed me in one way after another, until I am no longer capable of disappointment."

At length I was advised, by Dr. Nathaniel Kendrick,* to take an appointment from the Board of the Baptist Missionary

* Then, and for many years afterwards, the revered Principal of the Hamilton Literary and Theological Institution.

Convention of the State of New York,* as an evangelist in Jefferson and Oswego Counties. I thought favorably of this suggestion, imagining that such an appointment would increase my influence and tend to silence my opposers. I therefore went to the meeting of the Convention, about a hundred and forty miles distant. I had not mingled with the brethren long, before I found that some, whom I had counted as friends, were disposed to treat me with coolness. Though indorsed by such a man as Dr. Kendrick, whose weight of personal influence was everywhere recognized, yet my application was instantly met by a decided opposition. One must tell what he had heard, another explain his views of the gospel method, until, after a lengthy debate, in which some cried one thing and some another, it was resolved to refer the question of my appointment to a committee. This committee made an adverse report, and my application was rejected. Overwhelmed with grief and mortification, I started to fill an engagement to preach in Loraine, a distance of about one hundred and fifty miles. The Lord brought me safely on my way some fifty miles, when my horse sickened and died. I got a brother to take me to Oswego, and then I went on board a boat for Sackett's Harbor. Shortly after we had started, "there arose a mighty tempest," and for a while there appeared but little chance for any of our lives. But my own spirits were so depressed that I seemed to have little choice between life and death. I thought myself "in perils by sea, in perils by land, and in perils by false brethren." But God preserved me for greater joys and greater sorrows than any I had hitherto experienced.

For a short time the effect of my rejection by the Board of the Convention was very disheartening. I had hoped to secure, by an appointment, greater influence among the churches, the more positive countenance of some of the ministers who hitherto had been sitting on the fence, hesitating as to which side to get down on, and also to silence the active opposition of those who

* The object of this Convention is the raising and furnishing of funds in aid of feeble churches throughout the State.

had avowed their hostility to my course; but it was not long before I found that my difficulties in these directions were on the increase. The non-committal became outspoken against me, and those heretofore opposed became violent and abusive. My soul was in deep trouble, and I knew not which way to turn.

But in my distress I cast my burdens on the Lord. I sought to know the will of God. I cried unto the Lord; and, blessed be his name, very soon he made known his ways, and lifted upon me the light of his countenance. After spending one whole day in fasting and prayer, and continuing my fast till midnight, the place where I was staying, was filled with the manifested glory of God. His presence appeared to me, not exactly in visible form, but as really to my recognition as though he had come in person, and a voice seemed to say to me, "Hast thou ever lacked a field in which to labor?" I answered, "Not a day." "Have I not sustained thee, and blessed thy labors?" I answered, "Yea, Lord." "Then learn that henceforth thou art not dependent on thy brethren, but on me. Have no concern but to go on in thy work. My grace shall be sufficient for thee."

From that night I felt willing to sacrifice the good opinion of my brethren, as I had previously sacrificed the favor of the world, and swing off from all dependences but God. Up to this time I had concerned myself too much about the opinions of other and older brethren, distrusting my youth and inexperience. But the Lord taught me that he was my only infallible guide. I joyously acquiesced in his will; and from that day to this have rested in this divine manifestation. Ah! how reluctant we are to cleave to the Lord! How prone to cling to creature dependences! Since I have endeavored to seek divine direction as to all my fields of labor, I have learned that it is possible for me, generally, to gain as clear impressions of the will of God concerning my duty as though it was announced in audible tones.

In this manifestation of God's presence to me, he cast no reflections on those of my ministerial brethren who differed from me, but, in the most tender manner, bade me leave them to pursue their own way, and cleave only to him. Thus was I, cured of all yearnings for denominational promotion, led to make an unreserved consecration of all my powers to the one end, — the conversion of men to Christ; and made willing to labor on, through evil and good report, leaving my vindication till the day of judgment.

A year did not elapse before I saw plainly that God's plan was much better than mine. I found it far more delightful and profitable to my soul to be directed by God's providence, where, and by his Spirit, how to labor, than to be prescribed in my field, and dictated to as to how to conduct my ministry, by others. The Lord carried me from place to place, even where I had the least expectation of going. In my perplexities, I was driven to God in prayer for him to direct my steps, and mark out every inch of my path. And I have been led to understand since, that had not the furnace been heated seven times hotter than it was wont to be, the dross would never have been separated from the gold. My kind and heavenly Father did not give me one blow that was not needful, nor one thorn that was not required to keep me from being exalted above measure, through the abundance of my success in winning souls, and the many flattering expressions of those who sympathized with my work.

The churches with which I labored were, for the most part, poor, and not well informed in relation to their duty of supporting the ministry. Sometimes I would receive thirty or forty dollars at the close of a protracted meeting, and sometimes nothing. I made up my mind, when I started, to make no demand, to do nothing, to say nothing, in reference to the matter of compensation, but to leave it entirely with God and the people. Sometimes, after a hard, long, and laborious campaign, I would return home to my increasing family with little or nothing; and find the means I had previously accumulated fast wearing away, and my wife toiling day and night in taking care of our little ones. But I found good things mixed with these apparently evil things. My wife made no complaints, but cheerfully acquiesced in my convictions of duty. Besides, I was comforted in the remembrance of the charge and promise, "Trust in the Lord and do good, and verily thou shalt be fed." "Thy bread shall be given thee, and thy water shall be sure." I felt that I would prefer to live on bread and water, and do the work of an evangelist, — thus making full proof of my ministry, than to have all the good things of this world. I expected soon to wear out, and to be called to render my account. I realized, more and more, how deficient I was in knowledge, and prayed daily for wisdom rather than riches and long life, that I might honor God, and become wise to win souls. I often read God's offer to Solomon, and I believed that he would deal in the same way now as then, if his servants would plead in faith.

I prayed for the right text, for the best divisions of it, and a true understanding of it; and I have always found those subjects which I studied in those days, and arranged while on my knees, have been the most powerful for good; and I now believe that there is a kind of inspiration about sermons thus gotten up, which makes them "mighty through God to the pulling down of the strongholds." And knowing, as I did, at the beginning of my labors as an evangelist, that I lacked everything, I pleaded the promise, "If any man lack wisdom, let him ask of God, who giveth liberally." I made up my mind to preach against sin everywhere, in every form, and in everybody, and take the consequences. I knew I had no reputation to lose, and thought I had none to gain; hence I intended to stand up for Jesus everywhere, on all occasions, and suffer shame for his sake, bear the reproach of his cross, and count it all joy that I was thought worthy to suffer for his name.

I soon found that the state of a man's heart had much to do with his judgment, and to a great extent controlled his sentiments. A cold-hearted or proud-spirited minister could not be in sympathy with one who was led by the Spirit. I therefore never attempted to lead into the light by argument those who opposed themselves. Their eyes must be touched a second time, before they can see clearly. Jesus said to Peter, "When thou art converted, strengthen thy brethren;" and evermore, it seems that most persons need re-conversions, in order rightly to understand the truths of God's word, or the plans of his providence.

CHAPTER IV.

CONDITION OF THE CHURCHES THEN AND NOW.

Forty Years ago. — No Sunday Schools. — No Missionary Enterprise. — Few educational Institutions. — No Liberality. — Antinomianism. — Elder Benedict. — Influence of Evangelism. — Opposition of Hyper-Calvinism. — Spurious Conversions. — Sudden Conversions. — A doubting Piety. — Jealousy. — Men-pleasers. — Early Discipline. — Consolation. — Success. — Sympathizers. — Change of Public Opinion.

AT this point, perhaps, better than at any other, I may pause in my narrative to invite my readers to a consideration, more at length, of the condition of the churches and their spirit at the time when I began to labor as an evangelist, and of the contrast which the state of religious sentiment in this age presents. Truly, as I look back forty years, and think of the marvellous change that has come over the churches, I am ready to exclaim with wondering gratitude, "What hath God wrought!"

Forty years ago there were no Sunday schools. The mighty train of agencies and influences which now move along the track of Sunday school efforts, had no place in the programme of Christian enterprise. Now such institutions are regarded as indispensable appointments in every church; the noblest talents of the church are consecrated to the instruction of the teeming throngs of youth that crowd the gates of Zion; and by far the greater proportion of those who join the church are gathered from the ranks of the Sunday school. Among Baptists this blessed agency was almost unheard of, nor was there any other appointment designed to take its place.

Forty years ago the cause of foreign and home missions had

scarcely place in the arrangements or sympathies of the vast proportion of our churches. As a matter of course, there was scarcely a missionary or a conversion among the heathen, and but little money raised with which to send them. The missionary enterprise was then in its infancy, and battling its way through prejudice and ignorance to the consciences of Christian men. Since then our denomination has leaped to a front rank in the grand instrumentalities for the world's conversion. Our missionaries, home and foreign, are dotting the world. Multitudes of souls at home, and in heathen lands, have been led to Christ. Churches all over our western territory, and amid the valleys, mountains, and jungles of India, are monuments of our missionary zeal; and every year our churches are sending up increasing sums to the treasury of the Lord.

Forty years ago there was not more than one or two institutions of learning under the auspices of our denomination, and societies for the education of young men for the ministry were just struggling into life. Now both colleges and education societies are multiplying in numbers, or increasing in power in the older states, and springing up as by magic in the new.

Forty years ago the churches had no idea of the obligations and blessedness of Christian liberality. The ministers were compelled, for the most part, to engage in farming or other business pursuits, in order to eke out the beggarly salaries on which the churches were willing to starve them; and, in short, the entire spirit of Christian enterprise was wanting.

As we contemplate the amazing differences in these regards at the present time, and try to imagine the bearings of the mighty forces now in operation on the future of the world's conversion, I ask, Is there one intelligent Christian who would wish to annihilate these grand agencies, obliterate this glorious history, and place the churches and the denomination back into the condition it occupied forty years ago? It is not difficult to imagine what would have been the history of the denomination by this time, had the opinions then prevalent continued to maintain their ascendency. The history of these results is already written in the fate of those churches where the blight of religious apathy remained undisturbed. In the beginning of this century there were numerous Baptist churches in Maryland; a few years ago there were only seven, and of these outside of Baltimore it might truly have been said, "They have a name to live while they are dead." In certain parts of Eastern New York, the territory once held by Baptists has been taken up by other denominations, and the Baptist name itself has become a byword and a reproach.

In looking for an explanation of this wide-spread apathy and inefficiency among the churches in former years, it is readily found in the fact that they, nearly all, had drank in the spirit of Antinomianism. Opposition to works, as the name itself indicates, was a cardinal dogma, held with unflinching tenacity by the ministers and the leading members of the churches. This error, so fatal in its practical bearings, was the logical result of those hyper-Calvinistic tenets which constituted the staple of pulpit ministrations. Resolving all questions of religious experience into the decrees of divine sovereignty, believing that the salvation of the elect was determined by an eternal purpose, irrespective of agencies, our fathers taught that an attempt to instruct an inquirer, or plead with an impenitent person, would be a presumptuous interference with the inscrutable purposes of God. When God wanted to convict or convert a sinner, he knew where to find him, and how to do it, without the intervention of human effort; and in his own "good time" he would, in his own way, bring his elect into the fold. Accordingly, it was held to be wrong to exhort sinners to repentance, to exert any influence by way of encouragement to troubled hearts. It was counted an excellent sign of being led by the Spirit, if a person remained under silent conviction for years; and to indulge in constant doubts and fears of being accepted, was thought to be one of the brightest evidences of personal election. Parents studiously avoided religious conversation with their children; family prayer was rarely observed. In many instances the logic of the creed made parents doubt the propriety of praying for the conversion of their children, while the idea of teaching an unregenerate child to pray for himself was deemed an approach to sacrilege. The grand argument in all such cases was, — If my child, or neighbor, or friend is one of the elect, God will regenerate him without human intervention; and if he is not one of the elect, no human efforts will avail. These views prevailed throughout the States of New York, New Jersey, Pennsylvania, Delaware, and Maryland.

As a matter of course, in the scheme of such a theology, Sunday schools, missionary enterprises, and protracted meetings could find no place. In our day Christians have learned that Antinomianism is a caricature of the cardinal truths of the gospel. It is not necessary to deny the grand doctrines that are co-related to the central truth of the divine sovereignty, in order to justify the use of means. Let us understand only that it is a part of the divine plan, that his purposes are to be accomplished in answer to the prayers of his people, and as a blessing upon their efforts, and we enter at once into the mind of God, and find our highest inspiration in the confidence that "our labor will not be in vain," because the purposes of God cannot fail of being accomplished.

It is true there were some noble exceptions to this general condition of denominational sentiment. There were a few ministers who began to discern the connection between "the means and end." These noble men have nearly all passed away, but their memories are blessed. They come down as precious legacies, and their works do follow them in the accumulating forces which are now hastening on to usher in the latter-day glories of the Lamb. Elder Benedict was preaching in New York city all the Bible doctrines practically and successfully. His labors were abundant, and he reaped a plentiful harvest. Hundreds were converted under his ministry, and two large churches grew directly out of the results of his endeavors. He labored to the last, and fell in the midst of the harvest field, and went to his reward with sweat-drops of toil unwiped from his brow.

Many of the more intelligent ministers of the denomination began, along from 1820 to 1830, to take an interest in missions, Sunday schools, and temperance and anti-slavery reforms. These latter movements, as might be expected, found their bitterest opponents in those who affected such zealous anxiety for the undisturbed decrees of God. They were startled from their lethargy only by their hostility to the encroachments of these new measures. They became active, not to save souls, and elevate society, but to oppose those who had set themselves to promote "every good word and work." But as they had no conversions, and scarcely any additions to their churches, except as they were recruited by those who left churches where the leaven of Christian effort was beginning to work, they were soon destined to die out from exhaustion. And, as they exercised themselves mainly in finding fault with those who "had a mind to work" for God, they made me think of a goose who would sit all summer on a few round stones, hiss off any who might propose to supply her with eggs, and finally get up without hatching a gosling.

Now, I do not think that I am claiming too much when I say, that among the agencies which God has specially honored in breaking up this apathetic state of the churches, in bringing into the ranks of the ministry men earnest in winning souls, and into the ranks of the laymen men zealous in supporting all our benevolent enterprises, in laboring in Sunday schools, and in working for the conversion of sinners, the early efforts of evangelists, of men specially devoted to holding protracted meetings, are to be recognized as preëminent.

Shortly before I started as an evangelist, the Lord had raised up among the Presbyterians Charles G. Finney and Jedediah Burchard. And God, as we all know, has crowned the labors of these devoted men with marvellous success. They went forth weeping; but they have already returned rejoicing, bringing the sheaves of an abundant harvest with them. In addition to the number of individual souls that have been converted through their labors, who can fully estimate the influence which they have exerted in breaking up the set forms, the stereotyped prayers, which once characterized the Presbyterian denomination, and turning it out of the old ruts in which it had been heretofore content to trudge along?

It was impossible that men of this stamp could invade established usages, and assail cherished opinions, without encountering opposition and persecution. Men who preach the same sentiments, and adopt the same measures to-day, find themselves borne along on the current of popular sympathy; but this was not the case then. Besides, talk as we may about the eccentricities of some of these earlier evangelists, it required men of marked individuality of character and unwavering purpose, in order to attract public attention, and bear up under the fearful persecutions which every innovation must invariably encounter.

Among Baptists, at the time when I started out, there was no one man who stood forth as the champion and exemplar of revival measures. I felt that I was entering upon a path that had not been trodden before me. Since then and shortly afterwards, God raised up others, such as Jabez Swan, A. C. Kingsley, Lewis Raymond, men of God, who have done valiant things for the truth, and who, amid much obloquy, have toiled on, and until those who survive can to-day rejoice with me in beholding that grand revolution in the sentiments of the Baptist denomination which recognizes the preëminent value of that very agency which we ventured to employ when it cost us many sacrifices and sorrows.

One source of opposition to revival measures arose from conscientious misgivings as to the scripturalness of the system. The hyper-Calvinistic notions which had been instilled into the churches had wrought out a wide-spread misapprehension of the way in which God purposed to fulfil his own promises. The idea that God's people could do anything as a means of promoting a revival was scouted as an impiety. The ministers taught that the strength of the church consisted in "lying still;" that, inasmuch as regeneration was the sovereign work of the Holy Spirit, God would in his own good time effectually call those whom he purposed to save, and that the only duty of the church was to wait. If a church proposed to meet, and spend a season in fasting and prayer for the outpouring of God's Spirit, it was said that they were interfering with the divine prerogative; and the use of any special overtures to induce sinners to repent and give their hearts to God, was denounced as attempts at "man-made conversions."

It was not understood that God also was waiting to bless his people, and waiting, too, to "be inquired of by the house of Israel to do this thing for them." It was not understood that the way in which God would have his people wait upon him, was as the apostles waited at Jerusalem for the descent of the Holy Spirit, — with prayer and supplication. Christians seemed to have forgotten that "faith cometh by hearing," and that the apostles besought men to "be reconciled to God," even day and night, and "with tears." Thus the people of God had lost sight of the obligation of every disciple to do all he could to present the gospel to every man, and satisfied themselves with offsetting the untiring activity of the devil and his emissaries to compass the ruin of men, by harping on the inscrutable and unchangeable purposes of God.

Many thought me crazy when I urged the members of the church to go from house to house, and compel sinners to come in to the services of the sanctuary. The first persons whom I succeeded in starting out in this work, in the city of New York, went forth under the inspiration that this was God's method, and returned at night with their faces beaming with light and love, amazed at their success, and wondering what they had been dreaming all their lifetime before.

I remember an interesting incident in which a devoted servant of Christ — one, too, active and successful in winning souls in spite of his creed — was affected at one of my meetings in the city of New York during the year 1835. As I was preparing the way for the inquirers to come forward to be prayed for, brother Duncan Dunbar stepped up to me, and whispered in my ear, "Brother Knapp, it will not do to call sinners to the anxious seats in this city; the prejudices of the people will not admit of it." I replied, "I am not going to be crowded into the gutters by the prejudices of the people; I am going straight through, let the consequences be what they may." The invitation was then given; upon which some thirty souls came forward, weeping and begging for mercy. Brother Dunbar, seeing this expression, at once arose and seconded the appeal, when several others came forward.

Although the meetings which I held were crowned with the conversion of many souls, yet there were not a few good people who were afraid that these conversions were not genuine. It was said that the people were excited into professing religion, without understanding its meaning or feeling its power. For my own part, I never could see why men might properly become excited on other subjects, but must invariably approach the momentous question of salvation with all the proprieties of an imperturbable deliberation. It seemed to me that the record of the acts of the apostles is a history of excitements, under which the world was verily turned upside down.

Others, again, were opposed to sudden conversions. They said the seed must have time to germinate. They forgot that the word of God "was quick and powerful," and overlooked the facts by which God has illustrated the operations of the Holy Spirit. I preferred to take my examples of God's methods of converting men from his own inspired account, rather than to accept, as a specimen, the fossilized mummies which Antinomianism had embalmed. And in the New Testament records I learned that three thousand persons were "pricked in their hearts" under the preaching of one sermon, and were converted and baptized in one day; that the eunuch received the truth as soon as it was presented to him, and was baptized at once; that Paul was stricken down in a moment, and in a moment gave his heart to Jesus, and after three days' delay was remonstrated with for his tardiness in not being immediately baptized; that the jailer and his household repented, believed, and were baptized in one night. Believing that God was unchangeable in the laws of his grace, I did not see why similar manifestations of the power of God would not attend similar exercises of faith, prayer, and effort now. I saw nothing in the Bible which led me to believe that it was a part of the plan of God that in our generation men were to rest under silent convictions for six months, or six years, in order to make genuine and thorough their final conversion to Christ.

It was also very common, in those days, to teach that doubts and fears of being converted were marked proofs of sound piety. If a man spoke of "peace in believing," and was disposed to "rejoice with joy unspeakable and full of glory," he was looked upon as spiritually proud, and giving premonitions of a speedy fall. All such expressions were discouraged, and it was thought that the grace of God was specially magnified by doubting the willingness of God to bestow it. As a matter of course, therefore, young people, on coming into the church, felt themselves under a restraint, and it was no unusual thing for a recent convert to find his remarks or efforts the subject of cautionary animadversions from some of the brethren who were reputed for their soundness in the faith. Alas! in how many instances has the ardor of a young Christian been dampened, and his entire character dwarfed, and his influence deadened, by the croaking of some of these fearful Malaprops, whose only zeal seemed to consist in assuring the converts that "they must not expect to feel so happy or so interested always." In fact, the attitude of the church was that of distrust as to the genuineness of anybody's conversion. It seemed to be taken for granted that every applicant at the doors of the church must be either a hypocrite or the victim of self-delusion; and the main business of these wiseacres, these men who assumed to steady the ark of God, was to keep them out until one's piety could be demonstrated by its ability to survive all their refusals to encourage it. In this way were the lambs of the flock cared for, and this was the kind of nurture by which it was proposed to "feed the church of God."

Another class opposed me from feelings of jealousy. As my success increased, their hostility to my work gathered strength. Their own want of pulpit power, the absence of conversions under their preaching, made them envious of the blessings that rested on the labors of others, and they sought vent for their vexation by calling in question the reality and permanency of results in which they could claim no share. They feared that a powerful presentation of the truth, and a large increase of members as a consequence, would beget a distaste for their own ministry, and they loved themselves, their ease, their pride, more than the salvation of souls.

Others opposed my ministry because they disliked my peculiar methods of presenting the gospel. They thought the better way was to give no offence to any man, but to study to please all. The prejudices, the errors, the vices of men must not be assailed. It was better to charm with smooth words and fair speeches, to keep the more offensive truths of the Bible out of sight, to say but little about total depravity and hell torments, and not to make too free a use of the name of the devil, lest his Satanic majesty might be displeased, and get up a persecution.

I do not pass judgment on the sincerity or piety of many who would have preferred to pursue a more man-pleasing policy. I can only say that God had cast me in a different mould, and I felt that he had called me to do a work which men of that plastic type would not be adapted to perform. Besides, I regarded the tendency of the doctrine of expediency as dangerous, and subversive of the great truths of the gospel. Whenever Christianity shall become palatable to the tastes of unregenerate men, the "offence of the cross" will have ceased. The triumphs of the cross are not to be achieved by getting on the right side of men, but by keeping on the right side of God. Christianity is not a doll, that is to be dressed up in fine clothing, with silver slippers and gold rings, but is a stern and uncompromising assailant of all forms of worldliness, and gaining the good will of men only as it subdues them to the power of godliness. The gospel can never adapt itself to the preferences of sinful men.

Conquests for Christianity, on this principle, are practical surrenders of its principles to those it undertakes to oppose. This is essentially the policy of Romanism, which, in seeking to convert pagans to Christianity, transferred the rites of paganism to the services of the church, and thus converted Christians into pagans.

For my own part, I felt that, if I sought to please men, I should not be a servant of Christ. I thought it was as true today as of old, that "he who would live godly in Christ Jesus must suffer persecution." I continually heard a voice ringing in my ears, "Woe unto you when all men speak well of you." Under these convictions, I felt constrained to call things by their right names, to use most simple language, the most direct arguments, and most matter-of-fact illustrations. I went forth, therefore, placing no reliance upon literary pretensions, beautiful sermons, fine meeting-houses, large organs, and splendid choirs, but trusting in the willingness of the Holy Spirit to make effectual the simple, plain, and straightforward presentation to the understandings and consciences of men of his own revealed truths.

Such were some of the difficulties with which I was called to contend in entering upon the work of an evangelist. I was not surprised, nor disappointed, nor discouraged, as they continued to present themselves in my path. My early discipline prepared me to bear up under trials, and had taught me that it was "better to trust in the Lord than to put confidence in princes." I had nothing to hope, and nothing to fear, from man. All expectations or desires for honors from men were crucified; and I constantly prayed that I might not be left to the influence of such considerations. I took counsel of no man, but daily sought God as the guide of my ways. My labors, though ignored by the religious press for many years, resulted in the conversion of more during a given number of years than all the conversions reported by our missionaries in the home field.

In addition to the consolation of knowing that my labors for souls were not in vain, I had the satisfaction of receiving the coöperation and confidence of the ministers and churches with whom I held meetings, and, as a general thing, they became my fast friends. In this way, as I went over the country, public opinion was gradually changed. I shall carry to my grave the remembrance of very many warm-hearted brethren, who laid themselves on the altar with me, and wept, and prayed, and toiled for the conversion of the world. Many of these are now in heaven. Nor were those who gave me their countenance men of our own denomination only; but among others there were not a few who said, "It is the work of the Lord." Among these I may make special mention of the Episcopal bishop in Maryland, Dr. Taylor of Yale College, and Dr. Nott of Union College. Dr. Nott was an enthusiastic friend. His whole moral nature was moved by the power and simplicity of the truth.

In the mean time, as I continued to labor, other ministers caught the spirit of evangelism. Pastors began to preach with more power, and sought to do all they could for the salvation of their people; and God, who is faithful to his promises, gave them marked success. Many of them went forth from their own immediate fields to assist neighboring pastors, and adopted the measures which had proved so successful with evangelists. Thus the work extended all through the United States. Converts were multiplied by tens of thousands; while those churches which did not sympathize with these new measures died out, and those ministers who opposed the progress of evangelical effort are forgotten, or are remembered only as men who misinterpreted the signs of the times.

And at the present day, I am permitted, as I look over the increased ranks of the Baptist ministry, to recognize scores and hundreds of honored and successful laborers in the vineyard who were converted in protracted meetings; and to count by thousands, laymen, now active, benevolent, and laborious in every good word and work, who were brought to Christ in connection with special efforts and revival measures.

CHAPTER V.

ACCOUNTS OF PROTRACTED MEETINGS.

(1832–4.)

Union Meetings. — *Why discontinued.* — *Duty of Baptists.* — *Blessed Meetings.* — *An Answer to Prayer.* — *Departed Worthies.* — NORTH RUTLAND: "*The Bower of Prayer.*" — *Deacon Woodward and the Young Men.* — TURIN: *Universalism.* — *A Universalist Mother.* — *Threatened Suit.* — *Mr. P.* — CONSTABLEVILLE: *Barn and Pork House.* — *Colonel M.* — *A Drunkard's Wife.* — *A Vision.*

DURING the period between the years 1832 and 1834, I held meetings in all the principal towns in the Counties of Jefferson, Lewis, and Oswego, and in many towns in Cayuga County. Throughout these two years I usually called in the aid of all evangelical denominations, namely, the Baptist Methodist, Presbyterian, and Congregational. All labored together, and I was content to leave the division of the spoils with the pastors and churches after I had gone. But I found this method fraught with serious evils.

In the first place, the different churches were almost always sure to quarrel about their respective share of the converts. The churches, in these small country villages, were generally more or less feeble; and each felt that its very existence depended on these accessions. This contention would stop the revival, the wicked would triumph, and devils hold a jubilee in hell.

In the second place, my conscience was not at ease. I was commissioned to go and "teach all nations, baptizing them in the name of the Father, and of the Son, and of the Holy Spirit." I asked myself, "How can I give a good account of my stewardship, if I do not fully carry out my commission?"

I loved all God's children; I delighted to labor with them. Everything calculated to divide or interrupt our union was painful to my feelings, and for a long time my mind was unsettled. I thought much on the subject, and prayed for wisdom from above. At length the subject came up before me in this form: "Suppose I should die to-night, and at the judgment Jesus should call me to him and say, 'My servant, Jacob, have you carried out your commission, preached my gospel, discipled and baptized?' I should be compelled to reply, 'I have preached thy blessed gospel as faithfully as I knew how; have made many disciples; sometimes I have baptized, and sometimes I have not.' 'Why did you sometimes not baptize?' I imagined my Savior to ask; and I supposed myself obliged to say, 'Well, Master, my Pedo-Baptist brethren had adopted the recent custom of sprinkling, and I could not carry out thy commission without giving offence.'" I concluded that it were better for me to go to the stake, than be under the necessity of meeting my Lord and Savior with a lame reply like this. What if Jesus should answer me, "He that loveth father and mother, husband and wife, more than me, is not worthy of me"!

I therefore made up my mind to carry out my commission regardless of all consequences; nor do I love my Pedo-Baptist brethren any the less, nor do I value Christian union any the less. But I have become convinced that the true way in which to bring about Christian union, to incorporate all Christians in one body, is to do away with all the errors which now divide them; and when we have one faith, then we can have one church, one baptism, and one communion. All attempts to bring antagonistic elements together have been, and must ever be, abortive. "How can two walk together, except they be agreed?" In the meantime we should harbor no sectarian feelings, no prejudice against those of other names, see to it that no selfishness mingles in our devotions, appreciate all that is good in those who differ from us, and, as far as we can, work together for the conversion of the world.

And I think that if all Baptists would carry out the commission in the right spirit, and turn not to the right or to the left in all revivals, and on all occasions; baptize converts as fast as they believe; never cringe, never exult, and be a little more patient, all the children of God would soon be led to see their errors; abandon infant baptism, and adopt immersion; then we are all substantially one. Other minor differences might exist for a while, but in process of time they would vanish away, and the great end, for which so many pious hearts are yearning and praying, would be reached.

Although during this period I baptized comparatively few of those who were converted under my preaching, yet I baptized over eight hundred; being about the same number as was reported to have been baptized by all the Baptist missionaries of the home field within the same length of time. Notwithstanding this success, my work was looked upon with suspicion, and scarcely alluded to in the public prints. I was forty years ahead of the times.

I have never witnessed, before nor since, such exhibitions of divine power, such earnest holding on in prayer. Not unfrequently the people of God would continue till the break of day in supplication for the outpouring of the Spirit, or the conversion of particular persons. There were many remarkable instances of answers to prayer. The ministers, and many of the leading members, seemed to be filled with the Spirit of God; and in many instances, when brethren knelt around a convicted sinner, they would not rise until his soul had been set at liberty, and was rejoicing "in hope of the glory of God."

I remember one occasion in which a company of sisters repaired to a grove to pray. Three hardened young men followed them with the intention of disturbing their devotions; but as they drew near to the spot, the one in advance fell to the ground, then the next, and then the next. A company of brethren, apprehending trouble, had followed them, and came upon them as they lay prostrate and helpless. They lifted them up, and took them back to the anxious meeting, where they continued in great agony of soul, until they were converted to

God. One of them tried hard to resist the strivings of the Spirit, but at length, crying out, "O, my knees! must you bow for the first time?" knelt in prayer, and made a complete surrender to the sceptre of Christ. I ought to have mentioned, when these sisters saw these young men coming, they cried out mightily to God that he would smite them to the earth with his convicting power. Their prayers were answered. This occurrence took place in Orleans, Jefferson County, N. Y., in 1832.

At the close of this meeting I baptized sixty persons in thirty minutes.

By this time (1867), all the ministers, and many of the brethren, who labored with me in those days, are dead. Among them I may mention Elders Little, Warner, Clarke, Freeman, Cooke, Waters, Wedge, and Horr. Some of them prayed and toiled themselves to death. They died on the field of battle, with their armor on. How strange it seems that I am permitted to outlive them all, when I was expecting to be among the first to cross over Jordan, as I did more of the preaching, and performed the hardest part of the labor!

North Rutland.

Strictly speaking, an account of the meeting held in North Rutland, Jefferson County, does not belong to a summary of my labors as a formal Evangelist. "A meeting of days" was held, in 1832, with the Baptist church in this place, then under the pastoral care of Elder Little. Several neighboring ministers had been invited to attend, and preach by turns. I was among the number.

The spirit of the meeting was very precious; and I, especially, have reason to remember it, because the impressions made on my mind while here, went very far towards bringing me to a decision to devote myself henceforth to the work of an Evangelist. At that time, I was in a great conflict between inclination and conviction. I was feeling that God was calling me to go forth into the field, but the sacrifices appeared too great. I could not bring myself to consent to leave the endearments of home and depend for support on the precarious contributions of the churches with which I might be called to labor.

While being agitated with these reflections, I went to one of these meetings, and heard, for the first time, the brethren and sisters sing the hymn called "The Bower of Prayer." As I listened to the sweet fulness of this hymn, the tears fell thick and fast down my cheeks. I requested them to sing it a second time, and my tears continued to flow. One verse in particular seemed so appropriate to my case, and awakened so many recollections of my struggles, that I was completely melted into tenderness, and at the same time was exalted into the ecstasy of a precious and entire acquiescence in the will of God.

"To leave my dear friends, and with neighbors to part,
And go from my home, it affects not my heart
Like the thought of absenting myself for a day
From that blest retreat where I've chosen to pray."

At the end of the first week the pastors returned to their homes; and as yet there had been no special work among the unconverted. The brethren of the church were unwilling to have the meetings close without more marked results, and they continued to "wait on the Lord." In the course of the week following I returned to Rutland, and found a work of grace in the church and community of marvellous power.

During this meeting one incident occurred, so remarkable, that I would scarcely venture to relate it if I did not know it to be true. Deacon Spencer Woodward, of Bellville, a man of strong faith, and "full of the Holy Spirit," fell in with a company of hardened scoffers, as they were standing on the village "green," mocking the saints of the Most High. One of them had a cane, the head of which consisted of a piece of deer's horn: and as the deacon was passing, in order to cast derision on the services of religion, he was asking his young companions, to whom he was extending his cane, to come forward and lay hold on "the horns of the altar."

Father Woodward stopped, and turning to them, remarked,

"Young men, if you knew what you were about, I should think your damnation sealed, and should not think it worth while to waste my breath on your account; but you are ignorant of the things of the kingdom of God. On this evening you will be made to see the power of the Almighty."

He induced them to enter the meeting-house, though it was some time before sundown and there was no service as yet, and, leading them into a pew, and shutting the door (it was an old-fashioned pew with a straight back and a high door), told them that nobody would disturb them. "Now," said he, "brace yourselves, for God is about to come down in great power." He then knelt in prayer in the aisle at the pew door. He got hold truly of "the horns of the altar," and the "Holy One came down from Teram." The young men trembled like Belshazzar when he saw the hand writing on the wall. Some of them got down on the floor, and their knees knocked against each other and against the sides of the pew. Soon one of them sank down to the floor utterly helpless. One of his companions reached over and whispered to father Woodward, "Uncle Spencer, Jim is a dying." "Get some water," said father W., "and fetch him to; don't let him die." One of them ran for water, but his hands trembled so that he spilt half of it out of the pail before he reached the prostrate man. The deacon told them to lift him up, adding, "I told you that God was coming down; now prepare to meet him." Two of the stoutest of the young men took hold of him, but they could not lift him; their strength failed them. The deacon raised the young man up, his consciousness soon returned, and very shortly afterwards he was converted.

Some of the others, also, were led by this event to seek and find salvation. One of them, however, by the name of Coburn, was smitten down during the meeting that evening, and carried to Elder Little's house, where he remained till midnight, insensible. When he had sufficiently recovered his strength, he went home, swearing that he would not submit to God, even though he was sent to "hell" before morning. About a year after this he was found among the scoffers, during a meeting of days that was being held in the same town. Again he was stricken to the floor by the hand of God, while sitting in a prayer-meeting, and again he resisted the Spirit. Some time in the course of the following year I received information that this hardened young man was smitten down the third time, and in this instance was smitten by the hand of death. He was "driven away in his wickedness" — a fearful example of the possibility and danger of striving against God.

TURIN.

In the course of these two years, 1832–1834, I was called, in the providence of God, to attend a meeting of days in Turin, Lewis County, N. Y. At that time there was no church of any denomination in the village. The town was called "Satan's seat." The people had built one meeting-house, which was free for anybody to preach in, whether they preached truth or error.

A number of Christian people of different names combined together to get up a meeting, and then extended to me an invitation to preach. When I arrived I found a number of ministers of the gospel of different names there, praying together, and ready to lend a helping hand for the conversion of the place. Most of the men of business were infidel or Universalist in sentiment. I commenced preaching day and night, and opened prayer-meetings in different places. The people came in. The Spirit began to manifest his power, and sinners were converted.

But opposition soon began to arise and develop itself more and more. When speaking on the tendency or effects of Universalism one evening, I related the following fact which took place in that village: —

A boy, whose mother was a Universalist, stepped into a store one day, in the absence of the merchant, and took from the drawer all the money it contained. As he was going out at the front door, the merchant was coming in at the back door, and recognized him. The merchant, knowing him to be a bad boy, followed and caught him, and accused him of having stolen money from his drawer. The boy denied the charge, calling on God to witness his innocence; but the money was found in his pocket. The merchant asked him what he thought would become of him if he continued to steal, and lie, and call on the name of God. The boy looked him impudently in the face, and replied, "I don't care if I do lie and steal; there is no hell; mother tells me so." The Universalists did not fancy such a naked, unvarnished application of the tendency of their doctrines. So they stirred up the wicked, set the town in an uproar, and got out a summons for me, with the intention of breaking up the meeting and of being revenged on me. Squire P. agreed to carry on the suit free of charge; others subscribed five dollars each to meet expenses, and it was reported through the town that "Knapp had lied; had slandered a poor widow, and was going to be prosecuted."

I called a council of war, and after praying over it and consulting together, we unanimously resolved to go on, regardless of what any one might say or do, and trust events in the hands of God. I was then young, and had had but little experience in such matters. I entered the pulpit, told the brethren that possibly the sheriff might call for me before I had finished my discourse, and that if he did I should go to jail, and I wished them to go on with the meeting; and that, if I could get bail on the limits, I would open a protracted meeting there, and we would kindle a fire on both sides of the devil, and burn him out. These remarks aroused the brethren, and seemed to carry them back to the days of the apostles, and they cried unto God mightily.

But no sheriff appeared. On that afternoon, however, I received a note from my persecutors, stating that if I would make a handsome apology they would pass the matter over; if not, that the suit should go on; and that they would all come out that evening to the meeting in order to hear my apology. That night the house was crowded to its utmost capacity. All were excited to the highest pitch; some were praying and looking beyond all creature aid; some were cursing, and some were smitten in their hearts. I think my text for that evening was,

"And thou mourn at the last, when thy flesh and thy body are consumed, and say, How have I hated instruction, and my heart despised reproof" (Prov. v. 11, 12); and if I ever felt that I stood between the living and the dead, I felt so that night. The solemnities of the eternal world gathered around us, and settled on the whole congregation; some sank down in their seats, helpless, before I had finished my sermon. Not a dog moved his tongue. We spent a season in prayer, and several were converted on the spot; others were unable to get home without assistance. Colonel F., a dry goods merchant, could not stand on his feet; several of the brethren helped him to his house, and staid with him all night. He was brought into light and liberty before morning. Strange to say, his wife continued hardened, and was heard to say, repeatedly, that she would rather that her husband lose all his property than to have lived to become a Christian. If I am not mistaken, she was, notwithstanding, brought to give her heart to Christ some time afterwards.

From that hour the work rolled on until the most of the village was converted to God. The lawyer who offered to carry on the suit was among the converts. A Dr. D. and wife were converted. A wealthy man by the name of P., a confirmed Universalist, who had subscribed five dollars towards the suit, and who laid his hand on the Bible, and swore that he would cowhide any man who should darken his door to talk with him or his family on the subject of religion, was made a signal trophy of redeeming grace. His family likewise shared in the blessing. He stated before a large congregation, that when he was a Universalist he was angry with God because he would not let him live in this world forever. He said he knew God might if he would, but now he could rejoice in the hope of a better life beyond the grave; and he added, "Should it please God to call me from this stand, I could go rejoicing, without even returning to take leave of my dear wife and children."

The victory of the people of God in this place was complete.

The devil was vanquished. Error was driven like chaff before a mighty wind; and I learned, from experience, that it was "better to trust in the Lord than to put confidence in princes."

CONSTABLEVILLE.

Shortly after this meeting, I held another in Constableville, in the same county. This is a beautiful village, nestling among the mountains, in a fertile valley. The only house of worship in this place, at that time, was an Episcopal church; but into this, of course, I could gain no admittance. But the Christian friends in the community turned out, and fitted up a large, newly-built barn, and built a bower on each side, so that two thousand people could be accommodated. Here we conducted an anxious-meeting, separate from the congregation which was listening to the preaching. As fast as one was brought under the influence of the Holy Spirit, and could be induced to go, he was led to the inquiry-meeting. The ungodly called it "the finishing-off-room."

While we were in want of such a room, Colonel Miller, a wealthy gentleman, offered the use of his old store, which he was then occupying for the purpose of packing pork. It was thankfully accepted; and he politely sent his hired man to assist in cleaning and fitting it up. Though a perfect gentleman, he would sometimes indulge in a sly joke with his friends, in a pleasant way, about the ministers taking the anxious to his "pork-shop" in order to get them converted. But it pleased God to touch his heart, and that of his noble wife. They were brought into great distress. They continued to attend the meetings at the barn; came forward, and rose, and asked for prayers. I, with one or two others, went to their house, and spent the whole night with them in reading the Scriptures and prayer; but no relief could they obtain. Others were being converted, and they began to deem themselves forsaken of God.

One afternoon, as I was about to preach, he arose, and begged prayers for himself and wife, and stated that they were nearly in despair. The suggestion was made, that perhaps he had set up his will against going to the pork-room; if so, that room lay between him and the kingdom of God. He saw the force of the remark, and turning to his wife, said, "If you are willing to go down to the pork-room, I will go with you. It is a bitter pill, but we may as well die in one way as another; we cannot live so." She took him by the arm, and they walked down to the pork-room, bowed in prayer, and both, there and then, found peace, and returned to their home rejoicing. We had in this meeting a blessed time. Very many souls were converted; I cannot say how many.

I remember the case of a poor woman, the daughter of a silk-merchant in India, who had married against her parents' wishes. Her husband had become a drunkard, and removed to this country. Here he became a sot, neglected his family, spent all his earnings in strong drink, and left his wife and children to shift for themselves. She came six miles to attend the meeting, with a babe in her arms, leaving the other children at home with only potatoes and salt to eat. She felt that all of her prospects for this life were blighted, and that there was the more reason why she should have a good hope for the next. She soon found Jesus precious to her soul, and went home with a light heart, rejoicing in the love of God.

Another circumstance occurred in this meeting, which I will relate, leaving the reader to make his own comments. There was, in an obscure part of the town, a pious woman in lowly circumstances, who had been longing for the consolation of Israel, and praying for the outpouring of the Spirit. In the visions of the night, she saw two men come into the town, and with long poles stir up the pond, which lay on the outskirts of the place, until the water became quite muddy; that then a wind arose, and swept, with mighty power, over it, driving off all the disturbed sediment which had been brought to the surface; then the face of the water became pure and calm. When this meeting commenced, she saw two men whom she distinctly recognized as those whom she had beheld in her dream. And when she perceived that they were engaging in the work of the Lord, she interpreted her vision as a prediction of a visitation from God, which would stir up the depths of wickedness in the place, and purify and bless it with the winds of his gracious and resistless love.

CHAPTER VI.

ACCOUNTS OF PROTRACTED MEETINGS.

(1832–4.)

RUTLAND HILL: *Holding on.* — *Great Results.* — *An alarmed Professor.* — *A good Conscience.* — *"Old Fogies."* — *A new Church.* — LORAINE: *Suspension of Business.* — *Three Meeting-Houses.* — *A Mother's Command.* — HANNIBAL CENTRE: *A cold Beginning.* — *Universalist Reporters.* — *A drunken Apostate.* — OSWEGO: *Peter S. Smith.* — *Power of Earnestness.* — *A real Religion.* — *Restitution.*

RUTLAND HILL.

ABOUT this time I attended a meeting at Rutland Hill, Jefferson County, preaching in the Congregational church. I labored ten days,'and was blessed with only five converts. The place was overrun with infidelity and Universalism. In the evenings all turned out and filled the house. Many were somewhat affected, but they did not break down. In those days, ten days were thought to be a long time in which to protract religious services. Three days' meetings were considered all that could be profitably sustained.

During these ten days we had all worked very hard, and were greatly worn down. We had not husbanded our strength. I had preached three times every day; and the brethren prayed as long and as loud as they could, and some half dozen of them had kept it up day and night. We were all either hoarse or suffering from sore throats.

We took counsel of ourselves and of God, as to what course to pursue. We remembered the promise, "In due time we shall reap if we faint not." So we concluded to take God at his word, and "go forward." I went to the pulpit, and the helpers went to the anxious-room. About twenty inquirers were present. They induced them all to kneel down; one of the inquirers summoned courage to open his mouth in prayer. He was at once set at liberty, and broke forth into earnest prayer for the salvation of others; these, in turn, went to praying for themselves, and as "God turned their captivity," they, too, prayed for their friends, until the whole twenty were brought to rejoice in the Savior.

After I had concluded the preaching service, many of the unconverted, attracted by the voice of prayer, went into the anxious-room. Several of them fell on their knees, and cried aloud for mercy. The converts began to plead with the anxious until until all in the room were led to surrender their hearts to Christ. The brethren could only "stand still and see the salvation of God." The good work went on with increasing power, much as on the day of Pentecost. Infidelity turned pale, and Universalism gave up the ghost. It was a time of deep heart-searching among Christians.

One lady, a member in good standing in the Congregational church, came to me, and said she thought she was not a Christian, and wanted to know what she should "do to be saved." I told her to go to God and cry for help. She went to her chamber, in the same house in which I was boarding, and, falling on her knees, continued in prayer for the space of two hours, when a sister came to me, and expressed her fears that the lady was dying, and asked me to go up to her room, and see what could be done. I found her still in a pleading posture, agony depicted on her face, and her eyes turned towards heaven. She could scarcely speak above a whisper. At first I was alarmed, fearing that she might die, and that her death would be attributed to me. I was on the point of requesting her to cease her supplications; but this text broke upon my ears as in peals of thunder, "The bruised reed he will not break, and the smoking flax he will not quench, till he send forth judgment unto victory."

I then said, "God will not break the bruised reed, and God

forbid that I should quench the smoking flax; let judgment come forth unto victory." In a few moments her countenance changed, a heavenly smile came over her whole face, and she began to whisper, "Blessed Savior! sweet Jesus! all is well! all is well!" From that day, to the last of my knowledge of her, she testified her conviction that never till then had she seen the preciousness of Christ as her atoning Savior.

Soon afterwards, while standing by the water where I was baptizing, she began to tremble and weep, and turning to a sister, said, "This ordinance never appeared so beautiful to me as now. O that I could be buried with Christ in baptism!" Being informed of her remark, I replied, that "her wish can be gratified now, if she desires;" and one of the sisters putting on a robe that had been already used, I led her down into the water, and she was baptized straightway, and she went on her "way rejoicing."

The Congregational brethren in this place were "old fogies." They would invite neither Finney nor Burchard to labor with them: nor did they get reconverted during this meeting. They did not believe in young converts speaking or praying, for fear they might become proud. They thought the more doubts a person cherished, the better evidence he gave of being a Christian. I left all the converts to go where they pleased. But they had no encouragement to work in this church. The "old fogies" went poking along like an old lazy yoke of oxen, keeping a little ahead of the converts, and hooking them back lest they should go too fast.

Finally, most of the converts went down to South Rutland (called Tylerville), and commenced a meeting by themselves. At their request, I went to their help, and began to blow the gospel trumpet. I found an old Baptist church there, with scarcely "a name to live." We got the old brands together, and besought God to kindle them once more with the fire of his Spirit. I commenced baptizing the converts (about one hundred), and soon went to another field. As I was leaving them, I urged them to continue the work. The revival kept on for nearly six months, and a great number professed faith in Christ.

There was a physician in the place, who stood out against all the means of grace, and became so uneasy and unhappy, that he sold out his property, at a great sacrifice, and went to Canada. He said that "he could not go to his barn, but some one was praying in the hay-mow; he could not go to the woods, but some one was praying behind every brush-heap; that the women pestered his life out of him, tormenting him with their religion, so that he would rather live in purgatory." Well may we ask, "How could the wicked be happy in heaven?" "Verily, ye must be born again."

LORAINE.

In the autumn of 1833, I was invited to labor in Loraine, Jefferson County, N. Y. On my arrival, I called together the three churches of the place, namely, Baptist, Presbyterian, and Methodist, and told them that, in view of other pressing calls, I could not remain in the place long, and would not remain at all, unless they would agree to lay all their business aside, and attend day and night, and work for God as they would work for themselves in harvest time. The response to my appeal was quite cordial and unanimous. "The people had a mind to work." They suspended all business, and waited on the Lord in his courts. We had meetings three times a day — morning, noon, and night. On some occasions we continued all night, the lamps not being put out till daylight. While some left for a time, others came in, and in this way a steady stream of prayer was kept up all night long.

Farmers took their teams through their respective neighborhoods, and brought all to meeting who wished to come. Days of fasting and prayer were observed, and great searching of heart was instituted. Some gave up their former hopes, and sought Christ anew. When one meeting-house was filled, another was opened, until all three were thronged with eager congregations. In many instances, the saints resorted to the groves, and to private houses, to pray, in order that they might make room for sinners, who came "like doves to their windows" to hear the preached word. One meeting-house would be filled with the unconverted to hear preaching; another would be crowded with praying saints; and a third would be thronged with inquirers, for whose benefit an inquiry-meeting was conducted every day by Deacon Tenman, of the Congregational church, and brother Horr, a licentiate. Both these brethren accompanied me for several years after this, praying and conducting meetings for inquiry. These men were filled with faith and the Holy Spirit, and were "*helpers*" in the Bible sense of the word. It was difficult to tell in which of these meetings there was the greatest interest, for the presence and power of God were manifested in them all.

There were numerous displays of God's marvellous grace during this meeting.

A widow lady, living in the village of Adams, six miles off, had a son fourteen years old, who was serving an apprenticeship at French Creek. While on a visit to his home he heard of our meetings, and of his sister's conversion there. His mother desired him to go over to Loraine; he replied, "Mother, I did not come home to go to meeting; I came to visit you, and must soon return to my employer." She told him that his trade would do him but little good, if he should lose his soul. She finally commanded him to go, urging him to make himself known to Elder Knapp or Deacon Tenman. God prepared his heart as he journeyed on the way; and reaching the steps of the church, he stood by the door, weeping. At that moment the deacon was passing by, and noticed him. Putting his hand very kindly on the shoulder of the lad, he asked him what was the matter. He told his errand, and the deacon, taking him by the hand, led him into the inquiry-room, and asked all to pray for him.

After an affecting season had been spent in prayer, the lad rose up, and going to the deacon, told him that he wanted to go home. "What," said the deacon, "are you tired of the meeting so soon?" "No, sir," he replied, "but I must see my mother; I will come back again." He hastened home with a light heart, and rushing into the house, he fell on his mother's neck, and kissing her, exclaimed, "O, my dear mother, I thank you a thousand times, that you compelled me to attend that meeting! I have found the blessed Savior, and all my sins are forgiven me." This mother was like unto "Abraham, who commanded his house after him."

Hannibal Centre.

During this same year, I held a meeting in Hannibal Centre, Oswego County, N. Y. On entering the Baptist meeting-house, I found the building cold; the wood that had been brought in was covered with snow, and would not burn. The congregation was small, and their hearts as cold as the weather. A brother some time afterwards reminded me (though I had forgotten it), that after a few of them had prayed as well as they could, I rose up and remarked, that "such prayers as these will freeze us all to death."

But we held on to the promises, and the blessing came. The people soon began to flock to hear the word, and the house was filled. I pitched into Universalism as usual. And after all supposed I had exhausted my thoughts and my vocabulary, I announced that on a given night I should preach another sermon on Universalism. Two of the leading members of that sect came in to take notes for their newspaper. The power of God confounded his enemies, and vindicated the truth. Both of these reporters were converted. Elder Woodin was the pastor of this church.

A man by the name of K., with whom I had boarded in Springfield before my marriage, was then living some eight miles from this place. He had given way to the use of strong drink; his property was squandered, his family were reduced to want, his wife was dead, and he was excluded from the church. I had not seen them for years; and now that I was so near to them, it seemed to me that the departed spirit of sister K. was continually saying to me, "Look after my poor motherless children." This impression became so strong, that I induced Captain Bullen, an excellent brother, with whom I was boarding, to send a sleigh after them, and bring them to me.

While brother Luther Myrick was preaching, a daughter of sister K. came into the church. Though she had grown up, and was then married, I knew her in a moment, and began to plead with God for her soul. After the sermon was finished, and the anxious were invited forward, she rose up at once, and was converted before she left the house.

The son I did not see, but I sent for the father. I brought all my power to bear on him to persuade him to reform. I reminded him of his former respectable standing; of his loving companion, whose heart he had broken. I told him of the crucified Savior, whose blood he had trampled under foot, and warned him of the hell that awaited him; but all to no purpose. The devil had made such a cowardly sneak of him, that he dared not meet his drunken associates, and tell them of his reformation. This was where the shoe pinched. So the poor fellow went over the dam.

During this meeting scores were converted. To God be all the glory.

Oswego.

While I was living in Watertown, a messenger came from Oswego, N. Y., to urge me to go to that town, and assist brother Myrick, a Congregationalist minister, in a meeting already begun. There were some indications for good before I reached there, and the work continued to increase in interest and power.

Among many others, who bowed at the feet of Jesus, was Mr. Peter S. Smith, a brother of Gerritt Smith.* He was a splendid man at the bar, and a member of the vestry of the Episcopal church. When this man took a stand for Christ, the

* Gerritt Smith has been widely known, and will ever be remembered and honored as a champion of anti-slavery, and an exemplar of noble philanthropy.

tide of salvation seemed to sweep on with mighty power; many, who had hitherto ignored the work as mere excitement, began to think that there was a divine reality in it, and multitudes believed, both of men and women.

Of course here, as elsewhere, some, even professed Christians, opposed this way of laboring for God, and "some doubted." All was new to them. Nevertheless, it was impossible that earnest prayers should be constantly offered, that solemn and sometimes vehement sermons should be preached, and that the most touching appeals should be made, and the most awful warnings given, together with personal overtures to individual consciences, without producing an excitement and making an impression. I remember well a remark made by Judge Hart to a friend of his (neither of them professors of religion). I was walking behind them, one dark and dreary night, and heard the strange gentleman say, "Judge, what do you think of this excitement?" The judge replied, "I like it; it makes religion a reality." This was a word of great encouragement, and it implied a great deal.

A dry goods merchant, whose wife was a member of the Baptist church, was brought to see his lost condition; his distress increased daily until sleep departed from him. His agony became unendurable. At a late hour, one night, he sent out for brother Savage, the pastor, and myself to come over and pray for him. It was soon discovered that, in a business transaction, he had defrauded a man out of one hundred and fifty dollars. As soon as he had made mention of this, and of his purpose to make restitution, he found peace to his soul.

The number of converts at this meeting was counted by hundreds; they were scattered among the different churches, never to be gathered together again until the morning of the resurrection.

CHAPTER VII.

ACCOUNTS OF PROTRACTED MEETINGS.

(1834–5.)

AUBURN: *A Disturber.* — *Opposition.* — *Cowards.* — *Stage Ride.* — *A Surprise.* — PHŒNIXVILLE: *Church organized.* — ITHACA: *Conversion of Mr. M.* — BROOME STREET, NEW YORK CITY: *Hyper-Calvinism.* — REMOVAL TO HAMILTON. — *Reasons.*

AUBURN.

IN the year 1834, I conducted a protracted meeting with the Baptist church in Auburn, Cayuga County, N. Y. I felt somewhat embarrassed for a time in this place, because I had not been accustomed to preach in such a large town, nor such a fine church. But as I went on in my work, thoughts of these things vanished out of my mind. The new method of presenting the gospel captivated some and repelled others. Deacon Daniels, of Scipio, came into town on business, and coming in to hear a sermon, was so deeply interested, that he remained a whole week, and told his friends that he would not take the best farm in the town of Scipio for what he had learned during that week.

But the work was no sooner well under way, than the devil began to be disturbed. Opposition, not only in words, but in action, became stronger and stronger. One man, who declared that his damnation was sealed, always began to rave whenever a season of religious interest began to prevail in the place. He would go up and down the streets cursing and swearing, and doing all in his power to break up the meeting. He would constantly make a noise in the vestibule, thumping against the wall, and stamping up and down the stairs. On one of these occasions, a deacon stepped out and requested him to be quiet, or leave the house; immediately this son of Belial laid violent hands on him, and forced him headlong down the steps, and instantly ran off and swore out a warrant against the deacon for assault and battery. On the next morning the deacon was summoned to trial.

In the mean time the wicked had organized their forces, and began to threaten to ride me on a rail. They went so far as to go into the woods and cut a pole, and put it up on a corner which they knew I was accustomed to pass. This demonstration alarmed many of my friends, and some of them began to remonstrate with me; but I replied, "Don't be concerned; if they intended to do anything of the kind, they would have kept the pole out of sight." On the same night some of them came into the meeting, were smitten down by the power of God's truth, and had to be carried to their homes.

In addressing the congregation the next evening, I indulged in a little irony (as did Elijah before the priests of Baal). I told them that it was a hard thing to fight against God; that they were a faint-hearted set of fellows; that if they had even succeeded in getting me on their pole, they would have probably fainted, and let me fall and break my neck; and then, in a more solemn manner, I proceeded to press the inquiries, "Who hath contended with Him and prospered?" and, "If the footmen have wearied thee, how canst thou contend with the horsemen?"

When the time for the mock trial of the deacon had arrived, a party of fellows, of "the baser sort," started, in company with the deputy sheriff, to arrest me, pretending that they wanted me as a witness. On reaching my boarding-house, Squire Burgess, the gentleman with whom I was staying, told them that they could not see Mr. Knapp, and, finding that they insisted on forcing an entrance, called to him a large, savage dog, and informed them that he gave them just five minutes in which to leave his premises, and that at the end of that time, if they were not gone, he would set his dog on them. The faithful creature seemed to understand the demands of the occasion, and impatiently awaited the signal from his master; but before the time had expired, the cowardly crew thought discretion to be the better part of valor, and withdrew. Of course the suit amounted to nothing.

A goodly number were converted in this meeting, though it 'asted only about three weeks. In those days we had learned the importance of holding on until we not only "carry the battle to the gates of the city, but until we go up and possess it."

When I took the stage for Oswego, where I was at that time residing, I found myself seated with six gentlemen, five of whom were Christians. With them I had a delightful season of religious conversation; but on turning to the other, and introducing the subject of religion to him, I was met by a very frank request to "mind my own business." I replied that I was doing so; that it was my business to look after the salvation of souls, and that I meant to attend to it faithfully, and stick to him like a brother. I soon found that he was a confirmed Universalist. I finally suggested to him, that "if a few hours' conversation with Christians in a stage-coach was unendurable, how did he think he would stand it in heaven, where there would be millions of saints, much holier than we were then, and where all would be absorbed in holiness." He answered that he did not care to trouble himself on the subject. It was not long, however, before he called out to the driver to stop and let him get out, saying he would rather lose his fare, than ride in a coach with saints and be bored with their talk.

I was relating this circumstance, a few years afterwards, to a congregation in Schenectady, when, to my astonishment and delight, a gentleman arose, and stated that he was the man referred to; and he went on to say, that, from that hour, he had no peace until he renounced his Universalism, and found "peace in believing" in Jesus. As he trudged on in the mud, the questions which I had propounded began to ring in his ear. He began to realize that heaven must, of course, be a religious place, and the inhabitants of it must be engaged in speaking and singing of the praises of Jesus; that there would be no business, nor amusements, nor worldly conversation there; and that if he got in there, he would not be able to get out as easily as he had got out of the stage; and if he could get out of heaven, where else would he want to go? He saw the sinfulness of his nature, and his need of a regenerating change, in order to enter the kingdom of God.

Phœnixville.

In the autumn of 1834 I attended a meeting at Phœnixville, N. Y. At that time there was no Christian church in the place, and scarcely a person who professed the Christian name. I put up at the public house kept by Colonel Richards, who was a Universalist. The meeting was called by a few Christians of different denominations, who resided in the vicinity. The Spirit of the Lord came down with power, and in about eight days more than one hundred souls were hopefully converted, among whom were Colonel Richards, his wife, and daughter. I baptized fifty-nine, and, aided by neighboring pastors, organized them into a church.

Ithaca.

In the year 1835 I held a meeting with the Baptist church in Ithaca, N. Y. It continued forty days, during which time I preached night and day. The Baptist church was small, and in a low condition. In consequence of long-standing difficulties and violent contentions, the community was generally prejudiced against the church, and many, who otherwise would have been disposed to attend on its worship, had turned away in disgust.

This meeting was gotten up at the instance of our beloved brethren, Thomas and Bronson,* who, at that time, were sup-

---

* Rev. J. Thomas was killed by the falling of a tree across his boat, just as he came in sight of the city to which he had been designated as the field of his future labors. Rev. Mr. Bronson is still living, and laboring in Assam, a veteran in the missionary service.

plying the church, and afterwards went as missionaries to Assam, India. It commenced on the first day of January. God was pleased to bless our efforts. The Holy Spirit was poured out on the entire community. Saints were humbled, differences were reconciled, and the hearts of many, who had been alienated from each other, were subdued and reunited under the power of Christian love, and the impenitent were brought to repentance. I baptized into the fellowship of the church one hundred and twenty converts. Among those who professed their faith in Christ were some noted infidels. One instance of this class of conversions is worth relating. The wife of Mr. M. had been converted during the meetings. When she came out, and avowed her faith, he became exceedingly enraged. The providence of God cast him in my way one morning as I was about to leave the village. I commenced conversation with him concerning the interests of his soul. He did not hesitate to abuse me with his tongue, and withal threatened to cowskin me. I treated him kindly, broke him down on every position he took, and as I rose to go, offered him my hand. He refused to take it, putting his behind him. I, however, stepped round him, took hold of his hand, and gently squeezing it, said, "*Take care, friend M., lest you lose your immortal soul.*" God was pleased to cause these words to sink down into his heart like melted iron, and he began to walk the streets in great agony of mind. At length he went into the prayer-meeting, and unable longer to control his feelings, fell down on his knees, and begged the prayers of those whom he had despised and reviled. Casting his all on the mercy of God through Christ, he rose up rejoicing in hope, and shortly afterwards sent for me to return, a journey of seventy miles, and baptize him.

THE CITY OF NEW YORK, 1835.

In the spring of 1835 I was invited to preach in the Broome Street Baptist Church in the city of New York. Their house of worship was a small building located near the East River. I found the condition of the Baptist churches there to be, for the most part, in a low state. The blighting influence of hyper-Calvinism seemed to spread the palsy of inaction on all their desires to serve God. This church had been organized ten years, and though located in the midst of a large population, it had, at the time I visited them, only thirty-seven members. The themes to which they wished to listen were *the decrees of God*, *particular redemption*, *personal and unconditional election*, *eternal justification*, *perseverance of the saints* (going backwards or forwards), and *baptism*. The presentation of any other topic from the pulpit was deemed a heresy; and the most guarded pleas for Christian effort in the salvation of sinners was denounced as Arminianism, and more to be dreaded than infidelity.

The meetings soon became quite interesting. The Lord was in our midst. Many were reconverted, and entered into the work. But some, even of those who had been praying for the revival of God's work, began to be alarmed at the way in which he was answering their petitions. One good brother, fearing it was the work of man rather than of the Spirit of God, made up his mind to come out publicly and oppose it; but after making the matter a subject of special prayer, was induced to acquaint himself more intimately with the experiences of those who were seeking or professing salvation. And when he found that the inquirers ascribed their sadness and anxiety to their discoveries of their own sinfulness and helplessness in the sight of the violated law, and that they readily acknowledged the justice of God in their condemnation, and when he heard the converts ascribe their peace, and joy, and love to the all-sufficiency of the perfect righteousness of Christ, he saw that they were taught of God, and led by his Holy Spirit; and instead of rising before the people to oppose and denounce, he broke forth into strains of joyful approbation, and gave his soul up to an unreserved and practical sympathy with the work. The protracted meetings continued about four weeks; and as the church had no pastor, I remained with them a few months longer. The number that were baptized, during my stay with this people, was about two hundred.

But though urged to accept the pastoral charge of the church, with fair prospects of increase in numbers and influence, yet the condition of the world at large was ever before me. Millions were crowding their way to hell, and churches seemed to be sleeping over them. And though my wife was afflicted with feeble health, and my family was increasing in numbers, and in claims on my attention, yet I felt constrained with the over-mastering conviction that God had called me to go forth among the churches, and I dared not be "disobedient to the heavenly vision."

Removal to Hamilton.

Until this time I had, for the most part, kept my family somewhere in the region of country where I was laboring. At length it became apparent that it was my duty to secure them a comfortable and permanent home in some central location. After praying and reflecting for some time on the subject, I concluded to select the village of Hamilton, Madison County, N. Y.

Several considerations operated in bringing me to this conclusion. In the first place, the Baptist Literary and Theological Institution was located there. And I hoped that my style of preaching, and methods of presenting subjects, would be of some service to the students for the ministry, in enabling them to combine the simple and plain presentation of the Gospel with the advantages of literary culture and systematic training. In the second place, I knew that Hamilton was the seat of a strong prejudice against me, and one which, unless dissipated, would seriously affect the after ministry of the young men who would go forth from the Institution as the instructors and overseers of the churches. For a while after I took up my residence there, I was studiously denied access to the pulpit, and nearly every sign of denominational recognition. In less than two years, however, this prejudice was swept by the board, by the rising tides of public sympathy and confidence. In the third place, the village was reputed for its healthiness and the excellence of its schools.

My family was now pleasantly settled, and I was free from domestic anxiety, for God opened the hearts of his people, from time to time, so that we lacked for nothing that was needful for our comfort. Thus I was enabled to devote my entire time to the work of preaching, and laboring in protracted meetings. I was also highly favored in the matter of health and the power of endurance, so that I was able to preach from two to three times a day almost constantly, besides attending anxious and prayer-meetings.

I continued holding meetings both summer and winter, seed time and harvest, for some two years, principally in the middle section of the State of New York. And notwithstanding all my weakness and unworthiness, God abundantly blessed these meetings, and in each of them many souls were converted. A short account of a few of them may be interesting and profitable.

CHAPTER VIII.

ACCOUNTS OF PROTRACTED MEETINGS.

(1836.)

BRIDGEWATER: *A Lawyer.* — *A Ball.* — *A Case of Prejudice.* — *The Presbyterian Minister.* — BENNINGTON, VT.: *Thirty-one Years afterwards.* — WATERVILLE: *Distilleries.* — *Liquor Dealers.* — *Proposed attack.*

BRIDGEWATER.

IN 1836 a meeting was arranged in Bridgewater, N. Y., in which I was to preach alternately in the Baptist and Presbyterian churches. We began with encouraging prospects, and went on well. The interest increased day by day. Both churches worked harmoniously.

Among the converts was an eminent lawyer, who stated that, for the last eight years, remorse of conscience, and the unavoidable evils of this life, had been more than enough to counterbalance all the happiness which he had ever enjoyed, so that he had come to regard a state of non-existence preferable to that of conscious being. But since he had believed in Jesus, he declared that he had found true happiness, and he could say that it was a blessing to live even in this world, while his soul was made to rejoice beyond expression in the hope of living forever.

When this revival was at its height, the young people of the place arranged to hold a ball. On the night appointed, the people of God held an all-night prayer-meeting. They danced while we prayed. But the ball was not a success. They adjourned at a very early hour. Nobody seemed to be in a mood for sport. Many came over to the prayer-meeting, and several were converted before it closed.

There were connected with the congregation of the Baptist church a well-known gentleman and lady, who had not attended any of the meetings since I had begun to preach. Brother Simmons and Deacon Allen called upon them, and learned that they had heard, that Mr. Knapp had refused to come to preach in the place until a certain amount of money had been raised for him; and they thought, that if he preached for money, his preaching would do them no good. These brethren informed them of their mistake; that they had corresponded with Mr. Knapp concerning his visit, and had asked him to state how much he would expect for his services, and how his family was supported, and that Elder Knapp had replied, "that he made no charges; that he went wherever the Master called. If his labors were blessed, and anybody was disposed to contribute anything for the support of his family, it would be thankfully received; that no demand was made for compensation, not even for travelling expenses."

They expressed themselves very much mortified at being so greatly imposed upon by the devil's pedlers, and came at once to hear me preach. At the close of the first sermon they heard, the wife came crowding her way along the aisle, and, reaching out her hand to me, the tears streaming down her cheeks, she said, "Mr. Knapp, I wish to make a confession to you." I replied, "My dear woman, why do you wish to confess to me? I do not know you." She replied, "I have cherished wicked and unfounded prejudices against you, and I would not hear you preach; and now, under the first sermon I have heard you preach, God has broken my heart."

In consequence of his deep anxiety and exhaustive labors in this meeting, the excellent pastor of the Presbyterian church lost his health, and for a time it was feared that his reason would be destroyed. Sometimes he would preach when bordering on the verge of insanity; and never, in my life, did I hear from mortal lips the realities of eternal truth portrayed in language that seemed so inspired by the breath of God, and visions of the world to come. O, thought I, that ministers would always preach under such a near sense of the judgment, heaven and hell, and with less regard to the feelings, the frowns, and the favor of men!

Bennington.

In the autumn of 1836 I held a meeting in Bennington, Vt. The place being small, Christians of all denominations united in giving interest to the services. The word preached was made "the power of God unto salvation." The Spirit of God came down on the youth in great power. Sometimes fifteen or twenty would cry aloud for mercy at a time. The converts united with the different churches.

Thirty-one years afterwards I met a number of them in Elmira, who gave an interesting account of many who were converted at that time, and who have since been active and prominent laborers in the cause of Christ. Some became eminent business men, others judges, others teachers and preachers.

During this meeting the devil was disturbed. Accordingly, he stirred up a company of persons to do all they could to hinder the progress of the work. One night some one went up into the steeple of the church and took out the tongue of the bell. Much prayer was offered for the persons who were engaged in this transaction; and I ventured to utter a prediction that within one year from that time the young men, who had thus attempted to silence the voice of God, would be in hell. It was afterwards ascertained that two young men did the deed; and surely enough, in less than a year afterwards they both died, and died without hope. One of them arose from his bed in the night, and opening a door in the dark, fell headlong and broke his neck.

Waterville.

During the same year I conducted a meeting in the Whiskey-mill village of Waterville, N. Y. Here there were four or five distilleries in full blast. I came out decidedly against this soul-destroying business, and told the people that the only way in which they could save their capital, would be to wind up those concerns, and invest their money in enterprises that conduced to their moral and religious well being. One of them took my advice. The others kept on until they failed and sank into poverty.

Much opposition was manifested to my ministry here by the retail dealers in this damning traffic. They organized a club, and pledged their fidelity to each other to break up the meeting, cost them what it might. One night a gang came into the church with clubs and missiles of different kinds, such as pokers and crowbars, and seated themselves in a body. I had been informed that they intended mischief, and this bold and defiant bearing confirmed the rumor.

After the sermon was concluded I dismissed the congregation, and requested all who wished to pray to remain. Nearly all the Christian people tarried, and we continued in prayer until near morning. The gang of intended disturbers made no offensive movement, and finally, being "convicted in their consciences, they went out one by one." There was no further talk of disturbance. Large accessions were made to all the churches, and the public sentiment became changed from opposition to sympathy with the preacher and his measures. I had long before this learned that ministers could as easily control public opinion, as to allow it to control them. All that is needful is that they take a bold stand for the right, and trust in God for strength to maintain it.

CHAPTER IX.

ACCOUNTS OF PROTRACTED MEETINGS.

(1837.)

HAMILTON: *Fear of Men.* — *Co-laborers.* — *Results.* — *Day of Small Things.* — PENNYAN: *Large Accessions.* — *Commotion among the Infidels.* — *Meeting-house paid for.* — *A Case of Conviction.* — *A Legacy of Ministers.*

HAMILTON.

IN the winter of 1837 I held a meeting with the Baptist church in Hamilton, N. Y. I felt considerable embarrassment in undertaking to preach in this place. Here I had been educated, and here I had married. Withal, I was not insensible of the fact that in my congregation would be those whose habits of thought and feeling inclined them to criticise sermons. As to their literary and intellectual merits, I knew that I was not punctilious as to my modes of speech, and more anxious to reach the consciences of men, than to please their fancies or their love of display. Yet, after I had got well under way, I lost sight of all these things. The great things of God, and God and eternity, rolled up before me in such a light, that I was determined to know nothing among them save "Jesus Christ and him crucified."

The church was soon aroused. The students generally came in and took hold of the work with warm hearts. Several of the professors in the Institution were greatly enlisted. Especially may I make mention of the venerable Dr. Nathaniel Kendrick. He was a warm-heated, devoted servant of Christ, and was then ripening for heaven. Squire Payne, Deacon Payne, and Judge Olmstead were all in their element, entering with a holy zest into this their last revival season on earth. Very many souls were converted. All-night prayer meetings were held. The atmosphere seemed impregnated with a divine influence.

Among those whom it was my privilege to baptize as the fruits of this meeting, were my eldest daughter, now the wife of A. J. Bingham; J. R. Kendrick, now the pastor of the Tabernacle Baptist Church, in the city of New York; Samuel C. Griggs, then a poor boy, but now a successful book publisher in Chicago, Ill.; Mr. Kendall, now a well-known business man in St. Louis and Alton; Dr. Douglass, then a practising physician, and afterwards a professor in the Medical College at Cleveland, Ohio.

It was a very common remark among those who opposed me, that "Mr. Knapp was adapted to reach only a certain class, and that they were only the poorer and less influential." Such people did not seem to know that the poor of one generation become the rich of the next. If it were possible to enumerate all who were converted under my ministry, and afterwards became eminent in the various walks of life, and who have consecrated their attainments to the cause of Christ, they would, perhaps, learn the folly of despising the day of small things.

PENNYAN.

In August, 1837, I was called to attend a meeting in Pennyan, Yates County, N. Y. The Baptist church in this village was young and small, consisting of about thirty members. Through assistance furnished them from abroad, they had built a good brick house of worship. Their plea being urgent, I felt a strong inclination to comply, notwithstanding I was under engagements for every month in the year, except the month of August, which I had reserved for rest. But as I must go then, or not at all, I concluded to trust in God for strength, and to comply with their request.

Our beginning was small, and for a long time the prospects were dark. During the first eight days we did not hear of a single conversion. The unconverted began to rejoice over the certain prospects of our failure. Nevertheless the congregations kept on increasing daily, until the house was too strait for us. Soon it became apparent that multitudes were under conviction, and conversions followed by scores. Many of all classes were brought to bow at the Savior's feet. During the meeting, which continued five weeks, it was estimated, after careful inquiry, that about four hundred souls were hopefully converted to Christ. At the end of the fourth week, I baptized fifty-three persons; and at the close of the fifth week, there were baptized, by the pastor and myself, sixty-five more. Brother Ira Bennett, the pastor, after the meetings had closed, baptized twenty-nine more, making, in all, an addition to the church of one hundred and forty-nine. Besides these, many of those who were converted joined other Baptist churches in that region, while a large number united with churches of other denominations.

Pennyan was the seat of infidelity for that entire region, and, as might be expected, I soon encountered the opposition of persons who imbibed such sentiments. My life was frequently threatened, and I learned, after the danger had passed, that a drunken Universalist, armed with a knife and pistol, had sought to waylay me for three successive nights; but God delivered me out of his hands, by leading me to go to my lodgings by a different route each night, though, at the time, I did not recognize any particular reason for doing so.

One man, a hardened and abandoned infidel, left the meeting-house one night cursing God, and swearing that he would have nothing to do with religion, and that he would fetch his wife out, if he had to go through hell after her. Shortly after he had reached home he was taken ill. His skin turned as yellow as saffron; his tongue became so swollen that he could not speak a word, nor keep it within his mouth. On the second day after he was seized, he died. This remarkable event seemed to strike terror throughout the community. Nearly every person accepted it as a judgment from God. Consternation spread through the ranks of infidelity, and many of its open advocates came to me, pale and trembling, begging for the prayers of Christians, and were converted to God.

One incident, illustrating the special providence of God, ought to be mentioned. In the spring previous to our meeting, an infidel, from the State of Ohio, came along in the character of a temperance lecturer. After getting possession of the Baptist meeting-house for the purpose of advocating the cause of temperance, he made an appointment to lecture on animal magnetism, and in the course of his remarks on this subject, he took occasion to assail the Christian religion, and to extol the beauties of infidelity. At the close of this lecture he made another appointment; but on going to the house the next evening, he found the doors locked against him. The infidels of the town became furious; and knowing that the Baptists were owing three thousand dollars on their house, and were poor, they vowed that they would buy up the mortgage, and turn the building into an infidel hall. This threat awakened the sympathy and zeal of the Christians of other denominations, and they stepped forward at once with such liberal contributions, that the Baptist church was enabled to free itself from debt. In order to do this, however, notwithstanding this outside help, nearly every male member of the Baptist church pledged one half of all he was worth in order to clear the indebtedness. The protracted meeting followed, truth triumphed, hundreds of persons were converted, and infidelity was swept by the board.

Among the incidents illustrating the manner in which some persons strove against the Holy Spirit, I recollect the instance of a young lady, who, during the early part of this meeting, resorted to violent measures in order to drive away the convictions that troubled her. She was a person of considerable culture, and of high social position. At first she declared she would not attend the meetings any more; yet she continued to come, but, lest she should be recognized, sought to disguise herself in the clothing of one of the servants of the family. As her convictions increased, her proud heart became more and more rebellious, and she determined to exhibit her unwillingness in forms of decided opposition. On one occasion she told the hired man to array the horses with flowers and evergreens, and taking with her a company of thoughtless girls, in this style she rode up and down the streets, passing the church, and waving her handkerchief at me in the streets. When she returned home, she found the servant girl reading the Bible, and, snatching it from her, threw it with violence across the room, bidding her not to touch it. On the next day, as she was dusting the room, her eye fell on the book as it lay where she had flung it, and in her rage seized the broom, and struck this precious volume as it lay on the floor. At this moment a reaction set in, and unable longer to resist the striving of God's grace, she was at length constrained to yield her heart to Christ.

Among the converts at this meeting in Pennyan were two young men, who afterwards studied for the ministry, and became successful laborers in the Savior's vineyard. One of these was J. B. Tombes, who is now pastor of the Baptist church at Carbondale, Pa.; the other was S. M. Bainbridge, well known in Western New York, who, after preaching Christ with great success for nearly thirty years, fell asleep in Jesus, bequeathing the mantle of his service to his son, who has recently been ordained pastor of the Baptist church at Erie, Pa.

CHAPTER X.

ACCOUNTS OF PROTRACTED MEETINGS.

(1838.)

UTICA: *Bethel Church.* — *The First and Second Presbyterian Churches.* — *Conversions.* — *Baptist Cause.* — *A new Church.* — *Universalists.* — SCHENECTADY: *Union of Christians.* — *Union College.* — *Conversion of Students.* — SENECA FALLS: *A Re-conversion of all the Churches.* — BROOKLYN: *Baptist Cause feeble.* — *Pillars in the Church.* — *John N. Wilder.* — *Conversion of an Atheist.* — *Sisterly Remonstrance.* — *Deacon Colgate.* — *General Results.*

UTICA.

ALTHOUGH there had been much prejudice against me in the city of Utica, I was at length invited to preach in this place. I began in the Bethel at West Utica. It was a small building, capable of holding about four hundred persons. I commenced in February, 1838, and continued preaching night and day for about two weeks, during which time there were some conversions; many were awakened, and Christians were aroused to action.

The place becoming now too small to contain the crowds that thronged to hear the word, we were invited to the Broad Street Baptist Church, and to the First and Second Presbyterian Churches. After much prayer and deliberation, it was determined to take the Second Presbyterian Church. This selection was made because of its central location, and because it was not so large as to make a fair-sized congregation seem small. But the power of God came down, and the house was immediately filled to its utmost capacity. Salvation rolled on like a mighty river.

After continuing here for about three weeks, it was found necessary to remove to the house of the First Presbyterian Church. This vast audience-room was thronged every night; sometimes every inch of standing-room was occupied. Here I remained two weeks, making the period of my stay in Utica seven weeks. I preached one and twenty sermons, besides attending prayer and inquiry meetings.

The cases of pungent conviction were so numerous that we could seldom close our evening services before eleven o'clock, although as many as wished to retire at an earlier hour were seasonably dismissed. Throughout these arduous, constant, and abundant labors, my health was graciously preserved. At the close of the meeting, all who had experienced a hope during the revival were seated in a body, making a congregation of nearly eight hundred persons. Nor did this assembly comprise all who had been led to the Savior during the meeting; many there were who lived in the surrounding villages.

Up to this time the Baptist cause had been struggling along, able only, with difficulty, to maintain an existence. I had fixed my mind on the formation of another Baptist church from the very beginning of the meeting; and although many of the Baptists opposed the measure, yet there were some who were willing to make almost any sacrifice to accomplish this result, believing it would be for the glory of God.

Accordingly, towards the close of the meeting, these brethren met together, invited me to be present, adopted articles of faith, and took all other steps needful for their organization as a church of Christ. It began with only thirteen constituent members. I then baptized into their fellowship about seventy converts; and in about eighteen months' time, this church obtained a commodious house of worship, and have continued to this day a blessing and a glory.

Among the converts in this meeting were persons of all classes; many of them were merchants, doctors, lawyers, judges, and city officials. There were four attorneys who professed conversion in a single day. Many of the experiences were clear, striking, and marvellous. Religion was the serious topic of conversation in the market-places and along the streets.

Hitherto Universalism had held a strong hold in Utica. The sect had quite an influential congregation, a good meeting-house, and an able paper, edited by Rush Skinner, a man of considerable intellectual power and notoriety. I undertook to unmask the hypocrisy and expose the nakedness of the system. Shortly after this revival, the Universalists sold their meeting-house, and Skinner left the city. They have not been able to accomplish much since.

SCHENECTADY.

In the month of June, 1838, I was called to hold a meeting of days in Schenectady, N. Y. I began preaching in the Baptist meeting-house, but very soon the throng so greatly exceeded its capacity, that I removed to the Presbyterian Church edifice. Throughout the session of this meeting there prevailed a remarkable union of feeling and action between Christians of all denominations. Baptists and Presbyterians, Dutch Reformed and Methodists, and also Episcopalians, became deeply interested. Dr. Nott, and all the Faculty of Union College, were constantly in attendance and actively engaged. The Lord was pleased to bless his truth, not only to the salvation of many of the citizens, but also to the hopeful conversion of about eighty of the students, many of whom have since "addicted themselves to the ministry" in different denominations.

There were thought to have been between three hundred and four hundred instances of conversion, during this meeting; and though the Baptist church was destitute of a pastor, yet about fifty persons were baptized into its fellowship. This meeting continued about four weeks.

By this time my throat became so seriously affected that I was advised by several physicians to abstain from public speaking. But the calls for help were so numerous and so pressing that I could not see any stopping-place. I therefore continued on preaching day and night, that is, fifteen sermons per week, until by praying, preaching, and drinking freely of cold water, my complaint was broken up.

Seneca Falls.

After this I attended meetings in Clinton, Fayetteville, Elmira and Seneca Falls, in all of which I was greatly blessed in seeing many sinners turning to God. The meeting in the last-named place was especially fruitful in bringing about a new era of religious feeling in the village. Up to this time the churches were comparatively feeble and inefficient. Infidelity was stalking unblushingly through the streets. Its corrupting, blighting, and damning influence was felt throughout the entire vicinity. This meeting was blessed to the re-conversion of the churches, the arresting of the tide of infidelity, and the immediate salvation of many souls. More than one hundred were added to the Baptist church, and a considerable number to other churches.

Brooklyn.

I commenced a meeting of days in the city of Brooklyn, N. Y., in connection with the First Baptist Church, on the first day of December, 1838. The Baptist interest in Brooklyn was at that time quite feeble. The meeting-house was not more than half filled by its ordinary congregation. Shortly after I had commenced preaching, the congregation greatly increased, the members of the church took hold with great zeal, backsliders were reclaimed, and converts were greatly multiplied. It pleased the Lord to cause the truth to take hold of the consciences of several men of wealth and influence, and several of this class were converted. Still the city was not at first moved to any remarkable extent, nor was the house filled until I had preached nearly four weeks.

By this time, however, the work of the Lord had not only extended throughout the city, but began to be powerfully felt among the churches in the city of New York. During this meeting I baptized, in connection with the pastor, Rev. S. Illsley, two hundred and ten persons, and subsequently brother Illsley baptized one hundred more, as the fruit of this effort. The meeting continued seven weeks, and I preached one hundred sermons.

Since that time this church has had an eventful history. As the city has extended its boundaries, many have gone from this church to assist in forming other Baptist churches. At times it has been in this way greatly reduced in numbers and deprived of its strength; but in its darkest hours there have been a few faithful ones, who held on to the ship, until now she again occupies a position of great prominence in the religious agencies of Brooklyn. And the few to whose untiring and self-sacrificing zeal the maintenance of the church is to be, under God, ascribed, were for the most part brought in during this revival.

Among the interesting incidents that were crowded into this meeting, I will mention a few.

A Mrs. Wilder and her daughter, Mrs. Smith, requested prayers for their son and brother, John N. Wilder. He was a gay and worldly young man, boarding at the time at a hotel in the city of Albany, and had just fallen heir to a fortune reputed to be worth one hundred and twenty thousand dollars. This devoted mother and sister, believing that God heard the prayers of his people, preferred their request that the Christians in Brooklyn would pray that he might be speedily converted. Day after day would this request be made, and as often was it remembered in our petitions to the throne of grace. In the mean time his mother and sister were writing him letters full of earnest entreaty. Though there was no religious interest in Albany, this young man soon began to feel the influence of the special strivings of the Holy Spirit. He struggled to dissipate the feelings that were overpowering him. He took a trip to Providence and mingled in gay society, and afterwards took the stage to Rochester; but all this while prayer was going up in his behalf, and still his soul was troubled. His sins were ever before him, and he found no rest. Returning to Albany, he called first on Dr. Sprague, and then on Dr. Welch, and by these servants of Christ he was led to see his lost condition, and to put his trust in the righteousness of the Savior.

He united with the Baptist church, and devoted himself and his wealth to the service of Him who had redeemed him. Shortly afterwards he gave me one thousand dollars for Madison University. He identified himself with the various denominational enterprises, and was specially active in promoting the founding of Rochester University, subscribing ten thousand dollars towards its endowment. A few years since, he died, quite suddenly, widely known and highly esteemed as a zealous laborer in the vineyard of the Lord.

I remember a striking instance of the power of God in the conversion of an avowed atheist. He came to the meeting to hear me preach on atheism. In the course of my sermon, I remarked that "atheism was the little end of nothing whittled to a point. Since the atheist denied everything and admitted nothing, it was itself the little end of nothing." This remark arrested his attention and mortified his pride. He had regarded himself as specially intellectual, and capable of refuting all the ministers in the land. He could not brook the thought that he, a free-thinker, should be represented as a fool, and his creed reduced to less than nothing. So, in order to be revenged, he requested a Christian neighbor to ask prayers for the little end of nothing. The request was complied with; nor was it overlooked amid the multiplicity of claims upon our prayers.

On the evening of the third day, as we repaired to the lecture-room for the purpose of spending a season in prayer, who should rise up but this infidel? Pale and haggard, not having slept for three nights, and borne down by deep despair, he broke the silence of the spell-bound congregation by saying, "My fellow-citizens, you see before you the greatest sinner which God ever suffered to live. I have denied the existence of my Creator. I have ridiculed his Son Jesus Christ, calling him a bastard. I have studied the word of God in order to pick flaws and make out contradictions. I have cursed my Maker more times than there are hairs on my head; and as for you Christians, there has been nothing too bad for me to say about you; and all I ask in return is, that you will not treat me as I have treated you." He took his seat. I said to him, "My dear sir, do you not wish the prayers of God's people?" He answered, "No. Prayer can do me no good; I must be lost." I told him, "God is merciful; Christ has died to save the chief of sinners." He replied, "I know that; and this knowledge will be the keenest part of my sufferings. I have sinned against infinite goodness and unparalleled mercy. *I deserve to be damned, and I must be damned.* All directions to Christ as a Savior avail nothing. I have not made the first attempt at prayer, under the full conviction that prayer will do no good."

He passed another sleepless night, walking his floor, and contemplating his fearful doom. To him it was a night of terrors. But just as the gray of the morning began to dawn, some mysterious agency whispered in his ear, "Whosoever *will*, let him come and take of the waters of life freely." For the first time in his life he dropped on his knees, and pleaded for mercy through Jesus Christ. In a few moments his load was gone, and his soul felt the peace of believing, and unspeakable joy beamed in his face. He rose from his knees, clapped his hands, and shouted, "Glory, glory to God!" and but for the fear of making his neighbors think he was crazy, he said he should have sung out at the top of his voice.

Much complaint in those days was made because I ventured to cross the ancient landmarks, and got betimes out of the old ruts. I sometimes made remarks which did not always accord with every person's notions of propriety. Such expressions as the one just named, which arrested the attention of the atheist, were deemed highly objectionable. In consequence of this feeling, early in this meeting a couple of well-meaning sisters, finding themselves tried with my course in this regard, and thinking such expressions calculated to do much harm, came to me one day in the spirit of remonstrance. They assured me — and I believed them — that they were not of those who peddle for the devil, talking against ministers and their measures behind their backs. They opened their minds freely to me, and to me only.

I listened patiently, and thanked them for their good intentions, but told them that if they would keep on doing their duty, and working for souls, they would find out, before the meetings closed, that I understood what was the best way in which I could work for the Master. After two weeks they came to me again, and candidly acknowledged that the very things to which they took exceptions had "fallen out for the furtherance of the gospel," and that this would be the last time in which they would undertake to dictate to a minister who was zealously and successfully laboring for souls.

During this meeting the wife of the lamented Deacon William Colgate attended quite constantly, crossing the ferry from New York back and forth in the cold and piercing winds. Her soul became especially concerned for the conversion of her children, and before the effort closed, some of them were brought to Christ. Thus was opened the way for the great meeting in the Baptist Tabernacle in 1840, where the rest of her children found the Savior. On one morning the deacon requested me to go and see his eldest son. I found him trembling under a sense of his sinfulness. He told me that he could withstand anything but his father's prayers and tears. Before that day closed he yielded his heart to Jesus, and found peace and joy.

It would be impossible to trace all the results of this meeting. When it commenced the Baptist cause was weak and small; and it is not too much to claim that from this meeting sprang directly those agencies which contributed to the enlargement of Baptist influence, and the multiplication of Baptist churches in Brooklyn. Men of business, and wealth, and culture were brought into the fold, besides a host of young persons, who have since become pillars in different churches. The work extended through the city, entered the navy-yard, and rolled over into the city of New York. Brother Illsley, the pastor, labored to the last extent of his ability, and was a "true yoke-fellow." Deacons Corning and Lewis, and, I believe, all who then were deacons in the church, have long since crossed over Jordan, and the remembrance of their earnest and untiring coöperation is among my sweetest recollections. Never before, nor since, have I passed such a night as that in which I preached my farewell sermon to this people. It was a night made sleepless by reason of the ecstasy of my soul. It is not enough to say, that it was to me " the gate of heaven," for I seemed to have passed its threshold, and entered into the fulness of the glory that shall be revealed.

CHAPTER XI.

ACCOUNTS OF PROTRACTED MEETINGS.

(CONTINUED.)

ROCHESTER: *Gamblers.* — *The Mob.* — *Arrest.* — *Councils of the Wicked brought to Nought.* — BALTIMORE: *General Interest.* — *Church strengthened.* — *Washingtonian Temperance Movement.* — *Threatenings.* — *A later Meeting.* — *Letter from Dr. Fuller.*

ROCHESTER.

TOWARDS the close of the month of January, 1839, I commenced a meeting with the First Baptist church in Rochester, N. Y., under the pastoral charge of Pharcellus Church. Many of the saints of different denominations soon became interested in the work, and continued to lift up united supplications to God for a plentiful outpouring of his Spirit. Salvation began to flow. The house soon became too small for the congregations, and hundreds went away, night after night, unable to gain admittance. After hundreds had been converted, the Lord was pleased to break into the ranks of a gambling club, which held its rendezvous at one of the hotels of the city. They gambled night and day, and throughout the Sabbath. They practised deception in their games, and were banded together to decoy the unwary and fleece the inexperienced. They not unfrequently took as much as three thousand dollars in one night. A horde of lewd women was kept at this house, who were supported by this gambling fraternity. Young men by scores were being drawn into this whirlpool of destruction, and ruined in health, in pocket, in reputation, and in morals — ruined for time and eternity.

One or two of this company were converted, who felt it to be their duty to expose the secret machinations of this club (for their abominations were not generally known, as they occupied a dark room with double partitions). I considered it to be my duty to make known to the public the facts which had been disclosed to me. Accordingly, I gave notice to that effect. At the appointed time the whole city seemed to have gathered together. Thousands collected who could not enter the meeting-house. Most of the leading gamblers managed, however, to get in, having previously arranged, in case any secret was likely to be disclosed, to break out in open contradictions and blaspheming, until they should drown the voice of the speaker, and disperse the meeting. Prayer-meetings were appointed at different places, to be held at the same time, and earnest supplications went up to God from many believing hearts.

My text was, "The love of money is the root of all evil." When I came to speak on the subject of gambling, and began to make some disclosures of the diabolical schemes of this soul-destroying business, one of the leading gamblers rose up, and, in distinct tones, exclaimed, "That is a d—d lie." I immediately replied, "If you had kept still, sir, we should not have known that you belonged to the gang; a hit bird always flutters!" A gentleman, well known in the community, mentioned the name of the gambler so audibly as to be heard by the entire congregation. All eyes were fixed upon him. One of his companions, sitting by his side, began to pull his cloak, saying, in a low tone, "*Sit down! sit down!*" He sat down in the midst of a profound silence, and covering his head with his cloak, raised it no more until the service was closed.

I continued my sermon, and, with still greater pointedness and force, exposed the enormity of this enterprise, and poured forth the awful threatenings of Jehovah against evil doers. A few evenings afterwards, notices were placarded in all the public places, and on the corners of the streets, calling a meeting, to be held on a certain evening, in front of the Baptist church, for the purpose of considering the expediency of restraining "a certain Mr. Knapp." "All the friends of order are invited to be present." Evidently it was the design of the originators of this call to get together a lot of people of "the baser sort," for the purpose of creating a riot. No arrangements were made by the children of God to prevent it, beyond the appointment of prayer-meetings in various places. The evening arrived; the meeting-house was crowded to suffocation. From the basement earnest prayers were offered unto God, and from the pulpit his word was preached to a solemn and deeply-affected congregation.

In the mean time, a crowd of about a thousand men had gathered around the building in separate groups. One company was stationed in a back yard, armed with stones. At three minutes before eight o'clock, a stone came whizzing through the window towards the pulpit. Simultaneously with its passage came a flash of lightning, followed by a peal of thunder (this was in the month of February, and snow was on the ground). In about a minute afterwards, another stone came through the window, accompanied by another flash of lightning, and followed by a still louder clap of thunder. Scarcely had another minute elapsed before another stone entered the building, when instantly the heavens pealed out its thunder more terribly than before. The house where the people were assembled was shaken, and the earth trembled beneath their feet. Fear seized hold on the ungodly crew, and dropping their missiles, they hastened from the spot, as if they would hide themselves from the presence of God, lest he should "cut them off with a stroke."

Shortly after I had retired for the night, the house of Deacon Sage, where I lodged, was assailed, and several of the windows were broken, but no one was injured. The work of the Lord went on with increasing power; and though the ungodly raged, their counsels came to nought. A writ was served on Deacon Sage because he had said that what I had asserted about these gamblers was true.

The meeting at length came to a close, and I supposed that I should be enabled to leave the city without annoyance. A large company of friends had gathered at the house of Deacon Sage, between eight and nine o'clock, for the purpose of spending a season in farewell exercises of singing and prayer. Just as myself and a few others, who were to accompany me, were about to enter the stage, the agent called to inform us that arrangements had been made by these landsharks to insult me as I passed through the city. It appeared that it had been arranged that a band of music in a carriage, drawn by six horses, and a company of twenty men, headed by the chief gambler as marshal, who, rigged out in regimentals, was to ride a white horse, should follow us out of the city playing and singing "The Rogue's March" as a special compliment to me. They were already assembled in the yard of one of the hotels by which we were to pass as we went to the stage office, and on a given signal they were to sally forth.

The agent offered to convey us in a private wagon some ten or twelve miles out of the city, but after a moment's reflection, I told the company that I would not leave the city in any evasive manner; that I had done nothing of which I was ashamed, and that if these wicked men saw fit to sing "The Rogue's March," we would sing "Old Ship Zion." After singing and praying, and many tears, we entered the stage. As we came round the corner on which stood the Monroe House, the large gate was thrown wide open, and forth issued the crowd of desperadoes, striking up their favorite tune. While pausing in front of the stage office, a fierce, rough-looking man stepped up to the stage, and asked if Mr. Knapp was inside. I replied, "I am the man." He then ordered me to get out of the stage, without intimating in any way that he was a civil officer, or had a civil process to serve on me. I gave him to understand that I did not see any reason why I should comply with his request. He became enraged, and his gang, rushing round him, cried, "Hustle him out."

In a very few minutes thousands of persons had gathered to the scene. The city was in an uproar. Many were my friends, while others, who did not particularly sympathize with me, were indignant at this great outrage against public order and decency. The man who had thus accosted me became furious at my resistance and the remonstrances of the citizens, and putting one foot on the step and the other on the hind wheel of the stage, reached into the coach, and seizing me by the throat, attempted to drag me out. At this demonstration the uproar became indescribable. Some encouraged him in his violence, and some denounced him, while a company of pious women called for a room in the hotel, and fell on their knees in prayer to God.

At length some one informed me that my assailant was the deputy sheriff. I thereupon informed him that I knew not that he was a civil officer, and that if he would stand back and behave himself like a man, I would get out of the stage and go with him. He stepped back, and, getting out, I took his arm and walked with him to his office. The crowd rushed along with us, some before and some behind, some weeping and some cursing, and some praying. On our way I took occasion to warn the sheriff of the value of his soul, and entreated him to be prepared for the summons which would soon call him before the judgment seat of Christ. When we had reached the office, I suggested that before we proceed any further I thought we had better spend a season in prayer. I fell on my knees, and poured out my soul to God for this man and all his company. The room was full of people; some remained standing, some knelt; all were silent and solemn as eternity.

After serving the process upon me, Deacon Sage and Mr. Smith (the mayor of the city) stepped forward and became bail for my appearance at court. By this time the indignation of the people had become so intense, that the owner of the horses returned them to the stable, and thus the company was broken up. I went back to the stage, and started quietly on my way, counting it all joy that I was thought worthy to suffer for the name of Christ. In all this scene of uproar and confusion I felt calm, and enjoyed a sweet sense of the presence of God. I was excited only by a feeling of tender compassion for the poor deluded men who had sold themselves to the service of Satan.

In the October following, when my case was to be tried, I had an engagement to attend a meeting in Baltimore. Some thought I ought to meet my appointment, and some thought I ought to meet the suit; but after praying over the matter, I concluded to leave the suit in the hands of the Lord, and to proceed on my Master's business. Accordingly, I went to Baltimore; and when it became known that I might not attend the trial, my persecutors boasted great things, and entered into secret combination to suborn testimony against me. Before, however, the case came up, the judge was taken sick, and adjourned the court; and before the next court sat, the plaintiff was laid on a bed of sickness. Death stared him in the face; his conscience became troubled, and sending for Deacon Sage, he confessed that my statements were true, and that the half had not been told. About this time another of the company died an awful death. The suit went by default, this company of gamblers was broken up, and many of its members left the city.

Baltimore.

The meeting in Baltimore was commenced on the 3d day of October, 1839, in the Sharp Street Baptist church, under the pastoral care of S. P. Hill. The number then professing the Baptist faith in this city was small. Indeed, throughout the State of Maryland, Baptists were very few and feeble. The blighting curse of Antinomianism had well nigh effaced the visibility of the Baptist name. The meeting had not been held many days before the tokens of God's favor became manifest; still the interest did not rise very high until about the third week. By this time, the waves of salvation began to sweep with power along the tracks of the high and the low. During seven weeks I preached two sermons every week day, and three times on the Sabbath, and attended a prayer and inquiry meeting in the morning and evening of each day.

The influence of this meeting was not confined to the city of Baltimore. A new impulse was given to the Baptist denomination throughout the entire state; so much so, that, according to the statistics reported at the next association, the number of Baptists in the state had been doubled. Revivals broke out in all parts of the surrounding country, and the tide of religious feeling swept on even to Pittsburg, Pa., where, as I was afterwards informed by letter, more than three hundred souls were converted through agencies that had originated in this meeting in Baltimore.

The Baptist church in Sharp Street, at the commencement of the revival, was in debt for their house of worship to the amount of twenty thousand dollars; but very soon after the meeting closed, such had been the strength of their increase, that the indebtedness was at once removed, the edifice improved, and for several years afterwards the contributions of the church, for benevolent purposes, averaged over ten thousand dollars per annum.

While in Baltimore I was invited to address the Young Men's City Temperance Society. The lower part of the church was crowded with men, and the galleries with ladies. In the audience was a liquor dealer, who had come into the city for the purpose of renewing his stock. He had purchased his supplies, and his wagons were loaded ready for a start on the ensuing morning. As he listened to my discourse, the awful character of the business in which he was engaged was so profoundly impressed on his conscience, that he returned the purchases he had made, sent his teams back empty, and resolved henceforth never to traffic in this business, so destructive of the well-being of his fellow-men for this world and the next.

Another very peculiar providence of God occurred during this meeting, illustrating the way in which God can make the wrath of man to praise him. During the progress of the revival, several well-known drunkards had been converted. This fact had enraged the rum-sellers. On the evening in which I preached on temperance, two men, named Mitchel and Hawkins, together with other hard drinkers, were present. From the church they went to a grog-shop, whose proprietor began to indulge in outbursts of rage and cursing against me and my preaching. After a while Mitchel got up, and declared that he would not hear Mr. Knapp abused any longer; that he believed he was doing a great deal of good in the city; and turning towards the rum-seller, he remarked, "If you keep up this abuse any longer, I will never drink another drop in your house, nor anywhere else, as long as my name is Mitchel." But the enraged proprietor continued to deal out his anathemas; whereupon Mitchel, true to his word, then and there solemnly pledged himself to absolute and total abstinence thenceforth through life. Hawkins and others joined with him in the pledge. This was the origin of the Washingtonian temperance movement, which swept over the country with such wonderful power, and by which tens of thousands of drunkards were reformed, and thousands of families were made happy for this life and the life to come. To God be all the glory!

Throughout this revival my whole soul and my entire time were absorbed, yea, wholly engrossed, in my work. I had but little assistance. Brother Hill, the pastor, labored as exhaustively as his enfeebled health would permit; and besides him there were only four brethren who engaged heartily and efficiently in the movement. One of these passed to his rest while in the midst of his toil. But "the Spirit of the Lord God was upon me," and he made my strength equal to my day. My mind was fruitful, my health was perfect, the weather was favorable for the assembling of congregations, and the gospel was "as a fire shut up in my bones." Never before did I so fully understand the words of the Psalmist, "By thee I have run through a troop, and by my God have I leaped over a wall." After laboring incessantly from early dawn till nearly midnight, when my day's work was finished, and my responsibility was rolled off from me for the time being, I would feel as light as a feather and as nimble as a deer. In fact I had to restrain myself, lest people should fail to understand the spirit that moved me, as the daughter of Saul failed to understand David, when he leaped and danced before the ark of the Lord.

After I had been preaching for some time in the city, and the entire people had been moved by the power of the truth, I began to throw out allusions to the subject of slavery. The public mind grew uneasy and feverish. One day a number of gentlemen called at my boarding-place in my absence, and inquired of the lady of the house, whether I was not "a downright red-hot abolitionist from New England." She told them that she presumed that Mr. Knapp was opposed to slavery, but was not of that kind of abolitionists who would advise the slaves to rise and cut the throats of their masters.

On going to the church that evening, I found the house crowded at an early hour, and the yard and street filled with an excited people. As I was about to ascend the pulpit stairs, a good and influential brother took me by the arm, and asked me if I could not satisfy my conscience by passing the subject of slavery in silence, adding that there was much feeling on that subject in the community. I told him that I thought not. It was a warm night for the month of October; the windows were all up, and the mob was staring with piercing eyes on the pulpit. A number of ministers were in the pulpit when I entered it; and two of them were skulking down behind the desk, lest they should be hurt by any missiles that might be sent at me. I gave one of them a jog, and told him to sit up, for he had not religion enough to make him worthy of martyrdom yet; and then, turning to the mob, told them that when I entered the ministry I pledged myself solemnly to preach up Christ and preach down the devil; to bear testimony against all evil in everybody, and without respect of persons; and that I should do my duty if I knew they would kill me before I left the pulpit, and cut me into inch pieces, and roast every piece on a red-hot gridiron; and then I informed them of the mob which their master had gotten up in Rochester, which God had scattered by sending his thunder and lightning. They all quailed, and, dropping their missiles, heard the sermon in quietness, and went away peaceably. Had I taken this stand at the beginning of my ministry there, they would have driven me out of the city, or taken my life.

In the winter of 1857 I was called to Baltimore again to assist Dr. Fuller, and was then informed that about ten thousand souls had been converted as the direct result of the former revival; that four hundred were added to the Sharp Street Baptist church, and that five Baptist churches sprang from this meeting; that sixteen hundred were united to the Methodist churches; that hundreds of others joined the Episcopalian and Presbyterian denominations. In fact persons, in whose judgment I had confidence, assured me that nearly ten thousand souls were supposed to have been converted in connection with the agencies that took their rise from this revival.

On the occasion of my second visit in 1857, my success was not so marked; nevertheless, much good was done. Over one hundred and fifty persons were baptized by Dr. Fuller during the two months that I was there.

At this point it may be interesting to insert a letter from Dr. Fuller, in which he kindly refers to my labors in Baltimore.

"BALTIMORE, November 23, 1866.

"REV. JACOB KNAPP.

"My dear Brother: I was in South Carolina during the period of the blessed work of God in 1839; but some of the noblest and most devoted children of God in the city, I know from personal intimacy with them, were brought to Christ during that revival.

"At a much later day you spent some weeks here, laboring with the church of which I am pastor, and the Lord then blessed your work and labor of love in the conversion of many souls.

"I found great spiritual enjoyment and profit from my coöperation with you; and all the church loved and esteemed you most sincerely for your earnest, humble, and devoted piety, and for your unwearied consecration to Jesus and his precious truth.

"With sincere affection,

"Your friend and brother in the Lord Jesus,

"R. FULLER."

CHAPTER XII.

ACCOUNTS OF PROTRACTED MEETINGS.

(CONTINUED.)

ALBANY: *Apprehensions.* — *Coöperation.* — *Instances of Conversion.* — *Liberality and Revival.* — *A Prodigal Son.* — *A Stranger.* — *The Shad Story.* — *Preparation of the Grounds.* — *State Street Baptist Church.* — *Unsuccessful Pastorate.* — NEW YORK CITY: *Baptist Tabernacle.* — *A Wonderful Work.* — *A Devoted Merchant.* — *New York Herald.* — *An Infidel converted.* — *A Magdalene.* — *The Church in Perplexity.* — *Results.* — *Statement of W. W. Everts.* — HARTFORD: *South Baptist Church.* — *A candid Universalist.* — *The Fiddler at a Ball.* — *Zaccheus at a Baptism.* — *The Infidel Mocker.* — *The Rum-seller and his Victim.* — NEW HAVEN: *Union Meetings.* — *Yale College.* — *A Gambling-house.* — *Plots, and God's Interpositions.* — *The Billiard-room Keepers.* — *Students' Ball.* — *Church Caution.* — *Baptist Progress.*

AT the close of my meeting in Baltimore, I commenced one with the Pearl Street Baptist church, Albany, N. Y., then under the pastoral care of Elder B. T. Welch, for many years acknowledged as preëminent among the eloquent preachers of the country. The policy which this church had pursued differed somewhat from mine. It had placed a value on the external appointments of a church, which I did not; and I therefore had some apprehensions whether my plain, outspoken style of presenting the truth would be acceptable to such a congregation.

Very soon, however, the power of the Spirit of God was made manifest, and the brethren entered heartily into the work. Brother Welch labored with all the enthusiasm of his earnest nature; so much so, that sometimes I deemed it necessary to restrain him, lest he should overtask his strength. Converts were multiplied rapidly; many of them were wealthy and influential.

Among the trophies of grace then gathered, I may mention the names of William Newton, James Wilson, Clark Durant, Mrs. Governor Marcy; and though the governor himself did not openly profess religion, yet I have learned facts which satisfy me that he was deeply impressed, and, I hope, really brought to experience a change of heart. I heard that on one occasion, while in a large company, a young man was berating me, when Governor Marcy took up my defence, and, rising to his feet, repeated the substance of one of my sermons with such effect, that the tears flowed down his own cheeks and the cheeks of many of his hearers.

As near as I can ascertain, about fifteen hundred persons were added to the different churches of the city as the result of this meeting.

While the meeting was in progress, I received a letter from Dr. Nathaniel Kendrick, asking me to raise some money in aid of the Institution at Hamilton. I devoted a part of one afternoon to this object, and obtained seven thousand dollars. As an evidence of the relation of a revival to liberality, I may state that I called on seven persons, asked each for one thousand dollars, and was not refused in a single instance.

On one occasion, as I closed my sermon on "The Prodigal Son," a well-known lawyer, Salem D., arose, faced the congregation, and spoke substantially as follows: "I am that prodigal son. I have spent my substance in riotous living. I am in want. I will arise and go to my Father — not next week, nor to-morrow, but *now!*" and falling on his knees, he called on God for mercy. And his heavenly Father "ran and fell on his neck, and kissed him."

Another lawyer, from Greene County, being in the city, came to hear me preach. He was deeply affected, though he struggled to conceal his feelings. But his compunctions followed him home. His wife noticed that something was the matter with him, and finally induced him to tell her of the burden of his heart. Her heart responded to his, and they both knelt in prayer to God. While they were calling on him, he answered them, and they both rejoiced in the hope of salvation. While I was preaching in New York city, some time after this, he came to see me, and told me that when the light of God's love first burst upon him, only the fear of being thought crazy restrained him from going among his neighbors, shouting, "Glory to God!"

I learned some interesting facts concerning this meeting, of which I was ignorant at the time it was in progress.

There was, in the outskirts of the city, a shop containing some sixty or seventy men; one of them came to hear me preach, and, being somewhat of a wag, reported to his comrades that a man was preaching in the Pearl Street Church, who had said, that "it was as impossible for some sinners to go to heaven, as it was for a shad to come up the North River tail foremost, or climb up a greased barber's pole with a loaf of bread in its mouth, and a barrel of mackerel under its fin." This canard excited their curiosity, and so they resolved to come and hear a man who talked in that strain. But they heard nothing about shad. They heard God's truth, and before long thirty of the men professed their faith in Christ. My authority for this statement is Deacon Richardson, of Elizabeth City, N. J., who was himself one of the number.

As the results of this revival, about five hundred persons were added to the two Baptist churches of the city. Afterwards, brother Raymond and brother Swan held meetings in the city, and God greatly blessed their labors. I do not claim exclusive credit as the sole agent whom God was pleased to employ in bringing about these precious blessings. Brother Welch had gathered about him many families of high standing, who, though attracted at first by his wonderful eloquence, had received permanent impressions of gospel truth. This class my ministry would never have drawn; but being there, and prepared to receive the truth, God was pleased to make my preaching effectual to the salvation of many of them. Thus God works by different agents, and accomplishes one kind of result by one man, and a different one by another.

Not long after the revival in this city had closed, S. M. Fish and William Newton proposed to build another meeting-house, on condition that I would promise to open it with a protracted meeting. I consented to do so. The building was at once erected. It was located on State Street, near the Capitol. I preached the dedication sermon, and commenced a protracted meeting. The Master smiled on the effort. I baptized about two hundred converts, who, together with a few from the other churches, were organized, and recognized under the name of the State Street Baptist church.

The new church was very anxious to have me become its pastor. In compliance with their request, I subsequently removed my family to Albany, and remained in charge of the church one whole year. But I soon found that I could not do justice to the work of a pastor and of an evangelist at the same time. Moreover, God did not seem to smile on the undertaking. The church did not continue to prosper under my pastoral services as much as the blessings, which had attended my labors as an evangelist, had led it to expect. I have always thought since, that God intended to drive me out of the pastorate, and to shut me up to the one work of an evangelist.

New York City.

As soon as my meeting in Albany, in the winter of 1840, closed, I went to the city of New York. I preached in the Baptist Tabernacle, a building erected for Dr. Maclay, in Mulberry Street, near Chatham Square. This church was then in its infancy, and had just called W. W. Everts to become its pastor. I boarded with Deacon William Colgate, who became my warm and fast friend. He was a good man, full of faith and of the Holy Spirit. The house of worship being very large, and being centrally located, I had a fine opportunity of reaching the masses of the city. Very soon the house was filled to its utmost capacity, the aisles being crowded, the porches jammed, and the sidewalks overrun with people.

The power of God came down on the people wondrously. The old stereotyped prayers gave place to the most earnest and solemn pleadings with God for the salvation of souls. The ancient traditions of having converts come before a committee, and wait a month before they could be baptized, was made to yield to the apostolic example. For a considerable time the members of the church would meet in the basement for the purpose of listening to experiences, while I was up stairs talking with the anxious. As fast as they found peace in believing with all their hearts, I sent them below to present themselves to the church. Sometimes there were thirty or forty persons who thus presented themselves on an evening. On one occasion, the lamented Deacon Colgate, in his humorous way, took me to task for sending the converts faster than the church could receive them. Brother Everts and myself baptized ninety-six in one day; and so the work went on for ten weeks, day and night, without any cessation.

I generally preached at three o'clock P. M., and half past seven o'clock in the evening. The time from four to five o'clock, and from nine to ten and a half o'clock, was spent in prayer and conference exercises.

The whole city was moved. Business men would come in during the day and spend a little while, and come again in the evening. Very many of them were converted. More than four hundred persons were baptized into the fellowship of this church; and when it was fourteen months old, it had seven hundred members. Very soon the church bought the Presbyterian Church in Laight Street, and set off a colony. The pastor went with the new interest.

A lady persuaded her husband, who was a wealthy merchant, and an attendant on the Episcopal church, to come one evening to the meeting. During the sermon he became so deeply interested, that at its close he repaired to the lecture-room, rose for prayers, and went to his house rejoicing in the hope of pardon. He was soon afterwards baptized and added to the church. This man was so completely absorbed in the great things of the kingdom, that he gave up all attention to his worldly business for one year, and devoted himself to the one concern of saving souls.

The New York Herald sent a reporter to our meetings, who pretended to furnish an account of the services for each morning's issue. Anxious to make a sensation, so as to procure sales of the paper, he would give caricature accounts of all that transpired, making burlesque descriptions of the person of brother Everts and of myself, and of the administration of the ordinance of baptism, and setting forth perverted and distorted statements of my language. The boys would "hawk" the paper through the streets, crying, "Elder Knapp and the tariff." In this way the meeting was advertised among a class who otherwise might have never heard of it, for at that time this paper circulated very widely, if not exclusively, among persons who never attended the house of God. But by this means infidels, gamblers, drunkards, and libertines were excited with curiosity to see and hear a man, concerning whom the Herald was making so much ado. Many of them, who "came to scoff, remained to pray."

I recollect an instance of an infidel, who had not attended a church in ten years, and had taken an oath that he never would, ratifying it with a wish that, if he ever should, the roof might fall on him and kill him on the spot. But despite his oath he was constrained to come. He was seated well forward in the middle aisle; the house was packed, and the audience as quiet and solemn as eternity. The speaker, instead of saying the funny things that had been reported of him, presented the truths of God and a future life with warnings and entreaties. The man looked on either side of him, and found the people melted into tears; he looked up to see if the roof was falling in; he looked back to see if there was a possibility of getting out, but the jam was too close. He was compelled to remain. His sins rolled up before him, and he sat trembling like an aspen leaf. At the close of the sermon, he went down into the lecture-room, rose for prayers, and was converted before he left the house. Thus we see why the devil and wicked men live. Their wrath is made to praise God; but for the devil and the service of the New York Herald, hundreds who were converted would not have been reached. No religious notices, no entreaties of Christian friends, could have brought them to the house of God.

One woman of ill repute professed conversion in this meeting, and presented herself to the church for admission. Many voted against receiving her, especially the sisters. A committee was appointed to wait upon her. They became satisfied of the genuineness of her conversion. In reporting the case to the church, Deacon Colgate, who was on the committee, remarked, "Brethren, we have got ourselves into difficulty, and I do not see how to get out of it. We have been praying the Lord to convert sinners; we did not tell him whom to convert, and he has converted one whom we do not want." All felt themselves rebuked, and voted unanimously to receive her. She proved to be a consistent and exemplary follower of Christ.

Deacon Colgate very justly remarked, that "under my labors thousands were converted from among a class of the wicked who belonged to families in which were no helps to piety. Rather, such converts were exposed to every influence calculated to draw them away, while those who professed faith under ordinary means, were usually those whose education had been moral and religious; whose families were pious, or, at least, attended church, while they themselves, perhaps, had been nurtured in the Sunday school."

I am unable to give an accurate account of the numbers who professed piety in this meeting. Hundreds united with other churches, Baptist and Pedo-baptist. But among the trophies of grace were quite a number of prominent merchants and young persons, who are now pillars in the church of God. Several young men gave themselves to preparation for the ministry; among whom I remember brother H. Harvey, since eminent as a pastor and a professor of biblical literature; brother A. C. Buckbee, now a secretary of the American Bible Union; brother James S. Dickerson, now pastor of the First Baptist church in Pittsburg.

Under date of November 29, 1866, brother W. W. Everts, of Chicago, wrote me the following statement regarding the meeting in the Tabernacle church in New York: —

"Elder Jacob Knapp commenced his labors in the Tabernacle Baptist church in February, 1840, at a crisis in the history of the Baptist denomination in New York, and his labors contributed much to mark that crisis.

"The revival measures that had obtained throughout the state for many years, and especially since 1830, had been distrusted, especially by the leading Baptist churches of the city. The late Deacon Colgate, studying with great interest the revivals of the country, became increasingly anxious to take more effective means to promote them in the city. A chief reason for uniting with others in founding the Tabernacle church, out of the old Mulberry Street church, was, to try more vigorous means to promote revivals, and bring the gospel to bear upon the masses.

"After a few months of supplies, the writer was called as the first pastor of the Tabernacle Baptist church, and became at once connected with the spirit and aims of the new movement. Considerable interest was at once awakened. Through the autumn and early winter considerable numbers were added to the church, both by letter and baptism.

"In these circumstances, and to carry out views entertained in the constitution of the new church, Elder Knapp commenced his labors. In the course of that meeting, continuing several weeks, hundreds were added to the church. Nor did any serious reaction or discouragement follow that revival. Large numbers were added the following years; so that in three years the membership of the church rose from over three hundred to over nine hundred.

"This progress of the Tabernacle church encouraged revival measures and church extension throughout the city. The Laight Street church grew out of the Tabernacle church. Fruits of that revival are now recognized as leading members of many churches in New York and vicinity, and throughout the country. The old church herself has continued in the direction and greatness of her influence from the impulses of that period and revival. And the most efficient membership of that church, from that day to this, have looked back to that time, as the period of 'the right hand of the Most High.'

"W. W. Everts."

Hartford.

In the month of December, 1840, I visited Hartford, Ct. As soon as I had stepped out of the stage-coach, and put my foot on the pavement of its streets, I felt myself moved by a strong conviction that the Lord had "much people" to be gathered in this place, and that he intended to make my labors effectual in the accomplishment of a great work.

I commenced services with the South Baptist church, and boarded, during most of my stay, in the family of brother Albert Day. The power of God was very soon made manifest amongst us. Saints got up out of the way of sinners, and sinners came rushing into the kingdom. Brother Eaton, pastor of the North Baptist church, came and labored with us, and large accessions were made to both of the churches.

Hartford, at this time, was a stronghold of the Universalists, many of whom were converted. Among these I may make mention of the case of Mr. B. He was a candid man, and enjoyed the respect of the community. He came quite frequently to hear me preach. He was present on the evening on which I preached on the subject of Universalism; and so impressed was he with the statements I made, that he went home and promised the Lord that he would reëxamine the subject more thoroughly, and that if he found his views to be false, he would renounce them. He opened his Bible at once, and spent most of the night in reading afresh those passages which he had been accustomed to regard as proof-texts of the Universalist doctrine. He was astonished to find that they failed utterly to support the theory. He came to church on the following evening. My text on that occasion was, "Choose ye this day whom ye will serve." At the close of the sermon he arose, and turning round to the congregation, he exclaimed, "As for me and my house, we will serve the Lord." As he spoke, a wonderful change came over his countenance, and his face became radiant with joy. Turning to me, he said, "Last night I hoped that some one would throw you into the river, or get you out of the way somehow; but to-night I feel as though I could hug you!" Shortly afterwards he was baptized. He proved to be a consistent and useful member of the church.

The person who had been engaged to play on a bass viol at the opening of the services, was expecting, on one occasion, to leave the church during service for the purpose of performing on the fiddle at a ball. It was known to us that this amusement was set down for that evening, and much prayer was offered that God would arrest its progress. At the appointed time the musician left the church, and entering the ball-room, he informed the manager that Elder Knapp had just been praying that "the right arm of the fiddler might be palsied, and that the music might sound like the shrieks and groans of the damned in the vaults of hell." The fiddler took his stand, and the company arranged themselves on the floor; but before the first set was half through, the fiddler was seized with a tremor, and his arm fell palsied by his side. The music ceased, and turning to the manager, he exclaimed, "I am under conviction. My restoration doctrines will not serve me. I am resolved to seek the salvation of my soul, and I advise you all to do the same." The ball was broken up. The fiddler and the manager came directly over to the church. The musician made known his case, and was converted on the spot. Many of the young people came from the ball-room also, and very soon found the Savior.

Whenever a professed Universalist was converted, the other Universalists were accustomed to say that he was not a real Universalist. Finally, the brethren challenged them to select out one whom they would acknowledge to be sound in their faith. They made choice of one, and instantly the brethren united in making him a subject of special prayer to God. The result was, that he too came out and renounced Universalism, and gave his heart to God.

On one occasion, as I was baptizing some converts in the river, a young man climbed up a tree, and took his position on a branch that stretched out over the spot where I was standing with the candidates. I prayed that God would speak to that "Zaccheus," and make him come down, and that he would abide in his house. On the following Lord's day he was baptized in the same place.

At one time, as I was preaching, a young man began to draw my portrait on the back of a pew. All of a sudden his hand was seized with palsy, so that he was unable to lift it. He came out for prayers, and was hopefully brought to Christ.

A company of infidels were chopping wood near the city, and every evening one of them would come to meeting, and report the proceedings to his associates on the next morning, as a matter of amusement and ridicule. Once, as he repeated the sermon with comments, and was about to go through a prayer, something seemed to speak to him in audible tones, saying, "You wicked wretch!" His axe dropped from his hands, and he fell helpless to the ground. He was carried to his home, and brother Eaton was sent for to pray for him. He became a penitent and pardoned man.

One day, as I was passing by a rum-shop, the keeper of the establishment was dragging a poor, drunken creature out of his cellar, and kicking him into the gutter. I turned round, looked the rum-seller in the face, and exclaimed, "Where am I? Is this hell, and are these devils? Is this the way they treat each other?" I related this circumstance in public. The rum-seller was enraged, and swore that he would be revenged. He was about to be married, and the arrangements were all made for the ceremony. He collected a crowd, and started for the church with the avowed purpose of breaking up the meeting. On his way he was taken sick; he lingered a short time, and on the day appointed for his wedding, he was a corpse.

During my stay here, the South church called brother E. Turney to be its pastor. I preached his ordination sermon.

New Haven.

I closed my meeting in Hartford on one evening, and commenced another in New Haven on the next. There was then only one Baptist church in the city, and it was small and feeble. Brother T. C. Teasdale was its pastor.

The Lord owned and blessed his truth during this effort, and made the gospel the power of God unto the salvation of very many. Christians of all denominations came in, and took a deep interest in the progress of the work. Dr. Taylor, professor of theology, attended, and was heard to say, that he "thanked God that the gospel was being preached so faithfully." The students of Yale College were quite constant in their attendance; of these, seventy-one were converted. At the close of the meeting, they sent me a letter containing all their names, and one hundred and twenty dollars as a personal testimonial.

At first some thought that the interests of the cause would be better promoted by holding an additional meeting in connection with, and for the sake of, the students. Accordingly, the services of Dr. Kirk were obtained. But he had scarcely reached the ground, before he recognized the importance of maintaining an undivided interest. He, therefore, together with nearly all the professors, came to my meeting, and rendered hearty coöperation in conducting it. And I am bound to say, that seldom, if ever, have I found a more noble, unsectarian class of Christians, than were the Congregationalists of New Haven. Their piety, liberal-mindedness, and intelligence, won my highest admiration and affection.

In this city there was a noted gambling-house, to which, as I learned, many of the ungodly students resorted; especially the high bloods from the South. I regarded it my duty to expose this den of iniquity, and warn all against it. This exposure brought out several of the students, and all the hard characters of the city. Thirty-eight of the students entered into a solemn covenant that they would break up the meeting at the risk of their lives.

Arming themselves with clubs, bowie-knives, and other instruments of death, they came into the church, and stationed themselves in different parts of the house — some in the gallery and some below. As soon as the congregation was dismissed, they undertook to keep the people from going out. They blocked up the aisles, and refused to give way, resisting the pressure by a display of clubs and threats of assault.

I requested them to stand aside and let the people pass; but they stood their ground, and brandished their weapons. I then called for the tithing-men (as the law of the state required). As soon as these officers began to appear, the students cried out, "*Yale! Yale!*" (the sign word agreed upon), when instantly those in the galleries threw themselves over its breastworks, and slid down the pillars into the crowd below. A sharp scuffle ensued, and very shortly law and order prevailed. Some of the mob were carried off to the watch-house, were tried the next day, and fined.

After this, for four or five nights in succession, a mob would form on the college-green, and come down to the church about the time of dismissing the congregation. They avowed their purpose to kill me, and on several occasions I went to my lodgings surrounded by a body-guard. On one evening I exchanged cloaks with a brother, and passed out before many of the congregation had left the church. On my way home alone, I met several hundreds of the mob. Those in advance asked me if the meeting was out. I replied, "Yes; and unless you look sharp, Knapp will be gone." They started on the run, and I went quietly to my room.

The mob was finally broken up by the following remarkable

providence. One of them had sent me an abusive letter, threatening my life if I did not leave the city. On the evening of the day in which I received it, a number of the desperadoes came into the sanctuary, and seated themselves in the gallery. Shortly after I had commenced preaching, a rifle-ball was thrown at me; but hitting the shade of the lamp, it was turned out of its course. Some thought that it had been shot from an air-gun, but the possibility is, that it was thrown by hand. Brother Teasdale immediately arose, and read to the congregation the letter referred to. This letter called me "the prince of liars," because I had related publicly how God had broken up the mob in Rochester by sending thunder and lightning; and challenged a repetition of the scene. Deacon Sage, of Rochester, who was providentially present, rose and corroborated my statement. No sooner had silence been regained, than a flash of terrific lightning blazed through the house, followed by awful peals of thunder and torrents of rain. This marvellous coincidence effectually dispersed the mob.

Nevertheless, the thirty-eight who had banded themselves together to break up the meeting, did not abandon their purpose. They changed their tactics. They arranged to gain access to my lodgings, and, disguised, to seize me, gag me, and putting me into a carriage, to carry me into the woods, and there deliberate as to what further course should be pursued. But one of their number was seized with convictions, which led him to reveal to me the plot. Several of the brethren resolved to stand guard each night. The desperadoes, learning that the house was well protected, resorted to stratagem. One night, after I had retired, the footsteps of a man were heard clamping on the sidewalk. In a moment the door-bell was pulled with great violence. Occupying a front room, I opened the window, and asked what was wanted. A man at the door replied that he wanted to see Mr. Knapp. I said, "I am the man." He remarked that "a person, some little distance off, was under deep conviction, and wanted Mr. Knapp to come right away and pray for him." I told him to "tell the man that he must pray for himself, or he would go right down to hell." I understood the plot at an instant, and learned, on the day following, that a carriage was in readiness, and a company of men, to carry me away, and that this man had been paid one dollar to decoy me out of the house.

After this, two of the gang were converted, and one of them told me that "it seemed to him that he could not be happy even in heaven, in view of the many souls he had already sent to hell." He had kept a depository for the sale of infidel books, and had engaged actively in every effort to disseminate the poison of error.

The two men whose billiard-room I exposed, soon became interested in the meeting. One of them, T., came forward for prayers, in the spirit of derision, having been hired to do so. I had been told of his intention, and kneeling down near to him, I prayed for him very earnestly. In my prayer, I described the character of a gambler, and spoke of him as one "who, though once having a kind heart, could harden himself until he got past all feeling — until he could even gamble on the grave of his father, or on the coffin of his wife." This allusion troubled him, for he had recently buried his wife. At the close of the service he came to me, and asked "how much I wanted for my prayer," and offered to pay me handsomely if I would give him a report of it. This poor man was undoubtedly under serious impressions, and alarmed by apprehensions. When I took the boat for New York, he came to the wharf to bid me good by, and wept when I gave him my hand.

The other partner, Mr. B., professed conversion, and gave me a history which went to my heart. When he came to New Haven his family stood high in social position, being on intimate terms with that of Dr. Dwight. But yielding to his passion for gambling and strong drink, he had dragged his wife and children down to poverty and disgrace. How painful, alas! that we cannot retrace our steps, nor rid ourselves of the consequences of our wrong-doing! These consequences are not confined to the wrong-doer, but they involve his family from generation to generation.

While the meeting was in progress, the time arrived for holding the annual ball of the Junior Class in college, but owing to the great interest on the subject of religion, it was put off. Soon after I left, however, a meeting was called, and arrangements were made, and the time appointed for it. It was said by one of them, that "the ball should come off in spite of Knapp, the devil, or the Almighty!" But one of the managers was taken sick suddenly, and died. On the day appointed for the ball, his schoolmates followed him to the grave.

The Baptists in this place had fallen into the habit (quite common elsewhere) of requiring their candidates for membership to undergo a sort of probation before being baptized. They must first go before the deacons, or a committee, for examination, and then must wait a while before they related their experience to the church. Multitudes of converts were thus kept waiting for baptism.

Finding that the church were disposed to cling to their usage, brother Teasdale and myself came to the conclusion to tell them that we should carry out our commission, and that they could take them into their church, or leave them to go to other churches, as they might choose. Whereupon the church annulled their former resolution, and voted to receive the candidates on their experience. Several hundred candidates were baptized; though how many I am unable to state, as no record was kept. As the result of this work of grace, the Baptist cause was greatly strengthened; and socially, numerically, and financially, the Baptist interest has been much greater in this stronghold of Pedo-baptist Congregationalism since, than it ever was before.

CHAPTER XIII.

ACCOUNTS OF PROTRACTED MEETINGS.

(CONTINUED.)

NEW BEDFORD: *A Revival in the Summer.* — *A Caviller.* — *Power of Endurance.* — *Earnestness.* — PROVIDENCE: *Want of Coöperation.* — *Dr. Wayland.* — *Trial of Faith.* — *Increase of Interest.* — *Lawsuit.* — *Results.* — BOSTON: *Five Churches United.* — *Arduous Labors.* — *Plain Preaching.* — *Opposition.* — *Anxiety.* — *Protests.* — *A Mob.* — *A Passage of Scripture.* — *Eagerness for Salvation.* — *Closing Meetings.* — *Disparagement.* — *Personal Detraction.* — *J. D. Fulton's Account.*

IN the month of June, 1841, I visited New Bedford. The Baptist church was then under the care of brother Henry Jackson.

It was sneeringly remarked by some one, that we could do nothing in the summer; that our God was the God of the *winter*, and not of the *summer*. But the meeting had not progressed far before the pastor and myself were sent for to pray for this same person. We found him in deep distress, in view of his guilt and danger, for he had found out that our God was not only God of the summer and of the winter alike, but also the Judge of the quick and the dead. We remained with him for some time, and poured out our souls in prayer, and left him with a trembling hope in the pardoning mercy of God. His love and light continued to increase, and he became a professed follower of Christ.

Our meeting went on day and night, in increasing power, for about six weeks. Many were converted. Only a very little opposition was manifested, and all denominations took part in the good work.

Mr. and Mrs. Howard, wealthy members of the Episcopal church, invited my eldest daughter to spend a year in their family, and attend the Female Seminary with their daughters. The invitation was gratefully accepted.

During this meeting a gentleman of marked independence of character was awakened by the death of his wife. Shortly before her last moment, she was told that she could not recover. Immediately she sprang from her bed — resisting all efforts to restrain her — and falling on her face, cried, with her expiring breath, "O Lord Jesus, have mercy on my poor soul!" This man came into our meeting, anxious to become a Christian, but could not be induced to take the seat assigned to the inquirers. I asked him "why he declined." He said "it would do him no good." I told him "it might help to subdue his pride, and overcome the fear of man." He answered, "There is not the man on earth of whom I stand in fear." I replied, "Friend R., I will give you a problem to solve: you find a strong reluctance to taking this step, and you say it is not pride nor the fear of man that keeps you back: please tell me, to-morrow, what it is that restrains you." The next day he told me he had solved the problem; that I was right; that he did fear man more than he feared his Maker. That evening he came out for prayers, and found Jesus at once.

The weather was warm, and my labors intense. The people were amazed, and wondered how I met the demands made upon my strength. But I have always found the truth of the promise, "As thy days are, so shall thy strength be." Worldly people have been often at a loss to know how Christian women, for instance, can attend to all their household affairs, keep everything in order, take care of company, and go to meeting day and night for months together, and yet keep as bright and cheerful as a lark. It is really surprising what a small amount of sleep and food we can get along with, and how much we can endure, when we are filled with the Spirit. Machinery well oiled can be run day and night for years together with but little friction.

While preaching one Sunday morning in this meeting, I became so absorbed in my subject, and so earnest in its delivery, that my daughter rose up in her seat, extending her arms to catch me, as she thought I was surely coming over the pulpit. At the same time I ruptured a blood-vessel near the centre of the eye, and a blood spot remained in sight for a considerable time.

I found brother Jackson a kind-hearted, generous man, who entered into the spirit of the meeting with all his heart.

PROVIDENCE.

I began my labors in the city of Providence, R. I., about the 1st of November, 1841. I was called to the field by the Third Baptist church, of which brother T. C. Jamieson was then pastor. The other Baptist churches did not, as a whole, coöperate with us in this effort. But different brethren of the various churches came in gradually, one after the other, until the prejudices of nearly all were overcome. Some held out to the last; and in this regard, I felt the difference between the treatment I received here from persons of high distinction, and that which I had received from persons in similar positions in Schenectady and New Haven. In Providence I had no coöperation nor favor from such.

Dr. Wayland came in and heard me preach once; but I suspect that he was not very favorably impressed; for I was merely giving a sort of talk to the church, and withal his presence embarrassed me. Nevertheless, I was glad to learn that, in his instructions to his pupils as to the right kind of preaching, his views came nearer to my style of sermonizing, than to that of any other man. And, certainly, many of his published writings are in perfect harmony with what I have preached for thirty-five years; especially do I consider his sermon on *The Apostolic Ministry* as a model presentation of the gospel method of disseminating the truths of salvation. I have rarely come across the writings of any man from which I have derived more pleasure and profit.

For a time everything looked dark. Our faith was put to a severe test. I remember that one evening as brother Jamieson and I stood on the hill which overlooks the city, we reconnoitred the forces that seemed to be against us. There were in sight of us the First and Pine Street Churches, with their great resources of influence, if not openly opposing, at least withholding their sympathies, and practically giving us the cold shoulder. And in positive array, on the devil's side, were the Unitarian and Universalist churches, together with that motley crowd of the ungodly who disclaimed association with any religious society. I felt the cold chills running up and down my back, and hastened to my room, and sought a renewal of my strength in prayer. My constant cry was, "O Lord, gird us up for this conflict; let not our faith fail; put the whole sacramental host in battle array against the powers of darkness, and let thy great name be honored in the salvation of thousands of souls!"

I soon found that as long as my eye was fixed on Christ, there was no danger of my sinking; but as soon as it was turned on the waves that pressed around me, I began to go down. It was not long before the work broke out with great power. New conquests were made every day, and public opinion began to change rapidly in my favor. The doors of the Pine Street Baptist church were at length thrown open to me, and the house became thronged at once with the multitudes who were eager to hear the words of life. Many of the members of Congregational and Episcopal churches came in with us, and the work extended over the city.

The Universalists, as usual, became very much enraged. A good brother gave me some information, which I repeated from the pulpit, concerning a woman in that city, which further investigation proved to be incorrect, to the extent that they related to her husband instead of to herself. A wealthy and revengeful Universalist took the matter up, and induced the woman to commence a suit against me. It was privately arranged among "the fellows of the baser sort" to have the summons served on me in the church, after the people had mostly gone, so as to give me no opportunity to get bail, in order that they might have the satisfaction of sending me to jail over night. Accordingly, on the appointed evening, just as we were dismissing the second service, the deputy sheriff, in company with a ruffianly crowd, came in. As they attempted to force their way up the aisles, through the congregation that was going out, great confusion and uproar ensued. The sheriff was summoned to take care of his own company, and keep the peace. In the mean time I quietly slipped out, and went to my lodgings. On my way I met a gang of rowdies, and I experienced a repetition of the scene which occurred, under similar circumstances, in New Haven. In a short time I was called upon by the sheriff, in company with several Baptist and Congregational brethren, who went my bail. Afterwards I regretted that I gave bail: it would certainly have been more apostolic to have gone to jail, and I should have been brought into closer sympathy with the experiences of Paul and Silas, who had blessed seasons of meditation, prayer, and praise.

When the time came for the case to be tried I was doing a great work in Salem, Mass. I wrote to my friends that I could not leave it to attend the suit, unless they felt it to be imperatively important, but that I would leave the matter in their hands, and hold myself responsible for any settlement they might make. The affair was finally settled by the payment of one hundred dollars.

Before I left Providence scores of souls were converted to God. Twenty-three husbands, whose wives were members of the Third Baptist church, were converted and baptized.

Boston.

In the latter part of December, 1841, I went to Boston, in response to the invitation of nearly all the Baptist pastors in the city. I preached in the First Baptist church, then and now under the pastoral care of brother Rollin H. Neale; in the Baldwin Place Baptist church, of which brother Baron

Stow was then pastor; in the Bowdoin Square Baptist church, whose pastor was brother R. W. Cushman; in the Harvard Street Baptist church, brother Robert Turnbull, pastor, and in the Tremont Street church, over whose services brother Nathaniel Colver presided. The people of brother Colver's church mingled their prayers and tears with us, but their audience-room was, at that time, so small, that we could use it only for inquiry-meetings. I preached uniformly twice every day, afternoon and evening, and a portion of the time in South Boston before daylight. Even at this early hour the house was crowded, for the religious interest was so intense in the community, that almost any sized house could have been filled at almost any hour in the twenty-four. I conducted inquiry-meetings at ten o'clock, A. M., and continued in prayer and conversation until noon; and at the close of the evening sermon I held another inquiry-meeting of one hour or more in length. In this way I went on, day in and day out, preaching to great crowds, often an hour at a time. It is easy to see that my labors were without cessation, and very severe; nevertheless the Lord strengthened me for the work he had given me to do. I closed my labors in Providence one night, and began them in Boston the next; and preached, without intermission, three months, and in all one hundred and eighty sermons.

At the end of the first week there were two hundred inquirers in the seats for prayers. But it pleased God to reduce the size of the army, as in the case of Gideon, before he gave us the city.

I came out, as I had done elsewhere, against Unitarianism and Universalism, and all similar systems of error. I called things by their right names, and bore down heavily on the manufacture, sale, and use of all intoxicating liquors; nor did I pass over the open infidelity of the city. The consequence was a grand rally against the progress of the meetings. The first public assault appeared in the columns of a paper, whose editor was a man of intemperate habits. He denounced the meetings, and was especially hard on the preacher. This movement emboldened all the powers of darkness. Many Christian people ordered the paper to be stopped, but the ungodly rallied to his encouragement.

The opposition at length culminated in the gathering of a vast mob in Bowdoin Square, in front of the church, with the avowed purpose of breaking up the meeting. This movement had been anticipated, for it was publicly announced. Some well-meaning, but cowardly people, withdrew from the meetings, but the faithful held on in prayer. For a short time it seemed uncertain which way the scale would turn; but the prayers of that eventful night — a night never to be forgotten — brought the victory. The brother with whom I was boarding, unable to sleep, came into his parlor about midnight, and not knowing that I was there, knelt down, and in doing so, placed his knees on my prostrate form, as I lay on the floor in the agony of supplication to God. I afterwards ascertained that very many others had been passing that night in sleeplessness and in prayer.

A number of gentlemen, not professors of religion, who had contributed to the erection of the beautiful and spacious church on Bowdoin Square, not relishing my style of preaching, sought to intimidate the trustees into shutting the doors against me by threatening to give up their pews. They were not prepared to listen to such plain, outspoken, sin-killing, and devil-binding truths. Deacon Asa Wilbur at once stepped forward, and bought the pews of all who wished to dispose of them. A few came into his hands, but before the meeting closed more were in demand than had been given up.

A distiller, who had paid liberally towards building the house, as an expression of his contempt for the meetings, took all his family, one night, to the Museum; on returning home he was seized with a pain in the hollow of his foot, and before the doctor reached him he was dead. One of Paine's disciples sat up all night preparing clubs with which to break my head, but coming in to hear me, God broke his heart. The chief officer, who called out the Lancers to quell the riot and disperse the mob, confessed that his heart was in sympathy with the mob, and that he hoped they might succeed, though at the same time he was resolved to discharge the duties of his office. He was convicted of his sins, and became an inquirer after salvation.

The man who drew the plan of the house, and who was mingling sympathizingly with the mob, suddenly broke away from them, came into the prayer-meeting, and begged the prayers of God's people. On the last night in which the mob made a demonstration, they followed me to the house of Deacon Wilbur, and stood in the street in front of it. The deacon walked up to them, and addressed them as follows: "Gentlemen, Mr. Knapp is in the house; walk in; he will treat you in a gentlemanly way; or, if you wish it, I will invite him out here, and he will address you." They took off their hats, and waving them gracefully, responded, "Good-night, Mr. Wilbur," and quietly retired. From this point public opinion began to react in our favor, and the word of the Lord "grew mightily."

When the conflict of public opinion was at its height, and some were saying of me, "He is a good man," and others were saying, "Nay, but he deceiveth the people," a circumstance occurred of singular interest. Mrs. D., a refined and pious lady, called upon me one day when I was absent. While waiting for my return, she took up a Bible which lay on the table, and prayed that she might be directed to some passage of Scripture which would indicate my real character. She opened the Bible at random, and her eyes instantly fell on Psalm xci. 15, 16: "He shall call upon me, and I will answer him: I will be with him in trouble; I will deliver him, and honor him. With long life will I satisfy him, and show him my salvation." When I came in she told me of the circumstance, and read the passage in my hearing. Under these peculiar circumstances, the passage afforded me great comfort and encouragement. It melted me to tears. I knew that many of those who stood aloof from me, and looked askance at me, were my superiors in intelligence, culture, and ability. I felt myself to be a child, and unable to stand up against the multitudes, and their manifold influences of opposition, unless the Lord should uphold me. But with the conviction that he was on my side, I had no fears.

It will never be known, until the day of judgment, how many were converted in this revival. Two thousand persons were added to the churches composing the Boston Baptist Association during that year. Hundreds were added to churches of other denominations, and many came in from the surrounding villages and were converted. Indeed, there were instances of persons coming from distant parts, and taking rooms at boarding-houses, for the sake of attending the meetings, in order that they might obtain salvation. One lady, residing in New York city, came with this end in view. Some of her friends expressed surprise at her course, especially as she had a family. Her reply was, "If I had supposed that there were any means in Europe which were better adapted to bring me to Christ than there are here, I would have left husband and children, and have hastened there as quickly as steam could carry me;" adding, "What are all these little sacrifices, in comparison with eternal life?" I need hardly remark that this dear woman went back to her home a new creature in Christ Jesus.

Near the close of these delightful meetings we spent two days in special thanksgiving — one day in the Bowdoin Square church, and one day in the Baldwin Place. From ten o'clock until dark each day the time was taken up in the review of God's wonderful mercy and grace. Almost every heart was surcharged with gratitude to God for some particular blessing: parents, because their children had become the children of God; husbands, because their wives, and wives because their husbands, had given their hearts to the Savior; teachers, because so many of the scholars had become disciples of Christ; and pastors, because so many of their congregations had been added to the company of those who would "be saved."

An Episcopalian missionary from Africa, on hearing a man give thanks for what "God had done for his soul," rose up, and remarked that this very man had been a rum-seller in Africa, and had stood much in his way in laboring for the conversion of the natives; he desired to lift up his voice in thanksgiving that this man had now become "a fellow-helper to the truth." The churches were greatly strengthened in numbers and means of usefulness. Several of the places of amusement were closed, the attendance on them not being sufficient to pay expenses. Billiard-tables and bar-rooms were neglected; and you could scarcely meet a man in the market or on the street whose countenance did not indicate seriousness, and whose language was not subdued. The Spirit of God was poured out on the whole city, and all the people seemed to be affected by the power of his presence. The streets at midnight were deserted, and the stillness of the hour was disturbed only by the voice of prayer or the song of praise, as they were wafted from counting-house, garret, or parlor. It was during the progress of these meetings that the Tremont Theatre was offered for sale and converted into a Temple. In this enterprise Timothy Gilbert was the prime mover.

I have often said to myself, "O, if Christians were always as devoted and earnest, how soon would the world be converted to Christ!" But shortly after my departure a sad and disastrous reaction set in. I know that assiduous attempts have been made to hold me responsible for all the unfortunate scenes that followed these meetings; but it seems to me that it would be just as reasonable to charge on Paul's zealous and untiring labors at Ephesus, the blame of all the havoc which wolves made among the flock after he had left them.

In this instance the opposition to my ministry arose, not from without, but from within. Jesus was "wounded in the house of his friends." It did not culminate while I was on the ground, but broke out after I had gone to another field. The very men who had given me their countenance while laboring to give strength to their churches, enlisted their sympathies against me, as an apology for their want of success in taking care of the increased flocks committed to their charge.

The assault that was made against me was of a two-fold

character. In the first place, the value of the work itself was disparaged. It was alleged that the converts brought in under my ministry did not hold out. Now I know full well that it is in the order of God's kingdom that the chaff shall grow with the wheat, and I doubt not that many who have been brought into the church under my labors will not be admitted into the church in heaven. But in this respect I believe that a careful and statistical investigation would show, that the proportion of apostates and worthless professors has been no greater under my preaching than it has been under the labors of stated pastors. And it should be borne in mind that very many of those who had been brought in during the protracted meetings, had never received any previous religious culture, and found themselves embarrassed when brought into the atmosphere of refinement and culture. These persons needed of the pastors, and the older church members, solicitous watch-care; but, alas! in too many instances they were neglected, and made to feel the chilling repulsions with which aristocratic bearing and suspicious reserve met them as they crossed the threshold of the Christian church. If there is one thing which pains me more than another, that awakens in my heart anxiety as to the future of Zion, it is the growing desire of ministers and churches to gather their converts from the ranks of the wealthy and the intelligent. The church of Christ is no place for caste. There, if any where, the rich and poor should meet together; and there, if any where, if any discrimination exists, it should be an intenser anxiety to gather into the fold of Christ those who, by reason of poverty, neglect, and vice, are tempted to exclaim, "No man cares for our souls!"

But instead of a redoubling of diligences lest any of these lambs should "fail of the grace of God," measures were immediately inaugurated which practically left them to perish. Two of the pastors went off to Europe, and were gone several months. One church was closed, during most of one season, for enlargement and repairs; while the leader of another part of the flock, either from sympathy with my enemies, or from a want of personal adaptation to the work before him, let slip the opportunity of retaining the crowds that thronged his house when I left; and brother Colver's edifice was too small to accommodate a large congregation, and his brethren were straining every nerve to convert the Tremont Theatre into the Tremont Temple.

No wonder then if, in view of these discouragements, many fell away. And yet a somewhat careful calculation, by Deacon Asa Wilbur, has shown that during the four years succeeding my ministry in Boston, the five churches with which I labored excommunicated only "fifteen per cent. on their baptisms, and all the other churches in the Boston Association, taken together, excluded nearly nineteen per cent. on their baptisms;" while the "two churches in the city where Mr. Knapp did not labor, baptized (during these four years) one hundred and twenty-two, and excluded thirty-six, or twenty-nine per cent. on their baptisms." *

In the second place, a wicked and deliberate attempt was made, by some in high standing in the denomination, to destroy the public confidence in my Christian integrity. The leaders in this conspiracy are now dead, and I pass over their names in silence. Unable to fix the shadow of suspicion on my personal purity and truthfulness, these men set themselves to the task of investigating the quality and texture of my garments. It is very true, that neither myself nor my family, while in Boston, arrayed ourselves in costly and fashionable attire. All the habits of my life were based on a theory of rigid economy: my early necessities had schooled me into it. My income from the churches, on which I had a right to rely for the support of my family, did not warrant lavish expenditures, and, withal, having spent most of my time in the country, I was not up to the demands of Boston fashions; so that it is possible that in some regards my toilet, though always whole and cleanly, was

* See "An Examination of the Comparative Statistical Results of the Labors of Elder Jacob Knapp in the State of Massachusetts, by A. Wilbur," in Appendix I.

not in keeping with the tastes of many of the people who came to hear me preach.

Now these wiseacres affected to make the wonderful discovery that I dressed thus plainly for the express purpose of creating the impression that I was desperately poor, and wanted, by this means, to excite public sympathy and contributions. Whereupon learned doctors of divinity set themselves busily to work to find out how many pairs of stockings, and how many changes of underclothing, and how many pocket-handkerchiefs I brought with me into Boston, and how many I carried with me when I left.

No one was found who could say that I had ever asked for a penny of compensation, or begged the favor of a single garment. It is true, that when my wife and I were getting ready to come to Boston, we were so far affected with a regard for the reputation of the people there for fastidiousness, that we thought we were making unusual preparations for our visit; it is further true, that in some cases, finding further purchases needful, we did sometimes make inquiries where certain articles could be bought; and it is further true, that instead of always telling us, many kind-hearted persons would anticipate our intentions, by procuring them for us. At the time, I accepted such presents as spontaneous expressions of genuine good feeling, and never dreamed that any would lend themselves to an attempt to construe them into evidences that my main reason for becoming an evangelist was a desire to make money.

NOTE.

The following interesting account of Mr. Knapp's labors in Boston, are to be found in the "Life of Timothy Gilbert, by Rev. J. D. Fulton, Pastor of Tremont Temple:" —

"In Providence there was determined opposition to his efforts, on the part of several distinguished ministers. On the other hand, a document, speaking of him in the highest praise, was signed by over three thousand individuals, and forwarded to Boston, where an effort was being made to destroy his influence. On or about the 1st of January, 1842, he began his labors with the First Church, Rev. Rollin H. Neale, pastor, and preached there in the afternoon, in the evening at Baldwin Place, Rev. Baron Stow, pastor. On Monday, January 9, Mr. Knapp commenced at Bowdoin Square Church, where he preached both afternoon and evening. It was while here that he met his fiercest oppositions. Mobs gathered about Bowdoin Square as they gathered in the olden time about the synagogue in Lystra, and would have stoned Jacob Knapp, and have dragged him through the city, as the Jews persuaded the people of Lystra to do unto the apostle to the Gentiles. Never did chieftain bear himself more bravely, never did martyr walk more in humble reliance upon the promises of a covenant-keeping God, than did this fearless preacher. Citizens were stirred by his appeal and awed by his sublime courage. William Ellery Channing said, concerning him, 'Let the minister alone; a man who can stir Boston like that will do good.'

"Day after day the excitement grew more fierce and intense. At length it was reported throughout the city that Mayor Chapman had said that the preacher was imprudent, and might take the consequences of his own conduct. Immediately Rev. William Hague, though not a supporter of his measures, called upon the mayor, and informed him of the report, saying that the occasion made its appeal to every lover of religious liberty, and in such an emergency he should feel it to be his duty to stand beside the preacher, and share the consequences. The mayor replied, 'Sir, the report is not true, and all the power I have at my command shall be concentrated at Bowdoin Square to-night in defence of freedom of speech.' The crowds were dispersed.

"To the honor of the secular press be it said that with united voice they sustained the action of the mayor, and supported the ambassador of Christ through the terrible ordeal.

"There was no hesitation on the part of his friends. The church at Baldwin Place unanimously invited Mr. Knapp to preach in their meeting-house. The tide continued to flow in, and indications of the divine approval abounded. The spiritual strength of Mr. Knapp seemed literally renewed. He fired no blank cartridges, but delivered broadsides at close range into the ranks of the foe. The opposition roused him and encouraged him. The attendance upon theatres waned, that upon churches increased. On February 9, 1842, the 'Reflector' says, 'It is our privilege to do something more than merely report progress. The work has now attained to a degree of prevalence and power that renders it utterly impossible for us to convey to our more distant readers an adequate conception of what God is permitting his people to witness and enjoy in Boston. Every day brings to light facts and scenes of the most thrilling interest. Among the converts, which now amount to hundreds, there are persons from every class and of every description of moral character — old men with thin and silvered locks, with deeply-furrowed cheeks, and voices tremulous and feeble, who were long since given up by their friends as hopeless cases, are, like little children, praying and weeping, and talking of the infinitude of God's mercy and the love of Christ; and young men, glowing with energy and ambition, strong with health and hope, are proclaiming, with apostolic fervor, the truths which to some are a stumbling-block, and to others foolishness; children are in many instances rejoicing over their parents' conversion, and in many others, parents are blessing God for the conversion of their children. A family in which father and mother and five adult children were converted were led to Christ through the instrumentality of a single young lady. Her importunity led them to the meetings; her kind and correct endeavors dissuaded them from dropping the subject or avoiding the influence which was now creeping over them. She rested not till God and conscience had done their work, and the souls she loved were loved of Heaven.

"On Tuesday evening of last week, brother Knapp made 'Universalism' the theme of his discourse, and for two hours and a half held a vast and crowded auditory in almost breathless silence, while he tore up the foundations of the system, and scattered the whole fabric to the winds. Never did we hear such an array of facts — authentic, astounding, withering facts. We thought that even his Satanic Majesty himself, had he appeared there as a Universalist, must have quailed under them, and hung his head in shame.'

"A young man, a member of Mr. Skinner's congregation, led by curiosity, found his way to Baldwin Place. Strong in the faith of Universalism, he listened with candor, as one inquiring after truth; and the result was, that Mr. Knapp swept away every vestige of his Universalism, and, to use his own language, 'took away every shingle and clapboard of the building — left nothing but the falling rafters, exposing his naked soul to the peltings of the pitiless storm.' The revival was characterized by the apparent genuineness of the conversions. The converts exhibited a clear understanding of the evil of sin, the holiness of God's laws, the doctrine of justification by faith, and the necessity of entire consecration to God — topics on which Mr. Knapp dwelt with great frequency and power. Though some of the ministers treated Mr. Knapp coolly, the majority of the churches were heart and soul with him.

"On the first Sabbath in February, forty-two united with the First Church, fourteen with Bowdoin Square, nineteen with Baldwin Place, and twenty-two with Tremont Street.

"On March 2 this announcement is made under the head of 'Theatres:' 'The friends of morality and religion will rejoice to learn that the great theatre of Boston, the Tremont, is closed, and that noble granite edifice is offered for sale, and is likely to be converted into a house of worship. At the conclusion of a late entertainment, the manager announced that the theatre would be closed, and stated that within the last three months they had lost ten thousand dollars by keeping it open.' The rush was in a different direction. The churches were thronged, and Mr. Knapp went from place to place, like a general on the field of battle, giving aid where needed. A writer in the 'New York Evangelist' says of him, 'He preaches in his own style, saying some things that are not in good taste, yet no doubt doing execution.' A professor in one of our theological schools attended upon his preaching a whole Sabbath since he has been here, and on being asked his opinion, replied, 'He is a man of genius and power, and though his preaching is not always in good taste, yet no thief, or profane swearer, or drunkard, or adulterer, can sit and listen to him a great while without feeling that the constable is after him.'

"The work goes on in increasing power. New and striking cases of conviction are daily occurring among persons of every faith, and class, and character; wholesale dealers in ardent spirits have yielded to the Spirit of God, and abandoned the cursed traffic. A large distiller was found beside a vendor among the inquirers. Baptisms are occurring in the different churches every Sabbath, and the work is spreading through the commonwealth. March 9 the 'Puritan' has taken sides against Mr. Knapp, and three eminent divines of the straitest sect declare 'the sentiments of Mr. Knapp are substantially sound, *so far as they go*, but his violation of good taste is the great secret of his notoriety.'

"The 'Reflector' speaks of Sabbath, March 6, as furnishing a scene upon which angels would look with delight. 'Picture to yourself a crowded sanctuary, with its long centre aisle occupied from end to end with a dense double column of "new recruits" to the army, fighting under the banners of our King, and then receiving, one after another, the significant pledge of Christian affection, and passing round, one to the right hand and another to the left, until the last young soldier was greeted, and all duly enrolled with the sacramental host of God's elect. The work has been more powerful in the First Church, during the last week, than at any time before. It seems as if not a single soul among them all was to be left in a state of unreconciliation to God. Baptisms reported: First Church, fifty-eight; Baldwin Place, fifty-two; Free Church, forty; Bowdoin Square, twenty-seven; Federal Street, twenty-eight; Boylston Street, twenty-four; Charles Street, six; Independent, nineteen. Notwithstanding these results, the "New England Puritan" ridicules the labors of Mr. Knapp, saying, "The operations after the sermons are more objectionable than anything in the sermons themselves." Calling forward to the anxious seat is characterized by declaring that "the congregation is put into a rambling state and some fifteen minutes of confusion." "Against such machinery, so productive of wholesale delusion, so destructive to the modesty becoming women and children, and so calculated to lead all impenitent men to the conclusion that religion is promoted by trick and artifice, we feel bound to enter our solemn protest;" and all this because Mr. Knapp, at the conclusion of the sermon, was accustomed to come down from the pulpit and exhort the impenitent to come to Christ, and converts to tell what God had done for their souls. The third week of March closed his labors in Boston, with the blessings of thousands ready to perish resting upon him, and following him to Lowell, his next field of labor.

"In accordance with the request of the leading citizens of Boston, he repeated the Temperance Sermon in Marlboro' Chapel, which, two years before, in Baltimore, led to the reformation of J. H. W. Hawkins, and initiated the Washingtonian reform. At the conclusion of the address, all who had signed the total abstinence pledge, or were determined to sign it, were asked to rise; and the whole of that immense assemblage sprang to their feet. It was a thrilling scene, and proved the potency of the religion of Christ to promote a spirit of reform.

"The time of his sojourn drew to a close. In the 'Reflector' of March 23 there was a description of the closing scenes. 'The mornings of Thursday and Friday, March 17 and 18, were occupied with meetings devoted to expressions of gratitude for the distinguishing mercies of Heaven. These meetings were full of interest. Thursday evening he preached to converts in Bowdoin Square. Friday afternoon he preached to Christians at Baldwin Place; and though it was a week day, and in the hurry of spring, such was the enthusiasm, that every standing place in the house was taken, and multitudes went away. In the evening he preached to the impenitent at Bowdoin Square, and the solemn service was concluded with the parting and farewell of those parties who had labored with him.'"

"This was a most wonderful period in denominational history. The laity that upheld the hands of the ministry were unsurpassed in character, in talent, and in devotion. Every church was strong, because each church might, like the Sultan of the East, point to her stalwart men as the walls of her defence and the implements of conquest. It was at this period Daniel Safford introduced Rev. E. N. Kirk, D. D., to Boston. It was a remarkable happen-so, even if it were a happen-so, that Mr. Kirk followed Mr. Knapp so frequently. One was the John the Baptist, preaching repentance, and the other was the reaper. One was the blacksmith, the other the silversmith. Said Dr. Kirk, 'I delighted to follow Mr. Knapp, because he stirred the conscience, and made a great number ready to listen to the truth, presented in a milder form. They were too mad to hear him, they were under too deep conviction to rest content; so, many gladly came to listen to me who might have gone, unmoved, to perdition, had it not been for the sledge-hammer style of Mr. Knapp.' For this reason he followed him, in Baltimore, in New Haven, and in Boston."

CHAPTER XIV.

ACCOUNTS OF PROTRACTED MEETINGS.

(CONTINUED.)

LOWELL: *A Universalist Covenant Meeting.* — *A Cotton Mill an Inquiry-Room.* — *Fifteen Hundred Converts.* — *A Challenge to Universalists.* — *Its Acceptance, and the Result.* — *Physical Exhaustion.* — *An Aged Convert.* — *A Farewell Scene.* — *An Infidel Observer.* CONCORD: *Excitement among Christians and among Scoffers.* — *An Illustration.* — *Conversion of a Universalist Preacher.* — *Penitent Scoffers.* — *A Refusal to baptize.* — *Regrets.* — *Baptist Influence.* — *The Second Advent.* — *Statement of E. E. Cummings.*

LOWELL.

I CLOSED my meetings in Boston on one night, and began my meeting in Lowell on the next. The wonderful work of God in Boston prepared the minds of the people in this neighboring city to expect a similar manifestation of the Divine Presence among them.

The Universalists took the alarm from the start; and even before I arrived, their congregation had been convened, and asked to pledge themselves that they would not go to hear me preach at all. Since they expected to get to heaven by lying as easily as by praying, their pledges did not hold good. I was no sooner on the ground than they went to hear me in great numbers.

The Lord came down in power, and the work rolled on mightily. It very soon assumed such vast proportions that in one of the cotton mills the superintendent, who was a Universalist, found it necessary to stop operations. The operatives were nearly all on their knees, in prayer for themselves, or for their unconverted associates. In fact, the entire factory was an anxious-room.

It was afterwards estimated that about fifteen hundred were converted, as the result of this meeting of five weeks. The interest was shared among Methodists, Congregationalists, and Episcopalians, as well as Baptists, and all reaped largely of its benefits.

At the close of one of my sermons, I remember calling upon all in the congregation who were willing to live and die by Universalism, and risk their eternal all upon it, to rise up. One woman arose; but fear seized hold of her while she stood; a sense of her awful temerity overwhelmed her. She sank down on her seat, convicted by the Spirit of God. Shortly afterwards she confessed her sins, renounced her errors, and became a believer in Jesus as her only refuge.

During this meeting I found myself greatly reduced in strength. I had been preaching twice a day, for two weeks, in Providence; from thence I had gone directly to Boston, and there had preached twice and three times a day, besides attending inquiry-meetings, for the space of three months; and had gone thence, without intermission, to enter upon a similar siege in Lowell. In this way I had spent nearly seven months in unceasing toil, taxing my physical and mental powers to the utmost. Towards the close of my labors here, I would go from the pulpit to the lounge, and from the lounge to the pulpit; and yet, though growing consciously weaker every day, I was enabled to preach, apparently with as much effectiveness as ever.

Among those who came forward for prayers was an old man, of over seventy years of age, who stated that he had been brought up in "the land of steady habits," had lived a moral life, and had depended on his morality for the salvation of his soul. Now his eyes were opened; he saw his guilt and danger, but could see no remedy, and felt that he must be lost. Days passed, and he found no relief. He had not as yet summoned strength to make the first attempt to pray; finally he was induced to kneel, and call on God to have mercy on him, for the sake of Jesus. Christ appeared to him, in the greatness and fulness of his redeeming love, and his soul was brought into the liberty of the gospel. When he went down into the baptismal waters, he walked with the sprightliness of youth; and coming up out of the water, "he went on his way rejoicing."

When I came to take my departure from the place, the people flocked in crowds around me, each eager to give me a farewell grasp of the hand. The throng became so great that the track was blockaded, and the cars were unable to venture a start, lest they should crush the people who were crowding about them. As fast as the track was cleared in one place, it was covered in another by the surging crowd; and yet the greatest order and decorum prevailed. The air resounded with the songs of the rejoicing and weeping multitudes.

An infidel, who had not attended the meeting, riding along on horseback, looking on the scene, seemed to hear a voice, saying to him, "Behold how these Christians love one another." "How good and how pleasant it is for brethren to dwell together in unity." He trembled, and had he not held on to his horse's mane, would have fallen to the ground. He went home, asked for the prayers of God's children, and was converted to God.

Concord.

In September, 1842, I commenced meeting in Concord, N. H. The Baptist church was then under the pastoral care of brother Cummings. The interest rose quite rapidly, and went on with increasing power for some six weeks. The excitement became intense. The Universalists, Unitarians, and infidels became wild with the excitement of denouncing our excitement. A shrewd infidel had published an article before my arrival, in which he predicted that "Knapp would whip them all out;" and the reason he assigned was, that they "had *no hell* in their creeds." While this outcry against our meetings was at its height, I gave the people an account of an occurrence which took place in their own community, illustrating the propriety of strong excitement on the part of those who believe in the truth of Christianity. A short time before I had commenced the meeting; the beloved son of the Unitarian minister had met death under circumstances peculiarly distressing. During his vacation from college, he, together with several of his companions, had repaired to the Merrimac River in order to bathe; shortly afterwards one of them came back, running with the utmost speed, with the cry that the minister's son had plunged into the river, and had not risen to the surface. The father, with all possible speed, hastened to the spot, screaming along the way, "Help, help, help!" and stripping off his coat, leaped into the stream, diving now in one place and then in another, until he came in contact with the body of his drowned boy. Seizing it, he brought it to the shore, and instantly physicians and friends were eager in their attempts to resuscitate animation. But all was in vain. In the mean time the news had spread like wildfire, and the people from their dwellings, schools, stores, and workshops had rushed to the scene of the disaster. Sympathy and anxiety were depicted in every face; and as the wails of the agonized family broke on their ears, stout hearts beat thick and fast, and eyes unused to tears, were suffused with signs of genuine sorrow. All sorts of business, for that day, were banished from every mind. In short, the whole town was wild with excitement. I used this fact as the basis of an appeal to the congregation. Who would presume to say that these manifestations of excited feeling were not justifiable? I do not say excusable, but demanded by the exigency of the case? What would have been thought of any one, if, during the prevalence of this intense emotion, he had gone among the excited crowds with the sneer of a cynic on his lips, had ridiculed this ebullition as a ridiculous excitement, and denounced the anguish of the smitten parents as the ravings of insanity, and the tears of the sympathizing throng as the snivellings of folly? Such a man would have been looked upon as a cold-blooded wretch, whose only impulse was the malignant misanthropy of a devil. O, then, what more reason for excitement on the part of those who realize the lost condition of their fellow-men, and view them sinking into the depths of an endless hell! All seemed not only speechless, but for the moment breathless.

While I was conducting this meeting, the Universalists were busily engaged in completing their meeting-house; they were specially excited, lest everybody would be converted before they had got it ready for use. One day, while two of their leading men were talking about forming themselves into an organized church, one of them said, "When we form our church you shall be one of the deacons, and I will be the other. I swear I will." In one of my sermons I repeated this conversation before the whole congregation. The next day the Universalist minister, with one of their prominent men, called on brother Cummings and myself, to remonstrate with us for "abusing them." We received them kindly, and after a very brief conversation, I proposed that we spend a season in prayer. I called on each of them to pray, but they both refused. Then brother Cummings prayed, and I followed. Like Felix of old, they both trembled. The minister came out, publicly renounced his errors, professed conversion, and united with the Presbyterian church.

On one evening, while the anxious were coming forward for prayers, my eye caught sight of a tall, fine-looking gentleman, who was standing near the door. He seemed to be looking on the scene with an apparent air of mingled contempt and defiance. I said to myself, "I should like to see your proud knees bend at the feet of Jesus." I stepped up to him, and asked him if he would take a seat among the inquirers? He replied that he had "no objection," and at once went forward, asking me, at the same time, to pray especially for him — call him out by name. I learned that he was the son of Governor H., and the editor of one of the political papers in the town. I bowed in prayer, requesting all to unite with me at the mercy-seat (for, what he meant in sport, we meant in earnest). When we rose from our knees, the sweat was rolling off of him like rain, and his knees smote together like Belshazzar's. The moment the benediction was pronounced, he shot out of the door and disappeared. On the next morning he came into the prayer-meeting, and stated that, while prayer was being offered for him on the preceding night, his sins rose up before him like mountains; he realized the necessity of meeting the great question of his salvation immediately. Instead of joining his comrades, and repairing to a saloon, to drink champagne, as he had been in the habit of doing, he hastened at once to his room, and locked the door. He felt that the crisis moment had come, and that if he yielded that night to the convivial overtures of his companions, the Spirit of God would leave him, and his damnation would be sealed. He had been spending the night in prayer, and he had come into the meeting to say that "another day was dawning." He had made a full surrender of his heart to Christ, and was now rejoicing in the hope of pardon and eternal life.

After making this statement, he turned to Squire B., a young lawyer, who edited the other paper, and an intimate friend of Mr. H., and entreated him to go forward for prayers. He arose at once, and took his seat among the inquirers. He then beckoned to me, and offering me a five-dollar bill, said he had a confession to make. I said to him, "I do not want your money, but your soul." He replied, that he had stated in his paper that I "was preaching for money," knowing better when he said it. He insisted that it would be a relief to his feelings if I would accept his overture. Lest he should think I was needlessly sensitive, I yielded to his request. I then bowed in prayer. Very soon he made a surrender of his soul to the sceptre of Christ.

The conversion of these young men introduced the subject of personal religion into a large circle of the leading families of the place. Many of this class were led to indulge hopes of salvation. I was waited upon by three or four of these persons, and informed that some twelve or fourteen of their number wished me to immerse them, with the understanding that they intended to join the Episcopal church. I endeavored to convince them that it would be better for them and their influence if they would join a church whose sentiments on this subject harmonized with their own convictions. They inferred that

I did not wish to immerse them, except on condition of their uniting with a Baptist church; and they finally submitted to the ceremony of sprinkling at the hands of the Episcopal minister. I have always regretted that I did not yield to their request. If I had immersed them, I should have helped them to perform the initiatory and symbolic rite required by Christ of his disciples, and have devolved the responsibility of their future associations on their own consciences. Their influence, even though indirect, would nevertheless have been more in favor of the true baptism, and their own minds would have been satisfied that they had at least obeyed the Savior's first command, and had symbolized the great truths that make distinctive and glorious the Christian system, namely, death to sin, and resurrection to newness of life; faith in a buried and risen Redeemer, and a hope of a blessed resurrection from the dead.*

I am unable to state the number of those who were converted or baptized as the result of this meeting. But all the churches received numerous accessions. Before this, the Baptist cause had been weak. There was only one church, and that a small one. Soon afterwards a second church was formed, and brother Cummings became its pastor, and continued such until quite recently (1867). Very many in this town had never witnessed the administration of a primitve baptism; and as they stood on the banks of the river, and saw score after score buried in the likeness of the Savior's death, they were constrained to acknowledge the beauty and scriptural simplicity of the ordinance.

About this time there prevailed throughout New England great excitement concerning the second coming of Christ. Brother Miller sincerely believed that the world would come to an end, and that the Savior would appear in personal glory some time during the year 1843. He was going from place to place proclaiming his views, and many good people adopted

* Christ has commissioned his ministers to baptize men, on condition of their faith in him; not on condition of their joining a Baptist church, and conforming to all its usages of polity and worship.

them. In some cases the peace of the churches was disturbed by reason of divisions on this question. The believers in this new doctrine of the special and immediate time in which Christ would appear, were very zealous in asserting their convictions in all the church meetings, and making demands on the ministers to preach the doctrine. In lukewarm churches this pertinacity of zeal was resisted and resented with acerbity; but where the Spirit of God was enjoyed, those brethren who did not adopt the view, were nevertheless willing that those who did might sing, and pray, and talk about the coming of Christ without hinderance. The subject itself is a glorious one at all times, and the errors as to date, though deplored, were not allowed to become a root of bitterness.

I was accustomed to dispose of all approaches on this subject in my meeting, as I did in theirs, by reminding the people that the spiritual presence of Christ was an existing fact, and one which they could all enjoy at present, and was more desirable than simply his corporeal presence, under the circumstances in which we were placed. Were he to come in person, all opportunity for repentance would be at an end; and that it was of the utmost importance that all Christians labor with all their might to bring sinners into the ark of salvation, especially as they believed they saw "the day approaching."

So far from being annoyed by the presence of these people, I found them of much service. They formed themselves into singing clubs, and they would sing and pray with great earnestness. A number of them accompanied me from Concord to Boston, singing in the cars on their way.

These were golden days, sunny spots, heavenly seasons. The memory of them is precious; and the recollection of them will be among my unspeakable joys when I shall have passed over Jordan.

My dear brother Cummings has furnished an account of this meeting, which I take pleasure in subjoining to mine: —

"The first century after the settlement of Concord was not marked by any very extensive revivals. During most of this period the 'standing order' held almost undisputed possession; there was but one church, and one place of meeting.

"The Baptist church came into existence in a very feeble condition, and for nearly ten years held meetings in school-houses, remote from the centre of the town. At length a house of worship was built in a most favorable location; and though the church was then feeble, it continued gradually to increase, and enjoyed, in the mean time, some most precious revivals. But the Baptists had not a commanding influence in the town. The state of religion, and the position of the Baptist church, rendered the labors of an evangelist both desirable and hopeful. In the winter of 1841–2 my people enjoyed a very precious revival, and the Spirit continued in the church through the season.

"Rev. Jacob Knapp commenced his labors in Concord, September 14, 1842. My people, I believe, were in a good degree prepared to enter into the work, and the community at large were anxious to hear the man about whom so much had been said. Our meetings were full from the first, and inquirers began to multiply. The meetings continued every afternoon and evening for six weeks. The work spread through my entire congregation, leaving but one family unblessed. It also extended through the entire town, including many in each congregation, and some who were not connected with any religious society.

"Indeed, the whole community was shaken; and persons who were supposed to be the farthest from the kingdom of heaven, were brought to bow at the foot of the cross. Some rum-sellers came forward, and confessed their deeds, and gave up the nefarious traffic. The Universalist minister first attempted to ease his conscience by submitting to the ordinance of baptism in a distant town; but afterwards renounced his heresies, professed to be converted, and united with the Congregational church. There were some very interesting cases of conversions, among which was a young lawyer, of marked ability, who gave very clear evidences of a change, and who, now in the midst of worldly distinctions, still retains the hope he then cherished.

"The work spread through all the regions. Persons attended the meeting from adjoining towns, and returned filled with the Spirit, and God worked through them in the communities where they belonged. Almost every church in the association was revived, and had large accessions to their number.

"It was estimated that over five hundred were converted during the meeting; of whom one hundred and twenty-six united with the Baptist church, and about two hundred with all the other churches in town. Brother Knapp preached the plain, simple gospel — "Jesus Christ, and him crucified." There was nothing in the doctrine or illustration to which I could object. There was constant reference to our dependence on divine influence. This was the key-note in the closet, in the family, in the inquiry-meeting, and in the pulpit. God's power was sought, and it was manifested from beginning to end. It was a gracious display of matchless grace; and I can bear witness to the endurance of the fruits. It is true some went back, and walked no more with Jesus; but many have gone home to glory, and many remain to bless the church of Christ to this day.

"As the results of the meeting, the church was enlarged and strengthened, secured a commanding influence in the town, and in eleven years after this meeting a colony went out from the church, built a new church edifice, and are enjoying a good degree of prosperity. The Baptists now have two churches, in a good condition, and have as much influence among the people as any denomination in the city; and the protracted meeting in 1842, under God, had much to do in giving them this standing. To Him be all the praise."

CHAPTER XV.

ACCOUNTS OF PROTRACTED MEETINGS.

(CONTINUED.)

SALEM *and* MARBLEHEAD: *Enlargement.* — *Conflict over a Soul.* — *A Universalist Prayer-Meeting.* — *Leaving Town.* — WASHINGTON: *A small Band.* — *Coöperation.* — *Dance-Hall.* — *Pro-Slavery.* — *A remarkable Conversion.* — *College Students.* — *E Street Church.* — RICHMOND: *Conditional Invitation.* — *Respect for Ministers.* — *An unhealthy Piety.* — *Slavery Abominations.* — *A Slave Prayer-Meeting, and Bloodhounds.* — *Remonstrance.* — *Departure.*

SALEM AND MARBLEHEAD.

ABOUT the beginning of the year 1843, I commenced my labors with the Second Baptist church in Salem, Mass., of which brother Banvard was pastor. The house of worship soon became too small for us. The First Baptist church was unwilling to open their doors to me, so that we were compelled to go to a public hall. At once this place became thronged. In a marvellous manner did God display the power of his grace. Hundreds on hundreds professed conversion, embracing persons of every class and condition: men, women, and children, rich and poor, high and low, all came together under the common impulse of a desire for salvation.

I spent a portion of the time at Marblehead, preaching there in the morning at half past nine o'clock, and returning in time to preach in the afternoon and evening at Salem. I conducted the inquiry-meetings as usual.

At Marblehead a hardened Universalist came forward for prayers, weeping, and begging for mercy. He continued all night in distress. His old Universalist friends came in to allay his fears, and dissuade him from his anxiety, but all was to no purpose: the load of sins weighed down his soul in grief. In the mean time he was visited by some Christian friends, who prayed with him and for him. Thus it seemed as if the conflicting agencies of good and evil were set to secure possession of his soul. One company was striving to save him from destruction, the other to compass his destruction. But towards morning judgment came forth unto victory; the prayers of saints, the sympathies of angels, and the Spirit of the Lord, prevailed over the combined assaults of wicked men, lost spirits, and the arch-fiend. The man found peace in believing, and shouted aloud, and gave glory to God.

Many Universalists were converted during this meeting. The minister and many of his members became alarmed, and, to save their sinking ship, they opened a prayer and conference-meeting. They invited everybody, of all denominations, to come and take part, and feel free to express their views on the subject of religion. Among those who responded, was a man who was under powerful conviction. He rose up to express his feelings; he confessed his sins, and invited others to seek the Lord with him. While he was yet speaking, the burden of guilt was rolled from his heart, the love of God filled him with joy indescribable, and he began to speak forth, with such thrilling eloquence, that he was soon requested to take his seat. He reminded them of their unlimited invitation to all to come and speak what was in their hearts; but they persisted in their purpose to silence him, and finally put him out of the house. Many others, indignant at this treatment, followed him, came over to our meeting, and found salvation. In this instance Satan cast out Satan.

The whole city of Salem was shaken by the power of God. Bar-rooms, ball-alleys, and haunts of vice were deserted, and those who had frequented them turned their feet to the place of prayer, and sought and found salvation.

When the time came for my departure, a company of Christians chartered a train of cars and accompanied me to Boston.

Immense crowds from the city and the regions round about gathered around the depot, covered the track, and blocked up the cars. All the adjoining streets were thronged with a sea of human beings. An hour was spent in attempts to clear the track, and the voice of singing and of prayer resounded through the air. In this way we continued our journey. On reaching Boston, I made a few farewell remarks. Amid many tears and parting greetings I turned from them, they and I weeping because we might never see each other's faces again; and joying, because very soon we should meet where

"No farewell sound is ever heard,
Not e'en the word Good-bye."

As soon as I reëntered the cars for Providence I took my seat in a corner, closed my eyes, and gave myself up to the ecstasy of silent prayer and praise to God.

Washington.

Near the close of the year 1843, I was invited by a little band of brethren and sisters in Washington, D. C., consisting of eleven persons, — eight women and three men, — who had formed themselves into a church, to hold a series of meetings with them. The only other Baptist church was a small, inefficient affair, exerting no moral power in the community.

This small company hired a hall, agreeing to pay one hundred dollars per month for the use of it, with the understanding that we were to vacate it two evenings in every week, on which nights it was engaged for holding balls. M. B. Anderson, now President of Rochester University, was then acting as their pulpit supply. He continued with me nearly through my meetings, but was at length compelled to return to his studies. Dr. Chapin and Professor Douglass, of Columbian College, took a deep interest in the work. Some Christians of other denominations came in, and lent a helping hand.

This dance-hall proved to be well adapted to our purposes; the side-rooms served us for holding female, inquiry, and young people's meetings. The Spirit of God soon began to move on the souls of men, and the hall itself seemed to be pervaded with the divine presence. We had to vacate it two nights for the service of the devil, but the balls proved miserable failures. One lady, who had paid three hundred dollars for a dress to wear on one of these occasions, said that she was never so wretched in all her life as on that night. The managers called on the proprietors, and told them that if they did not get Knapp out of the hall they would never hire it again. But our brethren had taken the precaution to secure, in writing, a lease for a given time, and in this case the children of light were wiser than the children of this world. We had got the start of the devil, and we kept in the advance. During the two evenings in which we were out of the hall, we were invited to occupy the Presbyterian Church, and did so. By this means we gained new recruits, and gathered increased strength to renew the battle on the devil's ground.

After I got well under way, I came out against the sin of slavery; denounced it as an institution of the devil; and advocated the equality and universality of human rights. Dr. Chapin called upon me, and tried to dissuade me from alluding to "the peculiar institution;" and informed me that if he had known I was going to preach against slavery, he would not have given me his influence; that it would not have been safe for himself, nor for the college, nor for the church. I replied that I could not help it; he must pursue such a course as he thought duty required, but that I should not, and could not, change my course. I was bound to preach up Christ, and preach down the devil.

Happily the work had, by this time, come to such a pitch, and gone on to such an extent, that the doctor did not dare to set his influence against it; nor would it have availed if he had, for it was not in the power of all the pro-slavery D. D.'s, nor of all the devils in hell, to stop the mighty tide of salvation which was then sweeping through the city.

One man, who had prosecuted a gentleman from New England

for having an anti-slavery tract in his trunk, and cast him into prison, where he took cold and died, came forward for prayers. He was in great distress of mind. A number of us continued in prayer for him, though at first the idea of such a man being converted taxed our faith; nevertheless, we knew he belonged to the human family, and that Christ had died for even such as he. And, sure enough, he gave us hopeful signs that he became truly penitent and believing!

Several of the students in the college were brought under the power of the gospel; some of them are now ministers.

Our baptismal services were usually scenes of great interest. On one occasion I formed twenty men in a line on the banks of the Potomac, and locking arms, they walked with me abreast down into the water, the congregation on the shore singing as they went. On reaching suitable depth, I commenced baptizing them; and each one standing in the water till all had been "buried with Christ;" we then locked arms again, and returned to the shore amid the greetings of song from the congregation who had witnessed the scene. Among the spectators were members of Congress, and several foreign ministers; some were standing, some were sitting in their carriages, but all were deeply affected, and many of them to tears.

While baptizing one day, a young man, who had imbibed infidel views from his father, rode his horse into the water close by where I was administering the ordinance, in order, as he said, that he might have a fair view. As he witnessed the calm and joyous expression of the faces of the candidates as they came up, one after another, out of the water, a sudden sensation of trembling seized him, so that he was compelled to hold himself on his horse by main force. He went from the scene to his home, and did not leave it for three days. On the evening of the third day he came to the meeting and related the above, and besought the prayers of God's people. On the following Lord's day he was baptized in the same place.

I remained in Washington about seven weeks, preaching day and night. As the result of this meeting, movements were inaugurated before I left, for the erection of the Baptist Church on E Street. The number of persons brought into the church in consequence of this effort, including those gathered in by brother Sampson after I had gone, amounted to about two hundred.

Richmond.

While I was preaching in Washington, I was waited on by Elder Jeter and Deacon Thomas, of Richmond, Va., and invited to visit that city. They wanted me, however, to give them a pledge that I would keep silence on the subject of slavery. They remained at my lodgings till near midnight, arguing this point, but to no purpose. I had never made such a pledge, and I could not be persuaded to put on a muzzle simply because of the prejudices of that people in favor of slavery. They left me, as I supposed, with the intention of letting the matter drop. But shortly afterwards I received a letter from them, asking me to come on, and saying that I would be left to take my own course in regard to that particular subject, expressing the belief, however, that when I got on the ground, and learned the state of things, I would see the propriety of abstaining from any interference with their "peculiar institution." I concluded to go to Richmond.

On going on board the steamer we found the table covered with gambling cards, and the preparations completed for beginning a game. But very soon it was whispered around that "Elder Knapp and his wife were on board." The cards were gathered up and put out of sight, and Bibles and hymn-books were set in their place. I began to think that I had never seen ministers of the gospel treated with greater respect on the waters of the Eastern or Western States, and I imagined that I could guess the reason. I knew that the devil was an old philosopher and a wise manager, and that as long as he could keep ministers under his control, and induce them to indorse slavery, rum-drinking, and the like, he would treat them politely. Rum-sellers will not object to wearing out two or three hats a year in bowing to ministers, provided they will keep silent, and let them carry on their work of death. Slaveholders will be very complaisant and respectful to God's servants if they will but apologize for their system of iniquity, occasionally come out with a defence of the practice, and allow them to prescribe the topics which shall constitute the staple of pulpit ministrations.

When we reached Richmond we were met by a number of the brethren, and accompanied to the house of Elder Jeter, with whom we boarded. He was the pastor of the First church, Elder Magoon of the Second, Elder Taylor was preaching in the Third, and spending a part of his time in the service of the Missionary Society.

I commenced with the First church, preaching day and night to large congregations. The prospects continued to brighten, and very many were beginning to yield to the power of the truth. As soon, however, as I began to elevate the standard of piety, and to labor to bring the church up to the Bible idea of a devoted, working, holy people, I found that I was bringing my batteries to bear against an impregnable fortress of prejudice and error. They did not want a reformation; they desired merely a revival, a season of religious sensationalism. I felt that the Lord bade me proclaim a fast; but they had no idea that it meant the breaking of every yoke, and letting the oppressed go free. All of their fasting seemed to me like solemn mockery.

I could hold my peace no longer; the pastor was raising boys and girls for market, like so many calves and pigs; the slave-pen was within the city corporation, and there men, and women, and children, some of them members of the church, were bought and sold every day; husbands and wives were torn asunder; little children were dragged from the arms of their mothers; womanhood was denuded of its modesty, and girls were sold for lust. The whipping-post was close to the house of God, and the crack of the lash and the cries of the slave victims mingled with the songs of devotion and the voice of prayer

While I was there a band of colored brethren and sisters, moved by the Spirit of God, met together in order to sing praises and unite in supplication to the Lord. They were surprised by a set of devils (called officers of the peace!), and those who could not escape were dragged to the whipping-post, and lashed to laceration, for no other offence than daring to meet without the presence of a white man. Throughout the night the slave-hounds were on the scent for these victims, and the hours were made hideous with their howlings. It seemed as if I was in Pandemonium.

How could I ask God to hear the prayers of such a people? I knew that the churches and the ministers were involved in this system of iniquity. I kept verging out gradually on this great evil. I found those who had been brought up in New England, and other Northern States, among the most strenuous and bitter advocates of slavery. As I continued to preach, with increasing plainness, the Bible doctrines concerning human rights, and those which cut up this system root and branch, the leading members became more and more uneasy. Some would plead with me to pass over this subject, assuring me that, with this exception, my preaching was popular with the community, and that I might do great good if I would not dwell on this one theme. But I could not refrain.

At length, after having preached about three weeks in the First church, and about two weeks in the Second, I preached a sermon on the moral government of God, in which I showed that all the misery in the world arose from the violation of God's laws. Our failures to love God supremely, and our neighbors as ourselves, were infractions of his holy law; and that if we did love our neighbor as ourselves, we should not, for example, be willing to enslave him, any more than we should be willing to have him enslave us. The feeling throughout the congregation was intense; many came forward for prayers, and the work was rolling on with increasing power.

On reaching my room, I was visited by a committee, and requested to preach no more, unless I would promise to keep silent on the subject of slavery. They professed fears for my safety, and thought that the house would be burned down. I told them that I would risk my life if they would risk their house. I knew where the shoe pinched. The slaveholding members were afraid that their non-slaveholding brethren would get light and influence, and render the position of the slaveholding party uncomfortable; besides, they were in love with their darling sin. The issue, however, was squarely made. I had no choice, except to submit to their terms or leave. I decided to leave. We sent for our clothes, which were out to be washed, packed them up, wet from the tub, and started from the place by six o'clock the next morning. We shook the dust of the city from off our feet as a witness against them, and I have not seen Richmond since.

CHAPTER XVI.

ACCOUNTS OF PROTRACTED MEETINGS.

(CONTINUED.)

ERIE: *A Universalist Meddler, and his Fate.* — *An Irish Lad.* — *Nineteen Years afterwards.* — OWEGO: *Philetus Peck.* — *Dews of Grace.* — *A model Church.* — *A defiant Infidel.* — *Wilfulness.* — *Departed Worthies.*

ERIE.

IN the month of June, 1847, I arrived at Erie, Pa., then comparatively a new town. The Baptist church was struggling into existence, and was weak in every sense of the word. I reached there on a Saturday, and began preaching on the next day. There was a remarkable expression of interest at the start. On the close of the evening sermon the Universalist minister arose, in the presence of the congregation, and began to contradict what I had said. I spoke to him kindly, reminding him that as that service was not of his appointment, he had no right to interrupt its exercises, and requested him to be seated. He replied, that he had as good a right to speak as I had, and would speak as much as he pleased. Finding that simple remonstrance was of no avail, I dropped on my knees, requesting all the congregation to unite with me in prayer. I prayed very earnestly, and specially asked God that, "if this servant of the devil was within the reach of mercy, he might be converted on the spot; but if he was never to be converted, that his mouth might be closed, so that he would not be able to lead others down to hell." As soon as I arose from my knees he began to speak again, and I dismissed the meeting. The choir struck up a hymn, and I signified to the congregation tc retire.

He followed me to my lodgings, and declared "that he would attend my meetings every night, and that I could not help myself." I merely said, "There is a God in heaven who can help me," and entered the house. I neither saw nor heard more of him during my stay in the place. I was somewhat surprised, and so were others, at his sudden subsiding. It was generally supposed that he had left town; but after my return home, I received a letter from brother Smith, the pastor of the Baptist church, stating that this Universalist minister lost his power of speech on the very night on which I turned from him; that he had remained concealed, and that the Universalists had sought to keep these facts from the knowledge of the community; and that at the date of that letter, he was able to speak only just above a whisper. I have inquired after him occasionally, and have learned, from time to time, that he has remained speechless for at least fifteen years. I have recently heard that his power of speech is somewhat improving, but he has never since, I believe, attempted to speak in public. This statement can be corroborated by reference to some of the older residents of the town.

This man was a great talker, and was very flippant in his advocacy of his favorite dogma. And as the people were then in a plastic taste, he was capable of doing much harm in leading the youth astray. He was fond of challenging ministers to debate with him, using "great swelling words," and making a tumult; like the Philistine of Gath, he defied the armies of Israel.

Our meeting went on quietly after we had got rid of this troubler, and large accessions were made to the Baptist church, and also several additions to other denominations.

Among the converts was a poor Irish lad, whom, on a visit nineteen years afterwards, I found to be a man worth a large property, and devotedly engaged in promoting the interests of the Savior's cause, and in all things proving himself to be a pillar in the Baptist church, and zealously coöperating with his pastor, brother Bainbridge, whose father I baptized in Pennyan many years ago. The father was a faithful minister of Christ, and who, after serving his generation, dropping his mantle on the shoulder of his son, went up to his reward. O, how earnestly I pray that God will uphold and honor the steps of the son!

Owego.

Near the close of 1848, brother Philetus Peck, son of Elder John Peck, and the pastor of the Baptist church at Owego, N. Y., was summoned to the bedside of his mother, who was dying, the victim of an epidemic. His brother, Linus, then preaching at Hamilton, N. Y., was with him. In a few days the two brothers were smitten down with the same disease, and died. Linus was the younger of the two, had recently been married to the daughter of Dr. Nathaniel Kendrick, and was beginning his ministry under circumstances full of promise. Philetus had been for several years pastor of the church at Owego, and was beloved of all, having proven himself to be an able preacher, a great-hearted man, and a sincere and humble Christian. While the life of their beloved pastor was trembling in the balance, the church was holding meetings of prayer for his recovery. At one of these assemblings, the sad news came upon them that their pastor was dead. Overwhelmed with the grief that was inspired by the sincerest affection, the church prostrated themselves before God, and besought him to strengthen them to bear their great sorrow, and to sanctify it to their greater devotion.

The gracious dews of heavenly grace began to fall on them at once, and they sent a messenger for me to come among them immediately. I had just returned from a long tour in the east, and needed rest, but my heart went out to this smitten flock. I could not understand the meaning of Providence in taking away a man in the midst of his days and of his usefulness, who, by reason of his advanced views, was so eminently fitted to be a leader of the people. I went at once, and found the field white for the harvest, and waiting only for the reaper's sickle. The interest of the meeting was overwhelming. The church as a body seemed to lay their all on the altar of God. I was specially struck with the utter absence of social distinctions among the brethren. The rich and well provided were careful to invite their poorer brethren, and those living at a distance, to their houses, in order that all might have opportunity to share the blessings of the meetings. Never did I see elsewhere such an exemplification of the command, " Have not the grace of our Lord Jesus Christ with respect to persons."

The minds of the different brethren were as the mind of one man. They came together " with one accord ; " they all pulled one way ; they delighted to honor each other ; they worked with all their might.

I preached day and night for some six weeks, and nearly three hundred persons were added to the church, most of whom I baptized before I left.

I remember that a hardened infidel, who had been accustomed to curse ministers and churches, followed me to my lodgings one night, keeping up an incessant tirade of abuse. As I was stepping into the door, I remarked, " Well, my friend, I expect to see you on the anxious-seat before long." He turned away, exclaiming, " Never ! no, never." On the evening of the third day after this conversation, whom should I see in the seats before me but this same man ! As I approached him, he asked, " What shall I do? I am in deep trouble." I told him to pray. He said, " I cannot pray ; *I dare not* pray." I replied, " God is merciful ; go to Jesus, and ask him to forgive you." He replied, " I have damned him to his face, and how can I ask him for mercy. It seems to me, that the moment I attempt to pray, the devil will take me right down to hell." I told him to begin, and keep on praying, and the devil would not carry him far, for he wanted no praying souls in hell. He knelt, and made the attempt to pray. He would open his mouth, and as he was about to speak his courage would fail him, and he would sink down again. Throughout that night, and during a part of the next day, he continued in this horrible condition; at length he cried out to God to have mercy upon him for the sake of Christ. God came to his relief, and he broke forth in strains of joy as the consciousness of pardon and of hope beamed on his soul.

A young lady, educated in the Congregational church, talented and respected, but strong in her prejudices, was awakened to a sense of her lost condition. After much hesitation she came forward for prayers; but when asked to rise, and express her feelings, she replied, "I do not think it proper for women to speak in public." A colored brother, who was within hearing, remarked, "Well, I guess when you git the lub o' God in yer heart, you'll be willin' to speak." She darted out of the seat, and out of the house, remarking, "I am not going to be lectured by negroes." She left us, and went to the Presbyterian and Methodist meetings; but at the end of a week she came back, still burdened with anxiety and beclouded with darkness. She summoned strength to rise and speak, still something held her back. She told me that she was afraid that if converted in a Baptist meeting, she would have to join a Baptist church. Under this pretext she was allowing Satan to deceive her. With this frivolous, sectarian excuse, she was trying to think she had a reason why she should not give her heart to God. At length she saw that her pride was her great hinderance. She let go her sectarianism and her prejudices, and made an unreserved surrender of herself to the will of Christ; and in the joy of her heart she sprang to her feet, and proclaimed, in thrilling words, what the Lord had done for her soul. She wanted to go down into the river and be baptized at once, and could hardly wait till the church had voted to receive her.

Among the precious memories of those days, I recall the faces of father Pinney, and his dear wife and their sons, and brother Tenman, and many others. How earnestly these aged saints labored in the good work! how lovingly they loved all who loved Christ, and sympathized with all classes of men! They have gone home, and "rest from their labors, but their works do follow them." Ah, how short is life! "It is even as a vapor, which appeareth for a little time, and then vanisheth away." How pertinent the admonition, "Whatsoever thy hand findeth to do, do it with thy might."

CHAPTER XVII.

ACCOUNTS OF PROTRACTED MEETINGS.

(CONTINUED.)

CHICAGO: *First Church in* 1849; *in* 1857. — *Conversions.* — *Invitation to a Ball.* — *Wabash Avenue Church.* — *Wordliness.* ROCKFORD: *Removal to, in* 1849. — *A Year's Labor in Rockford.* CANTON: *In* 1851. — *A Mind to Work.* — *The Zeal of one Man.* — *Immediate Baptisms.* — "*Hell upon Earth.*"

CHICAGO.

IN the month of June, 1849, for the first time I visited the West. I spent a few weeks in Chicago, Ill., preaching to the First Baptist church. They were without a pastor at the time. I baptized about fifty persons, and searched out, and gathered into the church, several who had been members of eastern churches, but who had not identified themselves with the cause in this place. Among these were some who are now recognized among the most valuable of its members.

Subsequently I held two other meetings in this city, both of which proved great blessings to the community. The third meeting was held with the Wabash Avenue Baptist church.

The second meeting with the First church, about 1857, resulted in the conversion of many young men, among whom were the children of the late Judge Thomas,* of Dr. Boone, then mayor of the city, and of Hon. Charles Walker.

While this meeting was in progress I received a ticket from the manager of a ball which was soon to come off. When I entered the pulpit, I remarked that I had received an invitation

* One of whom is now the beloved pastor of the Pierrepont Street Baptist church, Brooklyn, N. Y.

to attend a ball that evening; and inasmuch as I had not attended one for more than thirty years, I thought I would go; that I would preach a short sermon, and wanted the brethren to continue in prayer till my return.

Some wag in the gallery slipped out, and went over to the ball-room, and told them that I was coming over there. One of the company said, "O, you are joking." "No," replied the young man, "I heard him say that he was coming at the close of a short sermon." I took brother Walker with me. Before we had reached the place some had left; and as we got there, some were going into the yard, and some were running up and down stairs. The young ladies were begging the gentlemen to take them home. Several, however, made a show of determination to keep up the dance. But they made bad work of it. There was music enough in the fiddles, but the fiddlers could not get it out. Their limbs trembled, and the dance was not up to time. I made a few remarks, spent a season in prayer, and invited them to come and hear me preach on the subject of dancing on the next Friday evening. Very many of them did so; and I hope that they were made wiser and better. I think that about seventy persons were baptized into the fellowship of the First church, as the result of this meeting.

Brother Edwards was preaching at the same time to the Second church, and a good work was done there.

My meeting in the Wabash Avenue church took place in 1862. The war excitement was running high, and the spirit of speculation higher. Many brethren of business could not find time to attend except on the Sabbath. Even brethren who had been converted under my ministry, or whose children had been, and who personally felt a great interest in me, were so engaged in their worldly pursuits, that they felt justified in excusing themselves from the work of the Lord. As might be expected, the work was not general. Still our labors were not without considerable fruit, and seed was sown that may yet bear a plentiful harvest.

Rockford.

In the month of October, 1849, I reached Rockford, Ill., with my family, and located them about four miles from the town.

The Baptist church in Rockford was quite small. They had a little wooden building, which might, by crowding, hold two hundred persons. Yet this was larger than the size of the congregation ordinarily required. The pulpit was being supplied by Professor S. S. Whitman, who lived in Belvidere. But his health was failing, and in a short time "he fell on sleep." I felt a deep interest in this little church, and consented to preach for them during the fall and winter. In the winter I preached forty sermons, in nightly succession, and rode home after each sermon.

In a short time we were crowded out of our small quarters, and secured the use of the Court House until the present commodious stone edifice was completed. I baptized eighty persons into the fellowship of this church. I remained with them nearly a whole year, until the new house was finished, and then they secured the services of Elder Ichabod Clarke, and I resumed my labors as an evangelist.

Canton.

In the autumn of 1851, I commenced a meeting in Canton, Ill. The Baptist church was under the pastoral care of brother W. G. Miner. There was no special religious interest in the community when we began, but the pastor and brethren took hold with a hearty good will, and the Spirit of God came down with great power. We gave the trumpet a certain sound, and the people prepared themselves for battle. Some squirmed under the truth, and quailed before the grape-shot which flew in every direction; sinners cried out for mercy, and crowded round "the anxious seats." The weather was very unpleasant, the mud being almost knee deep, and the roads nearly impassable; nevertheless the people met, and men and women kept pouring in from all the surrounding region. Two brethren kept their teams constantly engaged in carrying the people to and from the meeting. The house soon became too small for the throngs that gathered to hear the word. In one single day lumber was brought on to the ground, and addition made to the building, so that the crowd at night found the borders of our habitation enlarged for their accommodation.

As an instance of the zeal of the brethren, I will mention the case of an aged saint, who lived some distance from town, and became so interested that he built a little room in the place, so that he and his wife might enjoy all the services. He became so greatly concerned on account of his children and grandchildren, that he started on a journey, eighteen miles, in order to talk with them on the concerns of their souls. He induced many of them, and of their neighbors, to come to the meetings, and about twenty persons were brought to Christ in that neighborhood as the reward of his fidelity. How easy it is to do good, and how much good can be done by the feeblest instrumentalities!

It was our custom to follow close upon the heels of the apostles in the baptizing of converts. When one rose up, rejoicing in the blessed Savior, the church would vote him right in, and we baptized him. In one week brother Miner and myself baptized seventy persons, who, during the same week, professed to have experienced a change of heart. Before the work ceased, three hundred were "added to the church," and the number of communicants amounted to six hundred. This season was a memorable epoch in the history of Canton.

At its close, when my mind was wrought up to the height of a blissful experience of communion with God and heaven, I was compelled to pass a night, on my return home, at a little, low grog-shop of a shanty, which was the only lodging-place the spot afforded. Drunkards and swearers were congregated in the room where I was obliged to sit, and they made the night hideous with their cursings and obscenities. It seemed as if they were exhausting the vocabulary of blasphemy. Their language was the dialect of perdition, and the scene formed such a contrast with the rapture with which I had been exalted, that it seemed to me to be itself a hell upon earth. Twice, as I fell into a doze, I was awakened by their carousals, and for the moment I thought I was verily in hell; and I opened my eyes, expecting to see the devil himself. When fully restored to wakefulness, I lifted up to God the prayer, "Gather not my soul with sinners."

CHAPTER XVIII.

ACCOUNTS OF PROTRACTED MEETINGS.

(CONTINUED.)

ST. LOUIS: *Sparks from the One Altar. — Disparagement. — Great Ingathering. — Giving the Hand of Fellowship. — A new Church formed. — Its Dismemberment.* MIDLETOWN: *Pecuniary Inducements. — Hesitation about going. — Prayers for the Devil. — Obeying Orders. — Results. — Meeting in* 1864. — *Youngest Son converted.* LOUISVILLE: *Sensitiveness of the People concerning Slavery. — Apprehensions. — Signs of Success. — A Dream, and its Interpretation. — Notice to leave.*

ST. LOUIS.

IN the winter of the year 1858, I was invited to hold a meeting in the Second Baptist church, in St. Louis, Mo., then destitute of a pastor. Though the church was in a low estate, I found much excellent material in it. As soon as prayer and preaching were maintained day and night, the members began to be interested, and came up to the work with zest. Converts were multiplied. The other churches began to catch the spirit; especially was this true of the Third church, where a blessed outpouring of the Spirit was enjoyed.

Some one wrote an article in the Christian Times, in which he announced that other churches were enjoying a precious visitation of grace almost as great as that with which the Second church was being favored. The tone of the article was impliedly calculated to insinuate disparagement on my labors. He did not, or would not, see that other altars had been kindled from sparks from off the altar before which we were ministering, and that others were reaping a harvest which had resulted from the breaking up of the fallow ground in the first instance. We made no reply; for the work was all of God, and to him belonged all the glory. He that planteth and he that watereth are nothing; but God, who giveth the increase, is all and in all.

On the last day of my labors with the Second church I extended the hand of fellowship to one hundred and fifty persons. The scene was admitted to be among the most soul-stirring that had ever been witnessed in the city. In the first place, after arranging the candidates along the outside aisle, the members sitting in the centre pews, I gave to each the hand of welcome, and made to each person a few appropriate remarks; then the members of the church formed into line, and passed along the line, and shook hands with each of the converts; all singing beautiful revival tunes as they went through the ceremony of greeting. The house was crowded, and many shed tears, and many were pricked in their hearts.

Many of the members of the church, both old and new, were strongly impressed with the conviction that the time had come in which to form a new church. There was wealth and talent sufficient to warrant it, and souls enough to demand it. After I had left, and had entered on another field, a delegation came to solicit my presence and counsel in the enterprise. Though the Second church, as a body, did not seem to favor the movement, yet it seemed to me that the general interests of the cause would be promoted if its forces were divided (for I never did think it best to plant all the corn in one hill); besides, the necessities of that growing city made the starting of another church a duty. Brother Nelson had secured a good church building, in a good location, at a very great bargain. I therefore went, and called together all who were willing to embark in the enterprise. A church was organized at once. I remained with them some four months, and at the end of that time the additions, by letter and baptisms, numbered two hundred persons.

On my departure, I helped them to secure the services of a well-known and highly-esteemed brother for six months. At the expiration of that time, the demands made on him from other quarters seemed to call him away. Then followed seasons of discouragement and difficulty, which finally led to the disbanding of the church, and the return of the members into the other churches.

MIDDLETOWN.

In the month of March, 1859, I visited Middletown, Ohio. A good brother, more than twenty years before, had urged me strongly to hold a meeting in this town. He had offered to give me one hundred dollars over and above what the church might do, if I would only come. But on that account, as well as for other reasons, I would not go, lest I might, even unconsciously, be actuated by a mercenary spirit. For the same reason I declined a call to another place, where I was offered one hundred and sixty acres of good land in the State of Illinois by one man. I never answered his letter. I have always been anxious to go where I thought I could do the most good, without any regard to my compensation; and I have often found that where there has been the least prospect of being well compensated I have fared the best.

But at length I felt it to be my duty to go to Middletown. I found this dear brother's heart, house, and purse all open to do anything for Jesus. At the beginning of the meeting, I remarked, that I wished all to suspend their judgments about the preaching until they had heard twenty sermons; that I did not always preach alike, and often did not like my own preaching; and that, if at the end of that time they did not feel themselves profited, I would excuse them.

A man of distinction in the town, and professedly an infidel, said, as also did many others, that my request was quite reasonable, and that he would comply with it, and attend steadily. While many were sending in requests for prayers, he sent in one, to the effect that "the devil might be converted," adding, that he thought that if the devil was converted, others might be more easily reached. I read the request, and gave notice that, on a given night, I would preach a sermon, showing "why it was necessary that there should be a devil." The night came, and the house was crowded. This infidel lawyer was on hand,

and beginning to give signs of a concern which he could not conceal. A few days afterwards, I said to him, "Mr. D., you are a lawyer, and I am a minister. If I had an important case to be tried before a civil court, I should commit it into your hands, and follow your advice, because I know that in such matters your judgment would be better than mine. Is it not reasonable that you should take my advice in religious matters, seeing they have been the study and business of my life?" His answer was, "Well, that looks reasonable; I will do it." "Now," said I, "come out, and take the seat for prayers." He did so. At the close of the meeting that evening I begged him to pray with his family before he retired. He agreed to do so. As he sat by the side of his wife, who was a Christian, before the fire, the cross seemed like the weight of a mountain. He afterwards told me, that if he could have chosen between kneeling in prayer and throwing a thousand bank bills into the stove, he would gladly have done the latter. But, true to his promise, he bowed himself in prayer for the first time in his life, and there Jesus met him. His burden left him, and he rejoiced in the Savior. He has made a useful Christian from that day to this.

There were between seventy and eighty persons converted, and added to the church, during this revival. In a meeting with this church, at a later period (1864), about the same number were again brought into the church. In each of these, persons joined who were influential members of society. And now the church is a strong and able body.

This people, as have many other, became very dear to me, by reason of the precious seasons I enjoyed with them; especially because it was here (1864) that my youngest son, Luther, was born again.

LOUISVILLE.

Shortly after the settlement of brother W. W. Everts, as pastor of the Walnut Street Baptist church, in Louisville, Ky., I was sent for. This was in the year 1856.

I knew that, Kentucky being a slave state, I should be exposed to serious liabilities of difficulty. The prejudices of the people were very strong, and their sensitiveness quickened by reason of the political excitement that was then beginning to rage all over the country on account of this subject. But the remembrance of the blessed seasons that I had enjoyed with brother Everts, in Mulberry Street, New York city, kindled within me a desire to renew my intercourse with a brother whom I so highly esteemed. I persuaded myself that perchance the way would be smoothed before me, so that I should share in a marvellous display of God's grace. I therefore resolved to go.

Very soon there appeared to prevail throughout the city a seriousness on the subject of religion, and very many, especially the young, came forward for prayers, and converts were beginning to be multiplied.

I found the membership of this church to be composed of two classes, — earnest pro-slavery, and strong anti-slavery men; who, however, had come to the mutual agreement that nothing should be said on the subject of slavery, either for or against. A former pastor — a northern man — had sought to conciliate the people by preaching in favor of slavery; but the church, consistent with itself, had dismissed him. Brother Everts and myself, after consulting together, in view of this peculiar state of things, concluded that it would not be wise for me to come out against slavery at once. The attempt might jeopardize the meeting, and fail to do as much good as the same remarks might effect when I had gained a better hold on the people. Still I could not bring my conscience to consent to an entire silence on the subject. So I concluded to say nothing about it till near the close of the meeting, when God had given me many souls as seals of my ministry. I purposed to preach on the subject in one discourse only, and give such advice as my age and experience would qualify me to give and prepare them to receive.

By some means, however, my intentions got whispered around. The devil rallied all his forces among the slaveholding members, and excited the prejudices and fears of the people. They became uneasy, and were expecting that in my "next" sermon I would open my batteries on their peculiar and pet institution. On one occasion, I merely quoted the simple text, "Think not that I am come to send peace on the earth; I came not to send peace, but a sword." Instantly their pro-slavery sympathies took the alarm.

A change, which I had felt to be coming over the people, now became more marked than ever. A studied reserve and avoidance seemed to characterize the deportment of many; a cloud appeared to hang over the meetings; the wheels of salvation were clogged. My soul was bowed down. I prayed and fasted often. I sought to know the mind of God as to what course I should pursue. At length, one night I had a sort of dream, or vision. I saw myself standing on the edge of a raceway, filled with all kinds and sizes of fish. I stepped into the water, and found them so plentiful, and withal so tame, that they gathered around and touched my limbs. I was able to take up and throw them on the bank as fast as others could take care of them. While thus engaged, some one, whom I did not clearly recognize, went below and shut down the gate, when, in an instant, the whole school of fish turned round, and moved up, and glided into the main stream, and went off beyond my reach. I had caught but few, and my hopes were blasted. I awoke with a feeling of sadness; a premonition of trouble.

On the next night, after the sermon, a paper was handed to me, which contained a communication, signed by some of the deacons and leading members, expressing the opinion that the work was now well under way, and requesting me to retire, and leave the meetings in the hands of the pastor. Of course the gate was shut. I remembered my dream, and saw the interpretation thereof.

My indignation at the injustice with which I was treated, yielded to my grief at their own blindness and insensibility to the blessings which God was willing to bestow upon them. I thought of the many souls that might have been saved; and as

I realized how easily they might have been reached, and that now they were thrown off into the broad stream of death, my heart was melted in grief. The everlasting well-being of multitudes, the honor of the cause of Christ, had been deliberately sacrified to the Moloch of slavery.

Many of the church were indignant, and even some of the old Kentucky families wept like children, as they thought of this unkindness. The next day was rainy and gloomy. I crossed the river, feeling myself forsaken, sad, and desolate. I remained standing on the opposite bank in the rain, deliberating whether or not I should go back and open a meeting in some other part of the town, and see if God would not come to my help, and shake the city; but finally concluded to shake the dust off my feet, and turn my back on the place. I understood, better than ever before, the feelings of the Savior when he wept at sight of Jerusalem, and uttered his lament over its inevitable fate.

CHAPTER XIX.

ACCOUNTS OF PROTRACTED MEETINGS.

(CONTINUED.)

BOSTON: *Baldwin Place Church. — Changes in Nineteen Years. — Self-Examination. — Discouragements. — Union Church. — Great Work. — A genuine Convert. — Presence of God. — Tremont Temple Church. — Sinless Perfection, and the lack of it. — Conversion of a Universalist Preacher. — Farewell Sermon in Bowdoin Square Church. — A working Church.*

BOSTON.

IN the autumn of 1860, I was again invited to visit Boston, Mass. The request came from the Baldwin Place and Union churches.

I began with the Baldwin Place church. I preached day and night, and had good, but not crowded congregations. The lapse of nineteen years had wrought many changes. In the first place, the tide of population had set in on the South End; the surroundings of Baldwin Place were occupied by stores and warehouses, and foreigners. In the next place, many of those whose coöperation I had enjoyed had passed to their reward. Again, others had become lukewarm, and many had imbibed prejudices against protracted efforts, especially if conducted by outside agency; while others, though sympathizing with me and my work, had become too old and feeble to render me much assistance. Among these I may mention brethren Wilbur, Gilbert, and Hill. Withal the church itself was very much reduced in numbers and efficiency, having only two or three who were earnest and available co-workers; and these few faithful men were embarrassed by reason of the serious faultiness of one who occupied the position of a leader in Israel, but failed sadly to come up to the help of the Lord, and whose inconsistencies were beginning to awaken anxiety and alarm.

The contrast between this and my former visit brought great sorrow to my soul, but I resolved to consecrate myself unreservedly to God. I fasted and prayed day and night; I instituted a new and strict self-examination; scrutinized my motives; reviewed my whole course of labors, and prayed to know all my defects. I asked God to show me if the tone of my preaching had been too severe; whether I had indulged in a censorious spirit in my remarks concerning ministers or the people, especially concerning those who had opposed me. In short, I inquired of the Lord to show me what change in my course would be agreeable to his will, or was demanded by the different state of public feeling. I think I sincerely desired to know and do the will of God.

After trying to accomplish something at Baldwin Place, I became satisfied that it was not my duty to continue there any longer. I therefore gave them notice of my intention to leave, and forthwith began a series of meetings with the Union church in Merrimac Street.

Here the work of the Lord broke out with great power. "The people had a mind to work." Brother Chipman paid the salary of a brother, whom he engaged to devote his entire time in going from house to house, talking and praying with the people, and inducing persons to attend the meetings and seek salvation. He was also quite prominent in providing the support of a brother who preached in Globe Hall, and labored among the most degraded classes of the city.

The interest extended over to Cambridgeport and Charlestown. Very many of the most hardened sinners were converted, especially as the result of the meetings held in the hall. One man, who had been a pirate, and others, whose lives had been given up to unrestrained wickedness, were converted. There was one marked case. A man of more than ordinary talent, and of natural generosity, — one whom we could call "whole-souled," — and who had been a rum-seller for twenty years, and, as might be supposed, a confirmed Universalist, came into our meetings. Once he was in comfortable circumstances and respectable, but now his family were reduced to want, and he became a sot. He was deeply convicted, and on one occasion took three glasses of brandy in order to put an end to his misery. He went home, laid himself on the floor, and waited for death; but the distress of his mind was more powerful than the brandy. At length he was constrained to send for some one to come and pray for him. He became a very humble and earnest Christian, and was especially successful in bringing his former associates to listen to the preached word. He spent his whole time among tipplers, drunkards, and drunkard makers, striving to lead them to Jesus. He rose up early in the mornings, and went on from day to day. One day his wife told him that there was nothing for dinner. His faith in God was such, that he assured her that God would provide for those who were intent on doing his will. As he turned to leave, he espied a five-dollar bill which some one had thrust in under the door. On another occasion, his wife reminded him that the rent was due. He gave her a similar answer, and a few minutes afterwards a friend sent to the house money enough to meet the rent. In this trustful way he worked all winter. His daily wants were provided for, and he was busy in winning souls. It is needless to say that his labors were crowned with great success.

During this meeting I enjoyed very much of the presence of God. The brethren would set apart special days of consecration, and pray for the descent of the Spirit on those particular days; and on those occasions the very atmosphere seemed impregnated with the divine influence. No one could come into the room where we were without recognizing the presence of God. At times it seemed as if I was overwhelmed with the gracious fulness of God, and that my poor and limited faculties could bear no more. The tide of salvation rose higher and higher. Converts were multiplied by scores and by hundreds. Our place of worship became too small for us, and it was thought best for me to move to some other part of the city. I remember, with great satisfaction, the warm-hearted coöperation of brother D. M. Crane, the pastor. I labored with the Union church about ten weeks.

After some consultation I concluded to go to the Tremont Temple. The pastor of this church was about to be absent for several months, and the location being central, and accessible from all parts, rendered the opportunity very desirable. On Sundays I preached in the main audience-room, and during the week in the Meionaon, — a hall in the building, which will hold eight hundred persons. Many of the brethren and sisters who had worked in the Union church came with me to the Temple. Enough remained behind to keep the work going on there.

At this place I met with some who thought they had reached a state of entire sanctification. As for myself, I was never troubled with too much holiness; my difficulty has rather been the want of it. I encourage all to believe in the doctrine as much as they please, and practise it all they can. I have believed, for many years, that there was no law of God that we were obliged to break; no command that we could not keep; and, for months together, I have thought that my entire will was swallowed in the divine will, and my soul was filled "with joy unspeakable, and full of glory;" still, at times, I could detect in myself some lurkings of ambition for the honors of men, or of more regard to my own indulgence or interest than was compatible with a state of sinless perfection. In short, I have never reached a condition in my religious experience wherein I have come to regard the repetition of the prayer, "Forgive us our sins," as a superfluous or inappropriate utterance.

A man who had been preaching Universalism, and lecturing on temperance throughout New England, came into the Temple full of a resolution to expose my errors; but he had not been in the room long before he began to perceive his own. He resisted, for a time, his convictions, and though "almost," was not quite "persuaded" to renounce his former views. While in this vacillating condition his eyesight became dim; his strength began to fail him; he started for his boarding-place, and when he reached the house he was so bewildered, and his sight had so failed him, that he was compelled to call for help He passed a sleepless night, and made a solemn promise to the Lord, that if he would preserve his life until morning, he would publicly renounce his errors, and devote his life to trying to undo the evil he had done. He continued to be blind, or nearly so, during all the next day; in the evening he was in the meeting, and he arose, confessed his sins, renounced his false doctrines, and begged for prayers. He remained, however, in a despondent state of mind for two or three days. He seemed to think that even if God were to forgive him, he could never forgive himself on account of the injury he had done in leading so many astray. This reflection was the great sorrow of his heart. He could neither think nor talk of anything else. Even after he had obtained a sense of pardon, through the atonement of Christ, the prevailing state of his mind was that of self-reproach.

After preaching one evening on the subject of "Parkerism," I called on him to relate his experience, but the infidels in the congregation would not listen to him. Their master, the devil, dare not risk them under such an exposure. I was compelled to close the meeting. As he thought how much he had done to fit men for destruction, he "wept bitterly."

I preached in the Temple five weeks, and those who took note of the progress of the work, told me that, as the result of the two meetings, there had been five hundred souls converted.

I preached my farewell sermon in the large house in Bowdoin Square, in which, nineteen years before, I had been permitted to proclaim the truth of God, though surrounded by an infuriated mob.

Since then the Tremont Temple and Union churches have united, and now meet in the Temple. A noble band of devoted, self-sacrificing servants of God are there, devising liberal things for the spread of the gospel, and cordially coöperating with their beloved pastor, brother J. D. Fulton, in every good word and work.

CHAPTER XX.

ACCOUNTS OF PROTRACTED MEETINGS.

(CONTINUED.)

WILMINGTON: *A former Visit.* — *Present Meeting of great Power.* — *A new Church started.* — PHILADELPHIA: *The Bethel.* — *A floating Church.* — *Many Conversions.* — *The Fourth Baptist Church.* — *A happy Birthday.* — *Great Results.* — *Interesting Conversions.* — *Valuable Accessions.* — NEWARK: *Harmonious Churches.* — *General Interest.* — *Union Prayer-Meeting.* — ELIZABETH: *A Threefold Call.* — *A divine Answer.* — NEW YORK CITY: *A Contrast.* — *Business and Religion.* — *A Farewell Service.* — *Labors in other Places.* — TRENTON: *Baptism of Children.* — *Numerous Conversions.* — *A blessed Season.* — *Reflections.* — *Going to California.*

WILMINGTON.

IN the year 1844, I held a meeting with the Second Baptist church in Wilmington, Del., then under the care of the late Morgan J. Rhees, in which about two hundred souls were converted.

Near the beginning of January, 1865, I was again invited to the same church, at the instance of the pastor, brother James S. Dickerson. Brother Dickerson was converted under my ministry twenty-five years before, in the Mulberry Street meeting, New York.

I had not preached long before the meetings became very interesting. Every night witnessed new cases for prayer, and new instances of conversion. After dismissing the meetings the people were loath to leave, and all seemed intent in talking with the convicted and encouraging the converted.

At first the conversions occurred mostly among the women,

especially among the young ladies connected with the Sunday school. But very soon the young men began to be interested, and finally many from the ranks of the more advanced in age, both men and women, were brought to bow to the power of the cross.

This blessed work went on until two hundred were baptized into the fellowship of the church; and before I left the place preparations were made for starting another church, and a lot was secured with that end in view. Since then the new church has been constituted, and has a pastor.

PHILADELPHIA.

On the 22d day of October, 1865, I commenced a meeting with the Bethel Baptist church in Philadelphia, Pa. I found the pastor, brother J. M. Perry, to be a warm-hearted man, ready to do anything for the salvation of sinners. The church had a small congregation, because so many of the members did "business on the great waters." In fact it may be termed a floating church: its members are to be found in every part of the globe. Many of them belong to the United States navy, and are liable to be called away in the service at any moment, and likely to remain away for years at a time. Still there seems always to be a few on land, who are ready to labor to keep up the organization, and continue the power of the church to do good.

I preached in the Bethel five weeks, during which time seventy-five persons were baptized; and after I left the work, it went on under the labors of brother Perry, until nearly two hundred converts were added to the church as the fruit of this revival. Several of these were officers in the military and marine service.

On the Lord's day, December 3, 1865, I commenced a meeting in the Fourth Baptist church, under the care of brother R. Jeffery. Here I preached every night, at half past seven o'clock, having a prayer-meeting before and after the sermon.

In my journal, under date of the 7th of this month, I

say, "This is my birthday, and also the day of national thanksgiving. I preached in the afternoon on the 'Goodness of God,' and in the evening on 'God's love to man.' This has been truly a blessed day to my soul — the most happy birthday I have ever enjoyed. Have had great liberty in preaching. Three souls were converted — the first fruits of the meeting. All day long my heart has been overflowing with gratitude to God: first, for a good constitution; second, because I was born in a Christian land; third, for a fair education; fourth, for the experience of the new birth; fifth, because God has 'counted me worthy' putting me into the ministry; sixth, for the great success which has attended my efforts to win souls to Christ."

I preached in this church seven weeks. On the last Sabbath of my stay the pastor gave the hand of fellowship to ninety-three persons, eighty-seven of whom had been baptized during the month; and the work continued for several weeks longer, until two hundred souls were converted, and added to the church.

There were numerous instances of interesting conversions. One fine-looking German rose in one of the meetings, and in broken language, but eloquent in earnest simplicity, related how he had been educated a Romanist, but had been induced to read the Bible at the solicitation of his servant girl, a member of that church, and had from her learned of the way of salvation through Christ, and that he had come to that meeting with a determination to profess Christ at once. He came out clearly into the light, and remains to this day steadfast in his zeal for Christ.

A young man related that he had been a drunkard, and addicted to every vice, but had recently been led, by the preaching of Elder Knapp, to reform, and seek forgiveness of the Savior. Since then he had computed the amount which he had been accustomed to spend in drink, and resolved to dedicate that sum to the cause of Christ. He used to spend fifty cents a day for liquor, and he thought he ought now to devote as much for the spread of the gospel.

Among the accessions to the church in connection with this meeting were several persons of education and influence in the community, and in working power the church received great strength.

When I came to Philadelphia I was strongly in hopes that the way would be opened for my remaining until the whole city was roused up, and at least twenty thousand souls were converted. But I found the people of Philadelphia slow to move, tenacious of their own way of doing things, and satisfied to trudge along "in the way their fathers trod." Some other of the churches talked somewhat of asking me to visit them, but were so long in coming to a decision that I was unable to wait their movements. I closed my labors with the Fourth church, Philadelphia, on one day, and commenced on the next with one of the churches in

NEWARK, N. J.

There are five Baptist churches in this city. All move on in delightful harmony with each other. The several pastors agreed to unite in the effort, as far as their distances from each other would permit. I commenced preaching in the First church, brother H. C. Fish, pastor, and in the evening at the church of which brother J. M. Levy is pastor. This arrangement was continued for two weeks. I preached one week in the Fifth church, and four weeks in brother Levy's church. In all, there were converted, and added to the Baptist churches, between three and four hundred souls. Besides, the truth of God took hold of all the people, and churches of other names opened their doors, and commenced extra meetings, at which hundreds of persons were brought to Christ.

In the progress of this meeting all the Baptist churches met together, "with one accord, in one place, to make prayer and supplication." The Spirit came down with Pentecostal power. The pastors led the way, confessing their sins. The entire day, until three o'clock in the afternoon, was spent in mutual confessions and earnest prayers. At that hour I preached a sermon about *breaking up the fallow ground.* I preached again in the evening, having abstained from food all day. I felt no inconvenience by reason of my abstinence, but great elevation of soul in my communions with God, and great satisfaction in eating of the manna which fell from heaven.

While laboring in this place, I received a peculiar call from the people of the neighboring city of

Elizabeth.

I was invited, first, by a unanimous call from the church and pastor; second, from a company of unconverted young men; third, from a circle of young ladies who had not yet professed Christ. Though pressed with invitations to go to other places, these singular coincidences impressed me with the conviction that I ought to recognize this call. I therefore went, and preached two weeks, night and day. Nearly all the young gentlemen and ladies referred to were converted, besides many others. The faithful little band of God's people in this place were greatly strengthened.

New York City.

On the 24th day of March, 1866, I found myself about to commence, once more, a campaign in the city of New York.

I began in the Laight Street church, brother R. McDougal, pastor.

My return to the city, after an absence of more than twenty years, was very cordial. Fifteen ministers came to hear me preach on the first afternoon, and to bid me welcome. Several of them had been converted under my ministry, and three of them had been baptized by me. During my stay here, I was called upon daily by very many Christians from all parts of the city and state, who ascribed their conversions, under God, to my labors.

My heart was very much affected by these soul-stirring interviews. The goodness of God shone before me with a new lustre. I remembered the time when I first came to the city, and the distrust with which my labors were regarded, and the purposed neglect with which I was treated; and as I felt the contrast, my heart was melted in gratitude to God for the change, and that he had permitted me to live to see it. The entire order of things is changed. Nearly all the ministers who now occupy the pulpits of the city, and, in fact, of the denomination throughout the country, were converted in protracted meetings, or in connection with revival measures. If all things in the churches had continued as they were in 1834, I wonder where the supply of ministers would have come from. Rather, I may ask, would there have been churches enough to have engaged the few ministers that would have remained to us? I do not claim that the change is owing to my labors, but I do say, that the very measures which I introduced, and on account of which I suffered persecution, are now almost universally adopted and relied upon as those on which the blessing of God is most likely to rest. As these thoughts were revived in my mind by these kind assurances, I felt like appropriating the prayer of good old Simeon: "Lord, now lettest thy servant depart in peace, for mine eyes have seen thy salvation."

I continued preaching, every afternoon and evening, for four weeks. I preached, also, a few sermons in several of the other churches — the McDougal Street, Jersey City, Forty-second Street, and also for brother S. Corey.

Beginning, as I did, in the spring, just as business was becoming active, I found it difficult to engage the attendance of the merchants and of the clerks. As a consequence, the results were not as extensive as they might have been otherwise, for now, as in Paul's day, "faith cometh by hearing." Nevertheless our labors were not in vain. About ninety souls professed conversion, fifty of whom united with the Laight Street church, and the rest with the different churches in the city.

At the close of this meeting arrangements were made for a farewell service. It so happened that the day was stormy; rivers of water ran down the streets, and the wind blew a hurricane; nevertheless, a large congregation assembled at the church. After a sermon from myself, remarks were made by brethren Westcott, Corey, Weston, and Graves. Brother Westcott, in behalf of his brethren in the ministry, invited me to return the next autumn for a winter's campaign.

I will not attempt to recount the many kind utterances that came from the lips of these brethren; but if an angel had told me, thirty-two years ago, that in 1866 such a scene would have occurred, I should have inquired for a sign from heaven to confirm his testimony. Yet I gratefully bless God that he has permitted me to have so great a share in producing the changes that have come over the spirit of the ministry and the churches; and even if my name were to be blotted out of the record, and the memory of me fail from the earth, I could labor just as earnestly for the triumph of the truth as it is in Jesus; and in its progressive triumph I could rejoice, yea, and greatly rejoice, for Christ is all, and what are we but his ministers? I say this in all humility, for I know my weaknesses better than my brethren do, and feel daily the need of the grace of God to keep me from falling.

I ought to add, that I received a cordial and sympathizing coöperation from brother McDougal, the pastor of the church.

During the remainder of this year I spent considerable time with the churches in Cohoes, Bloomingdale (New York City), Waverly, Elmira, and Homer, N. Y. In each of these places I was permitted to rejoice over several converts; but none of the meetings were marked with incidents that were different from those which I have related as having occurred elsewhere.

TRENTON.

On the 7th day of February, 1867, I entered upon my labors with the Central Baptist church in Trenton, N. J., brother T. S. Griffith, pastor. I found the church prepared for my coming. Conversions occurred every day. On a certain Sabbath, brother Griffith baptized seventeen children belonging to the Sunday school, and an invitation was given to all the Sunday school children to be present. A vast congregation assembled. The candidates were dressed in white, and the solemn impression made on the minds of the youthful spectators will never be effaced.

On the Sabbath following seventy persons received the hand of fellowship, and the material and moral power of the church was greatly increased.

The meetings continued throughout seven weeks, the interest gradually increasing to the last. I enjoyed the labors with this dear people greatly. There was no friction, no complaining about measures, no disposition to find fault with the plain and outspoken presentation of the gospel. As the result of my labors here about two hundred persons were added to the Central church, and about one hundred to the First church.

Reflections.

In the foregoing accounts I have made mention of only some of the many meetings which I have held during the past thirty-five years. It would have required volumes to contain a history of them all. I have omitted to allude to some, because the memory of distinct incidents has faded from my mind; I have passed over others, because the incidents, though interesting, did not differ materially from those which I have related as occurring in other places; and I have remained silent concerning others, because I could not give a fair statement without alluding to circumstances which would reflect on others, some of whom have passed beyond the reach of human censure.

I am now an old man. I have outlived the generation of my early associates. Multitudes of those who have professed conversion under my labors have gone to the judgment before me, and the influence of my labors will be projected into the future after I shall have gone to my account. I realize that my life has been burdened with fearful responsibilities. The destinies of multitudes, dead, living, and yet unborn, are linked with the influences I have exerted.

As I have commended others to the mercy of God through Christ, so I look to the same source for the pardon of my sins, and the overruling of all my mistakes. And though deeply conscious of my failings and errors, I am, nevertheless, sustained with the conviction that God has made me the agent for the accomplishment of great good; and I trustfully look forward to the gracious recognition of my Savior when the results of my life-work shall be summed up.

I thank God that he has permitted me to live to my present age, and continued me in good health, my "eye not dimmed, nor my natural force abated." At my advanced stage of life many ministers have felt themselves compelled to retire from active service, and guard themselves against their increasing infirmities, but through the goodness of God I am permitted to labor for souls a little longer. Of late I have felt constrained to go to California, and it may be that I shall not be spared to return; but before the eyes of the reader will fall on these pages I expect to reach those distant shores, and be preaching the gospel to the people of the setting sun.

CHAPTER XXI.

MISCELLANEOUS FACTS.

Numbers converted. — Baptized. — Answers to Questions. — Number of Meetings held. — Of Sermons preached. — Of Converts who became Ministers. — Amount of Compensation.

Number of Conversions.

FOR a time I endeavored to keep an approximate account of the number of persons who professed conversion in my meetings, but after my reckonings took in more than one hundred thousand cases I gave up the attempt. They came in such crowds, from all denominations; so many united with other churches, and so many were reported in meetings commenced by me after I had left, and so many were strangers from distant towns and states, sojourning for a few days or weeks where I was preaching, and so many other meetings sprang from those I was holding, that I found the attempt to number Israel an impossibility, and suspected that it might be a sin. I must, therefore, refer the answer to this inquiry to the statistics of the Judgment, which will be more accurate than my most careful endeavors could possibly make it. I abandoned the effort to reckon numbers more than twenty years ago.

Numbers Baptized.

I have baptized only a small proportion of those who have been added to the churches in connection with my labors. 1st. Because many united with other denominations. 2d. Because, as a general thing, it seemed desirable and proper that the pastors with whom I labored should administer the ordinance.

3d. Because, specially, I have always felt that "Christ sent me, not to baptize, but to preach the gospel."

Up to the year 1845 I had baptized about four thousand persons, and since then about a thousand more.

Answers to certain Questions.

A brother, who had heard that I was thinking of preparing an account of my life, has requested me to give a statement in regard to certain inquiries. I indicate his questions, and give such answers as I am able.

1. Number of meetings which I have held to this date, July, 1867.

Answer. About one hundred and fifty.

2. Number of sermons which I have preached.

Answer. About one thousand three hundred and sixty.

3. Number of persons converted under my labors who have entered the ministry.

Answer. I cannot speak with accuracy on this subject. Many young men, whose names I have forgotten, have come to the conclusion to become ministers months and years after I have lost sight of them. I am constantly meeting persons, now preaching the gospel, who inform me that they were brought out in meetings which I have held. I can recall several.

There were six young men, converted in the Tabernacle church, New York, at my meeting, who became ministers: brother A. C. Buckbee, now Secretary of the American Bible Union, in California; James S. Dickerson, now pastor of the First Baptist church, Pittsburg, Pa.; Sidney A. Corey, now pastor of a Baptist church in New York city; H. Harvey, formerly Professor of Biblical Literature in Madison University, and lately pastor of the Baptist church in Dayton, Ohio. Of the names of the other two I am not sufficiently certain to justify me in reporting them.

Besides these, I remember the names of brother J. R. Kendrick, now pastor of the Tabernacle Baptist church, New York city, who was converted at Hamilton; J. B. Tombes, pastor of the Baptist church in Carbondale, Pa.; S. M. Bainbridge, well known in Central New York, now deceased; H. Hutchins, for many years, and yet a pastor in Brooklyn; B. Griffith, Corresponding Secretary of the American Baptist Publishing Society, Philadelphia; Franklin Wilson, of Baltimore; J. B. Jackson, now Professor of Biblical Literature in Chicago College of Theology; Professor Roberts, of Burlington University, Iowa. Besides these, I remember the names of Raymond, now of Kansas; Clark, of Newark, New Jersey; Bywater, of St. Louis; Wilbur, of Iowa; Fisher and Waterbury, of New York.

A student in Union College told me that he knew the names of twelve young men, converted in my meetings in Schenectady, who had entered the ministry. I have been informed that about this number of converts in Yale College, during my meetings in New Haven, became ministers. There were five young men converted in the Utica meeting who became ministers.

I can speak of about forty, converted in five meetings, who entered the ministry: In Schenectady, 12; New Haven, 12; Tabernacle church, New York, 6; Utica, 5; Baltimore, 5. Total, 40.

4. Amount of compensation.

Answer. During the first seven years of my labors as an Evangelist my salary averaged $300 per annum,	$2,100
From 1839 to 1843 (four years) it averaged $2,000 per annum, ...	8,000
During sixteen years of labor in the West it averaged $380 per annum, ...	6,080
During the remaining ten years it averaged $500 per annum, ...	5,000
In all, during thirty-six years, it has amounted to . .	$21,180
Divide this amount ($21,180) by thirty-six years, and my annual compensation has averaged	$588.31
Deduct, for annual travelling expenses, say	88.31
and I have realized, per annum, ...	$500.00

VIEWS ON VARIOUS SUBJECTS.

I.

HONORARY TITLES.

I CONSIDER the custom of conferring titles of distinction on ministers of the gospel to be wrong.

1. In the first place, the explicit language of Holy Scripture forbids it. Elihu said, "I know not to give flattering titles; in so doing my Maker would take me away." When there arose a dispute among his disciples as to who should be greatest in the kingdom of heaven, "Jesus called a little child unto him, and set him in the midst of them, and said, Verily, I say unto you, except ye be converted and become as little children, ye shall not enter into the kingdom of heaven. Whosoever therefore shall humble himself as this little child, the same is greatest in the kingdom of heaven." Matt. xviii. 1–4. Again, Jesus said unto his disciples, "Whosoever will be great among you, let him be your minister; and whosoever will be chief among you, let him be your servant." Matt. xx. 26, 27. Christ presented his own example as the model, after which all his followers should copy. "I am among you as he that serveth." Luke xxii. 27.

How much more dignified and godlike is the spirit here inculcated and insisted upon as the condition of our entering into the kingdom of heaven, than the foolish strife and unholy rivalry among men as to who shall be the greatest. The very spirit of emulation involved in this anxiety, is essentially contrary to that spirit of humility and meekness which the gospel enjoins.

It is said that the title, D. D., only means a doctor or teacher of divinity; then why not confer it on all who teach divinity, and thus make no distinction? But many desire it because it makes a distinction, and many experience heart-burnings and jealousies because they do not get it. Thus the practice is a double-edged sword; it cuts those who receive the honor, and those who feel themselves slighted because they do not receive it. The church of Christ should discountenance whatever tends to foster such states of mind.

2. In the second place, no body of men have the right to confer it. Christ never gave such authority. None of the apostles did. Their example is against it. Who ever heard of Rev. Mr. Paul, D. D., or of the Right Rev. Simon Peter, D. D.? These titles originated, not in the apostolic church, but in the spirit of vaulting ambition, which culminated in the blasphemous assumptions of the church of Rome.

3. In the third place, the reception of the title is unworthy of the dignity of the ministerial office. Our ministers need not come down from the sacred hill of Zion, and kneel before the sceptre of civil or literary power in order to receive titular distinctions, whereby they may be known as ministers of the meek and lowly Jesus. This practice is virtually a repudiation of the authority of Christ, and a weak and wicked subserviency to the maxims of this world. It is well known that, in many instances, these titles are bought and sold, as were the pardons and indulgences of the church of Rome; and it has come to be regarded no longer a sign of the worth or learning of its recipient. In numerous cases the very association of this title with certain names involuntarily excites the mental inquiry, How did they get it? In some cases ministers of the gospel have fallen so low as to solicit the Board of a College to bestow on them the title. In other cases the minister resorts to indirection. His friends move in the matter. Nor will it be denied that in many cases the College Board have as much regard to pecuniary returns as they do to the deservedness of the candidate. There are many D. D.'s in modern times who cannot preach a sermon without murdering the queen's English, and whose chief distinction in the ministry is their want of success in winning souls.

I know there are many on whom the title has been conferred to whom these remarks do not apply, and who would prefer to dispense with it, if they know how to get rid of it. I am aware that there are many able and worthy men who have been dubbed with this title, and these are the very men who care the least about it.

For my own part, I consider it more honorable to a minister of Jesus Christ to be pelted with stones, smitten with clubs, and hooted through the streets, — as were Whitefield and Wesley, — than to receive all the titles which civil governments or schools of learning can get up or confer.

Finally, it is my heart's desire and prayer to God, that the time will soon come when all Christians, and all Christian churches, will be content to stand on one common level; to esteem each other better than themselves, and seek honor only from God, and lay what he bestows at the Savior's feet.

II.

THOUGHTS ON MINISTERIAL POWER.

IN order to become successful, a minister of the gospel must be possessed of an ardent love of the work. He must have such an appreciation of it, as a high and holy calling, that he will look with indifference upon every other pursuit. His love of Christ and of souls must serve as a magnet to draw away his interest from all worldly callings. It must be an inspiration to propel him forward under all discouragements, and to lead him to "count not his life dear unto himself, that he may finish his course with joy, and the ministry which he has received of the Lord Jesus." He must be able to say to all worldly allurements, as did Robert Hall when urged to accept a position of greater emolument than that of a Baptist preacher: "As for your honors, I desire them not; and as for your riches, I despise them."

2. To be successful, a minister must seek for immediate success. It is a favorite method with some ministers, in order to account for their failure to a achieve anything for Christ, to say they are sowing the seed, the fruit of which another will gather. But he that would accomplish much for his race must "serve his own generation." He must know that sinners are dying, and, unless converted, going to hell. The men of this generation must be brought to Christ through existing agencies, and the minister must specially feel that he is concerned with the care of the individuals whom God has put under his charge.

A man who has no success in saving the souls of those to whom he ministers, or in gathering in the people of the place in which he preaches, may seriously question whether God has called him to the work. It does not seem reasonable that God would give a special call to a man to go and labor in a field during the harvest, who had no elements of adaptation to do the thing unto which he thinks himself called. I am sometimes asked, "What are the evidences that a man is called to preach the gospel?" I answer, first, a single and strong desire for the work; second, indications that he knows how to preach; third, evidence that he can get any body to hear him; fourth, success in winning souls to the Savior.

3. Another condition of a minister's power, is an exclusive devotion to the specific duties of his calling. In this way his profiting shall appear unto all. His work is too important to admit of a rival, and his time too short to be made still shorter by wasting it in matters foreign to his calling. What would be thought of a foreign minister of state who should turn aside from, and neglect the interests of his government, in order to amuse or profit himself? If the apostles had taken such a course they would have insured the failure of Christianity, and perverted its entire spirit. They could not find time to attend to the distribution of the charities of the church, and referred the charge of that matter to others, in order that they might devote themselves wholly "to prayer and the ministry of the word."

It is true that they sometimes worked at business callings in order to provide for their daily wants; but this they did only in subordination to their high calling, and in order to insure the preaching of the gospel, and the preaching of it with greater effect among the people whose salvation they sought. But they tell us that they were naked and hungry, and suffered the loss of all things, lest they should hinder the gospel of Christ.

I have now been in the ministry forty years, and in looking back, can see clearly that if I had never lifted my finger in order tc promote my worldly interests, it would have been better for me and for my family. I could have escaped many occasions of personal unhappiness, and have greatly added to my power to do good. If a minister of Christ have faith in God, and make it his whole concern to serve him, God will take care of him. At times his faith may be tried, but if it does not stagger under the pressure, he will find God to be as good as his promises: "Trust in the Lord and do good, and thou shalt dwell in the land, and verily thou shalt be fed." "Thy bread shall be given thee, and thy water shall be sure." And if we are sometimes brought into close quarters, we shall be enriched by the experimental knowledge that the "the trial of our faith is more precious than gold."

4. If a minister would have power, he must aim in his preaching to reach the consciences of his hearers. If he preaches so as to improve the literary tastes, or quicken the intellectual faculties, or gratify the æsthetic tendencies of his hearers, he may succeed in accomplishing the end in view, but he will not succeed in saving souls. If he aims at saying smooth and beautiful things, he may be able to do so, and thus gain the admiration of men who value culture in the preacher more than they do pungent presentation of truth; but while ministering to the literary gratification of his hearers, he may, at the same time, be making their damnation more sure.

Some preachers pride themselves on their metaphysical acumen and theological accuracy. They have more to say about the philosophy of religion than about its facts; and the force of their ministry is expended in theorizing about the methods of truth, rather than in enforcing the reality of it. They demand a faith based upon the apprehensions of reason more than upon the testimony of God. The result is, that they talk about things they do not understand, and their hearers either become listless or sceptical. The devil is well satisfied with such kind of preaching. He is willing that men's minds should become mystified about theories so long as they allow him to control their hearts.

The successful preacher must be practical. He must make religion appear to be a thing that has something to do with the moral convictions; that appeals to them, and demands the immediate consecration of them to the claims of God.

5. The preacher must study adaptation. It is seldom that preaching produces saving results, except it takes effect at the time, and brings a person to speedy action. Consequently the preacher cannot appreciate too highly the importance of *timing* his subjects. It would be very unwise to come out on a cold church and congregation with a sermon on the awful terrors of everlasting damnation. Their feelings would be shocked, and their pride would array itself in rebellion; but let him first remind them of their "first love," and call on them to return unto it; let him inquire why Jesus has been to them as a wayfaring man that turneth aside for a night, and tell them much of the greatness of God's love to them. In this way, if they are Christians indeed, the hearts of his hearers will be melted. Then let the preacher speak of the terrors of the law, and the Christians will be aroused to labor for souls, and the wicked will quail under its power.

6. The power of the pulpit depends very much on the style of language employed in the presentation of the truth. A plain, clear, correct, and common-sense way of "putting" the thing before a congregation is the only effective method of interesting and reaching the masses. The apostle says expressly that he did not "come with excellency of speech, which man's wisdom teacheth;" and "if I seek to please man, I am no more the servant of Christ." The language employed by the holy apostles is the model of all succeeding preachers. It is the language which the Spirit of God has seen fit to employ as the vehicle of divine truth. Smooth and ornate diction is not in keeping with the gravity of the great truths contained in the Bible; and a highly-wrought style is unworthy of their dignity, and evidence of the utter want of appreciation on the part of the preacher of the momentous issues involved, and the impending danger of those who do not receive them. From all such stilted, or dry, or tinsel displays, the common people will evermore turn away unimpressed if not disgusted. To many persons much of the language of the pulpit is an unknown tongue: and Paul says, "I had rather speak five words with

the understanding (that is, to the understanding of others), than ten thousand words in an unknown tongue."

7. The man who has power in the pulpit is a man of strong faith. There are many preachers and churches who are afraid to venture on the promises of God. They are afraid to go to work for the salvation of souls unless a sign be given them, lest they should be mortified by a failure. Thus they let months and years pass on, and souls go down to death while they are waiting for indications. God honored Abraham above all men because of his great faith. Paul, in speaking of the different gifts, says "one has the gift of faith." For the want of faith the Israelites were doomed to drag out forty years in the wilderness, and not one of the unbelievers was permitted to enter into the promised land. All of the mighty conquests recorded in Scripture were achieved by faith. But unbelief cuts off communication with God. It shuts up heaven, and paralyzes all our efforts to do good. "Let such an one know that he shall receive nothing at the hands of the Lord."

8. In order to have power as a preacher the minister must have knowledge. First of all he must know God; must be in sympathy with his plans, and in communion with him. Secondly, he must know himself, so as neither to overrate nor underrate himself. He must know somewhat the direction in which his own power lies. Thirdly, he must be well versed in the Bible, so as to prove himself to be "not a novice," but "a workman that needeth not to be ashamed, rightly dividing the word of truth." Fourthly, he must have a good knowledge of human nature.

If a man is well versed in these things he will not fail to make his mark. He will become powerful for good, even though he may not have much of that knowledge that puffeth up. Nevertheless mere scholastic knowledge is good, and the more a preacher has of it the better, provided always he have the other kinds of knowledge and grace, and sense enough to make his attainments subordinate and illustrative of his consecration to the one aim of winning souls.

A man who does not study, but spends his time in ministerial gossiping and loafing, can never excel, however great his genius or brilliant his intellect. All of our powers are strengthened by their use.

9. Another element of ministerial power is the spirit of love. No amount of learning, no degree of genius, nor measure of eloquence, will atone for the lack of that genuine spirit of sympathy which has its origin in love. A people will bear plain dealing from one who can rebuke with much long-suffering and kindness. They will overlook many defects in execution on the part of one of whose sincere affection for them they feel assured. There is eloquence in love: it lights up the face with its radiant beams, and transmutes the glistening tear into a precious pearl. It magnetizes, enkindles, and subdues.

10. Finally, the preacher that would have power with men must have power with God. He must be filled with the Spirit; and so greatly filled, that all other rivals for the control of his being shall be expelled. Much is said in the New Testament of "being full of the Holy Spirit." The apostles gave thanks to God, who always made them to triumph. Luther was powerful only as God was with him and in him. Wesley and Whitefield were eloquent and powerful because they were crucified to the world, and because "Christ lived in them." I know of no reason, in the divine economy, why, if there be an equal degree of seeking for it, there should not be marked and numerous evidences of divine effectiveness in ministers now as in former times. God is as willing to give the Holy Spirit to them that ask him now as he was formerly. And the promise still holds good, "If any man will do His will, I and my Father will come to him, and make our abode with him."

III.

HOW TO GET UP A REFORMATION.

I USE this phraseology, because it is the very language of those who are novices concerning this subject, and make so many complaints against special measures.

God works by means, and by appointed and established means. His Spirit is hovering over all of our cities, towns, and country places, ready to respond to a faithful use of the means at all times. "The set time" in which to favor Zion is always when "her sons take pleasure in her stones, and favor the dust thereof."

Is it not proper to excite an enthusiasm on the subject of foreign or home missions? And would not God be pleased to have us get up a revival in the interest of education or of temperance? Why, then, is it not equally proper to put forth special efforts to promote the salvation of souls?

But how shall a revival be brought about? Not, as some would imagine, by a resort to eccentricities and sensational appeals. It is probable that some such agencies may conduce to bring people to listen to the truth of God, but of themselves they are powerless and hurtful.

The great necessity in promoting a revival is the outpouring of the Spirit of God. Until the Spirit be poured out from on high, the most pungent truths, the most tender appeals, and the most attractive manner, are in vain. Everything will remain as hard and as dead as a stone wall (and sinners are dead) until infused by the quickening influence of the Spirit's power.

Consequently, our first work is prayer. Earnest, importunate, believing prayer, must be made. The history of the first protracted meeting after the ascension of Christ, was doubtless designed as a pattern for all succeeding ages. There was not a sermon preached until after the Spirit had descended; but then, under the preaching of a single sermon, three thousand souls were "pricked in their hearts." If we preach at all before the direct influences of the Holy Spirit are felt in the hearts of the church, our preaching should be directed to the church; we should labor to have them see wherein they have sinned and departed from the living God, and to induce them to return unto their first love. In short, the people must sanctify themselves before the Lord. Caleb and Joshua said, "If the Lord delight in us, he will give it us;" and if we would go up and possess a town or a city, we must become so humble, and so penitent, and so holy, that God will delight in us.

"If I regard iniquity in my heart, the Lord will not hear me." It is our sins which separate us from God; and it is our iniquities which hide his face from our sight.

When the Holy Spirit comes down in power, it visits the hearts of the community, and they are inclined to come in and hear the preached word. It was not the preaching of Peter which brought together the crowds, but the Holy Spirit, which came down in answer to prayers, continuously and unitedly offered by the waiting disciples.

The Holy Spirit likewise indites the prayers and sermons. When God's ministers are filled with the Spirit, there is a kind of inspiration about their sermons, which makes them "mighty to the pulling down of the strongholds;" a sort of inspiration in the conception and expression of their thoughts, and in the method of their delivery. Those who have imagined that I have depended for effect on eccentricities of speech, or tactics of management, have utterly misapprehended me, and done me great injustice. My reliance has been upon the power of God's truth, made effectual by his own Spirit, and the hearty coöperation of the church, as "workers together with him."

I can conceive of a difference between a revival and a reformation, and desire only the former. But in all my efforts I have labored assiduously to bring about a *reformation.* I have sought to do a work which should abide — a permanent element of power and blessing after I had passed on to other places. Accordingly, I have earnestly sought to pour all of God's truth upon the consciences of men; to bring up the church to a proper understanding of the Bible standard of Christian character and Christian effort. I have found many who like the excitation of a revival, but have no relish for the labor of a reform. Such want a pastor or an evangelist who leaves them in the undisputed enjoyment of their sinful indulgences. They prefer sons of consolation to sons of thunder, and want the minister to say soft things softly. They have no idea of having the gospel plough driven through the church, breaking up the fallow ground, cutting all the ligaments that bind them to the world and to the service of Satan. Their religion is a white-gloved religion. It can attend sociables, donation and surprise parties, and enjoy a good religious time generally, in which they can outdo the world, and keep close upon the heels of the devil. They like to feast, but not to fast; they are delighted with singing, but have no taste for prayer.

But this is not the apostolic sort of revival. The practices of church members who dance, and frolic, and are absorbed in worldliness, have been as much in my way of promoting a reformation as drunkenness, profanity, or infidelity; yes, as all put together. In laboring for reformation, it has been my custom to expose all the sins of God's people. He says, "Lift up thy voice like a trumpet; cry aloud; spare not. Show unto my people their sins, and the house of Israel their transgressions."

If the work drags, I preach on some subjects which are applicable to both saints and sinners; appoint a fast, requiring all who join in it to abstain from all business and all food during the twenty-four hours. Sometimes we have held three or four such seasons in one meeting. Thus, by prayer and fasting, by preaching and exhortation, by humiliations and confessions, we have sought the Lord, until he has "come and rained righteousness upon us."

The church needs to be stimulated as well as depleted, or else they will sink and become despondent. They must be encouraged to take God at his word, and to hope in his mercy, and expect the fulfilment of all his promises; so that they must be taught to use at once all means to bring in sinners, and labor and look for their conversion. The sooner and the more they work, the sooner and the more they will be in sympathy with Christ, and be filled with the Spirit. That pastor who is the most successful in securing and keeping up the coöperation of the church, will be most successful in producing and keeping up a perpetual reformation. This was the secret of the success of John Wesley.

When the church is aroused and consecrated, and the presence of the Spirit realized, then pour on God's truth, *hand over hand;* now thundering out *hell and damnation*, until the mountain is covered with fire and smoke, and the people tremble; then ascend Calvary's bloody summit; bid the smitten people "Behold the Lamb of God, who taketh away the sin of the world." Preach Christ crucified; knock out every prop on which sinners lean. Sometimes the prop is one thing, sometimes it is another. It may be Universalism, or Unitarianism, or morality. No matter what it is; let not one remain, — and see to it that the soul build on no other foundation than that which is already laid, which is Christ Jesus.

This is a momentous work, demanding the utmost exertion of the laborers for God. It behooves them to keep alive and active the conviction of the solemn fact, that all who are not reached soon, will very soon be beyond the reach of all the means of grace. It is now or never. "Knowing the terrors of the Lord, we persuade men." "When the commandment came, sin revived and I died." So said Paul. And Jesus asks, "How can ye escape the damnation of hell?" Human sinfulness, helplessness, and danger must be plainly enforced in order to give effect to the arguments of the cross.

Men in all ages are liable to go to extremes; and though the present generation of ministers have made many improvements on the past, yet I think the tendency now is to make the gospel pleasing to the tastes of unconverted men; and as the result of this desire is to give "none offence," the doctrines of human depravity, of the enmity of the carnal mind against God, the necessity of the new birth, and the certainty of eternal punishment to the finally impenitent, are not made as prominent, or dwelt upon as much as formerly. Indeed, I find some churches which do not wish to hear anything about them. But the truths of the Bible are adapted to the condition of man in all ages and circumstances, and any deviation from this standard is dangerous.

There are two methods of carrying on a successful revival of religion. One is, by calling in the aid of an evangelist, and making a special effort to enlist and arouse the entire community.

But when this plan is not practicable, let the pastor of a church, in connection with his most spiritually-minded brethren, seek in prayer the outpouring of the Spirit. Then let them seek out the most seriously disposed persons in the congregation; when one person is converted set him to work to win others, and endeavor to give every member of the church something to do. The more each one works the more he will have a mind to work, and the more he will find to do. Let there be a short lecture from the pastor, followed by prayer and pertinent remarks by the brethren and converts. In this way the whole leaven of grace will continue to work until the whole lump is leavened, and an entire church or community is permeated with the power of the gospel.

Formalists and hypocrites may say what they please against excitement, but from the earliest days of God's communication with men there have been seasons of religious refreshing and declension. There was a declension before the flood, and a revival under Abraham; a declension in Egypt, and a revival under Moses; a declension before the days of John the Baptist, and a revival shortly after Christ. And so it has been from that day to this, and so it will continue to be, so long as man is what he is, the devil is what he is, and God does not change.

Indeed, the history of the apostles is a history of excitement; deeper, stronger, and more lasting than we have ever had since. The history of the church is the history of strong and purifying excitements.

IV.

COMPLAINTS AGAINST SPEEDY ADMISSIONS CONSIDERED.

LET it be distinctly understood that the word of God and the example of the apostles are our only guides in this matter. No creeds, catechisms, laws, by-laws, usages, or customs of modern churches, ought ever to be allowed to come into competition with the teachings of Holy Writ. It is always safe to follow its directions and examples as to the method of promoting the advancement of the kingdom of God. "To the law and the testimony; if they speak not according to this word, it is because there is no light in them."

2. What was the custom of the apostles on this subject? Peter, on the day of Pentecost, commanded sinners to "repent and be baptized;" "and they that gladly received the word, were baptized; and the same day there was added unto them about three thousand souls." Now it is evident to any unbiased mind, that all who believed on the Lord Jesus Christ on that occasion, were baptized the same day; yes, before they left the spot. Acts ii. 38–41. The jailer was not only baptized on the same night in which he was converted, but in "the same hour." Acts xvi. 33.

When Philip opened his mouth and preached unto the eunuch Jesus, as they were riding along in the chariot, the eunuch said, "Here is water, what doth hinder me to be baptized?" Philip said, "If thou believest with all thine heart, thou mayest." And on the declaration of his faith, "they went down into the water, both Philip and the eunuch, and he baptized him." Acts

viii. 38. Now it is evident that in this case baptism was not delayed until the eunuch reached home, but he was baptized immediately on the declaration of his faith.

In the case of Cornelius and his house, we read that while Peter was preaching the Holy Spirit fell on those that heard, and that Peter immediately commanded that they should be baptized in the name of the Lord Jesus. Acts x. 47, 48.

Likewise it appears when the Lord had opened the eyes of Lydia, as she was praying on the banks of the river, that she was baptized therein, before returning to her home.

The case of Saul of Tarsus is the only one recorded in the New Testament of a person whose baptism was delayed after conversion. He was not baptized till three days had elapsed; but there were reasons which make his case evidently exceptional. 1. There was no administrator at hand when he was converted. 2. Jesus bade him go into the city, and await further instructions. 3. As soon as Ananias was informed of the case, he sought out Saul, and as soon as Saul was told that his next duty was to be baptized, he instantly obeyed. 4. The delay of three days seems to have been an occasion of regret to Ananias; and, 5. As it was, Saul did not either eat or drink, after his conversion, till he had been baptized.

It is very evident that the apostles in no instance demanded of a candidate a probationary trial, nor even a metaphysical analysis of the workings of their minds under conviction, as prerequisites of baptism. They simply required a sincere expression of repentance of sin and faith in Jesus Christ.

But it may be said that the apostles, being inspired men, could tell who were converted and who were not. To this I answer, there is no evidence that their inspiration related to this subject. On the contrary, it seems that they did not ground the reception of members on any such supernatural recognition. They confess themselves to have been disappointed in some cases, and allusions are frequent to those who fell away.

Again, it is urged that there was little danger of persons confessing Christ in times of persecution. I ask, what reason had the three thousand to expect persecution, and what evidence is there that they recognized an apprehension of it? On the contrary, it is more probable that multitudes, in view of the marvellous descent of the Spirit, were inclined to think that the new religion was about to become immediately popular.

If ever there was a time in which extra precautions should be taken against immediate receptions, it was at the Pentecost. 1. It was a time of great excitement, in which the fanatical would be very likely to show themselves. 2. There was little or no time or opportunity for reflection; so that the impulsive could be easily betrayed. 3. It was a time of great ignorance of the real nature of Christianity. Multitudes were less informed of the elementary principles of Christ's kingdom than are the simplest of modern Sunday-school children. 4. Many of the converts were from all parts of the world, sojourners in Jerusalem only for a few days, destined to go back among peoples who knew not Christ, and where they could not enjoy the privileges of an organized church. Notwithstanding all these incentives to precaution, the apostles understood the commission to require of them the instantaneous baptism of all who professed their faith in Christ.

The caviller may say again, there is no harm in their waiting. So say Pedobaptists, when convicted of the unscripturalness of infant baptism, "There is no harm in the ceremony." But I think that every deviation from the divinely-prescribed method of building up the kingdom of Christ is full of harm. In this particular case, the habit of delay is injurious to the piety of the convert, grieves the Holy Spirit, by calling into question the genuineness of his work, begets a spirit of unbelief in our prayers, and opens up a wide door for innumerable departures from the word of God. If in one instance we may depart from, and attempt to improve upon, the pattern given us, we may do so *ad libitum.* And yet there are many Baptists (thank God their number is diminishing every year) with whom usages and customs are everything, and the authority of God nothing. The laws and by-laws of some such churches are all in all; but the laws of Jesus Christ and the apostles are of no account. They seem to think that the apostles were very imprudent, and those who seek to copy after them are dangerous men.

And especially ought it to be remarked, that this agitation about receiving members invariably retards a revival. Every baptism imparts new courage to the church, and becomes an element of conviction to the unconverted. But when this duty is deferred, all these good influences are retarded. Suppose, when Peter heard the three thousand cry out, "What must we do?" he had said, "Don't get excited; keep cool; go home and read your Bibles:" and then suppose that the rest of the disciples had set in with their admonitions, "Examine yourselves; don't be deceived; ascertain whether you can hold out; and, above all, remember you won't always feel as you do now:" suppose some such procedure, and I leave it to the men who advocate this policy to compute how long it would have taken for Christianity to have achieved the triumphs which made the first Christain era so illustrious.

3. Baptism is the act of putting on Christ. "As many of you as have been baptized into Christ have put on Christ." When we have renounced the world, the flesh, and the devil, why defer putting on Christ? Why not put him on at once? As did the primitive Christians in this matter, so let us do. A new-born soul is a babe, whose mother is the church; and where is the place for the babe, but in the warm and fostering bosom of its mother? What would you think of the policy of putting the tender infant up garret for a week, a month, or six months, in order to see whether it would hold out? If there is ever a time when the child needs nursing and tender care it is when it is just born.

This hesitancy to receive newly-born souls is an evidence of something wrong in the churches, disqualifying them to extend a fostering care to the babes in Christ, and thus rendering them unwilling or unable to bear the labor and risk of receiving those who are genuinely converted, on account of the risk of taking in the few who may not be.

In this way converts are discouraged at the start, and instead of finding cordial welcome, they find themselves to be objects of distrust. The very consciousness of being distrusted depresses the ardor of effort, makes them afraid to express their difficulties, turns them to seek that sympathy in the world which is refused them in the church, and furnishes them a relief from the restraints which they would feel in the church, and an excuse for yielding to temptation. It rarely happens that persons who have been kept off from the privileges and responsibilities of the church relation for a period of several months, or even weeks, are ever brought into the church at all; partly because the church loses sight of them, and partly because they themselves become either indifferent about uniting with the church, or fearful of a rebuff if they should make the attempt to do so.

4. It is not uncommon for churches to ascribe the backsliding of newly-received members to the wrong cause. They say, "It is because they were taken into the church too soon." I say, it is because they are not taken care of when they are in.

In the first place, converts experience a chill from coming into contact with cold, formal, and worldly members. Every spirit begets its own likeness. Let me know the character of the church, and I can tell what prospects there are of the converts holding out. If the older members are running off to the theatre, or the dance, or flirting about at parties, or think more of attending religious festivals than church prayer-meetings, ought it to be a matter of surprise if the new members become like unto them?

I have always observed that those in the churches who have the least piety affect the most care about receiving members. They act as if they were hoping to atone for their sins by their extreme conservatism. They will ask as many questions of a candidate as if they were examining him for ordination. I have also noticed that those who were the most zealous in saving souls generally receive the converts with greater cordiality, and are more ready to take upon themselves the burden of watching over and encouraging them than are those who exhaust their zeal in trying to keep them out.

In the next place, churches frequently kill off the converts by not giving them a chance to work. In many churches there are no organized plans of Christian effort, and the members have no church help to "exercise themselves unto godliness." The convert is thrown upon his own individual resources. In many cases, however willing to work, in his inexperience he does not know what to do, or how to set about doing anything, so that he is timid, and hesitates, lest he shall be deemed froward. Besides, much time need not elapse before he can find out that a few are not indisposed to monopolize the offices and honors, while others seem to find their chief exercise in repressing the ardor of any who might wish to do more than themselves. Converts are usually in a plastic state, and are peculiarly sensitive to first influences that are exerted on them on joining the church. Multitudes receive a set back then, from which they never recover.

Very many make much of the kind of experience a candidate may be able to relate; but facts abundantly prove that "experiences" are uncertain reliances. Many who told bright experiences live inconsistent lives, and many who stumbled and bungled in their narration prove, by consistent conduct, that the root of the matter was in them.

Many are also much opposed to the baptizing of children. I know of one little girl, converted in the Sunday school, whose parents refused their consent to her being baptized on account of her youth, who one day brought her Testament to her pastor, and asked him to mark out the passage which tells how old a person must be before he could be baptized. The only answer that can be given to such a question is one which admits that a child who is old enough to repent and believe is not too young to be baptized.

V.

THE UTILITY OF ANXIOUS-SEATS.

THERE is no intrinsic virtue in an "anxious-seat." There is no merit in taking it. There is nothing in the thing itself that can place God under obligation to save. Nevertheless there are advantages in the use of this institution.

1. It serves as a test of character. Many people think that they are not ashamed of Christ, but when called upon to give a public expression of their feelings, they recognize and evince a strong unwillingness to expose themselves to such an avowal. They are afraid of the comments of the ungodly; and besides this, they become conscious of a resistance to the overtures of the gospel, that springs from a hatred to Christ, an unwillingness to make the surrender, of which they were hardly conscious before. Thus many have become amazed at the discovery of their carnal enmity, and have been brought to realize, more fully than ever, the necessity of their being born again.

2. It is a public committal. When once the step is taken, it is more dishonorable and more mortifying to go back than it is to go forward. The more obstacles that can be put in the way of receding the better. God frequently helps men to a right decision by bringing them to a crisis, in which the retreat is more disastrous than a forward movement. Thus was it with the children of Israel, as they came to the Red Sea, with the hosts of Pharaoh behind them. Consequently all the barriers that can be put in the way of the anxious, to prevent their going back, should be piled up behind them; and all inducements to strengthen their resolutions, and to make them strive to enter

in at the strait gate, should be employed, for "the kingdom of heaven is taken by violence, and the violent take it by force."

3. It is a convenient way of making a public acknowledgment of our need of Christ. The language of the Savior is emphatic: "Whoso shall confess me before men, him will I confess before my Father and his holy angels." "He that shall deny me before men, him will I deny before my Father and his holy angels." The blind man not only prayed publicly to Christ for the opening of his eyes, but was called upon to answer this question: "What wilt thou that I shall do unto thee?" Why did the Savior ask that question? Clearly, he wished him to ask again, in order to make him emphasize his wants before all the people, that all might know that Christ had opened his eyes.

In like manner all sinners must come out and confess their need of the healing virtue there is in Christ. The woman who *secretly* touched the garment of Christ was brought out before all the people, and rebuked for her hesitancy to appeal to the Savior publicly.

4. The effect of such an example is an encouragement to other convicted souls. A man who thinks he is willing to do something for Christ, can do no less than this simple service. He may not have the tongue of eloquence to exhort, he may not have abundance of wealth to pay missionaries, but can quietly and humbly take a position before a congregation, which evinces his sincerity and earnestness. Thus one can be the means of bringing others to a right decision by the force of example.

5. The effect of taking such a step is also an encouragement to the minister and the church. By this means they know that their labors are not in vain. They see that their prayers are being answered.

It may be asked, however, "What authority have we in the teachings or examples of the Bible for anxious-seats?" Answer: I have shown that the principle of publicly avowing our desire for salvation is recognized by Christ. I am not tenacious about the way of carrying out the principle, whether an inquirer rise on his feet and speak, or whether he take a seat assigned for those in his condition. I prefer the latter course on several accounts. Some persons are timid (especially ladies), and shrink from speaking for the first time before a large and promiscuous assembly. They can quietly walk forward to an assigned seat much more readily. Again, the interest of the meeting is ascertained and concentrated. Scores may rise from their seats and sit down again, and be unnoticed, and the church fail to appreciate the extent of the feeling. Besides, the anxious become more accessible to the acquaintance, sympathy, and instruction of the minister and brethren. In many cases the mere act of coming forward has brought no relief; but once forward, the anxious soul comes in contact with some one who takes an immediate interest in his case, prays for him, converses with him, follows him up, and thus he is saved.

It should be borne in mind that while the means of grace are divinely appointed, such as the preaching of the gospel, prayer, singing, baptism, and the Lord's supper, the measures in detail which are to be adopted in applying these agencies are left to be determined by the varying circumstances and exigencies of the time, and place, and people.

Hence, while the act of preaching is an imperative duty, it is a matter of discretion or circumstance whether we preach in a dedicated building, an ordinary dwelling, a barn, or the open field. We may preach throughout one hour or two hours, fast or slow, loud or low.

It is the duty of Christians to pray, but the style or method of our praying need not be the same in all cases. We must baptize, but it is left free to decide, according to circumstances, whether we shall baptize in a river, a lake, the sea, or a fount. Only in all cases let it be remembered that we are to "let all things be done decently and in order."

VI.

HOW TO INSTRUCT INQUIRERS.

ON this subject the Bible is our guide. Peter said to those who asked "What must we do?" "Repent and be baptized." When the jailer asked a similar question, Paul answered, "Believe on the Lord Jesus Christ." Jesus said, "Come unto me, all ye that are weary and heavy-laden, and I will give you rest." These directions are substantially alike. No man repents without believing. No man believes in Christ without repenting, and no man comes to Christ without doing both; and baptism is the symbol and profession of this moral experience.

Thirty-five or forty years ago, Baptists, Presbyterians, and Congregationalists would tell inquirers to go home, read their Bibles, reflect upon their condition, look within, dig deep, and be not deceived. They enforced a process of introspection, rather than the idea of looking out from themselves unto Jesus. The Methodists would tell them to put their names on the "class" paper, and become probationers for six months. In many cases they would find a kind of relief in the notion that they had a period of six months in which to become Christians; but before the allotted period had expired their interest would die out, and they would find themselves where they started, with this difference, that they were more hardened, and less likely to make another effort.

In contradistinction from all such usages of delay and hesitancy, the apostles called upon men to make an immediate surrender of their hearts to God. They required the exercise of repentance and faith on the spot. They made no provision for delays, and clearly implied that this very hesitancy was a resistance of the Holy Spirit, and an act of hostility to God. Any other instruction seems like tolerating impenitence, unbelief, and a rejection of Christ.

Is it not amazing that ministers of the gospel should betray such ignorance of the Sacred Scriptures, and be so regardless of inspired directions and apostolic examples? Yet despite such bad counsels, many made out to stumble into the kingdom; while others would guess their way along in darkness for years, and after a while would get some glimmers of light. I am amazed that while the other denominations named are coming nearer to the Bible standard, that our Methodist friends should hold on to their old tradition of putting all of the inquirers on a probation of six months. I think it is the worst thing in their whole system, and have been hoping and praying that they would correct the evil.

There are numerous influences which operate on inquirers to embarrass their efforts after salvation. Some are holding on to their companions, and are unwilling to give them up for Christ. Others are depending on something which they have done, or intend to do, instead of depending on Christ alone. Some are unwilling to abandon an unlawful business, or to give up their unlawful gain. Others again have contracted bad habits, such as the use of tobacco, wine, rum, whiskey, or dancing. Every person is willing to give up something, but not the particular idol which they worship. They make reservations, and say, "Pardon, O Lord, thy servant in this one thing." But Christ says, "Whosoever doth not forsake all that he hath, cannot be my disciple."

If persons, who have been converted, are in a backslidden state, now hoping and now doubting, it is safe to bring them to the same test that you do an inquirer. The great necessity is to bring every soul to trust in Christ solely and implicitly, and to serve him unreservedly, and leave all consequences with Him, who, with Christ, freely giveth us all things. It is ours to serve God; it is his to save.

We are all directed to pray. The apostle told Simon to "pray God, if perhaps the thought of thy heart may be forgiven thee." God "will have all men to pray everywhere." The mercy-seat should be the sinner's first resort. O, how strange it is that the soul should be so loath to come to Jesus, the sinner's friend, and his only "helper in time of trouble" — to him who has done for him more than any other being, and stands ready to save!

No two persons under conviction are exercised precisely alike. There are diversities of operations, but the same God "worketh all in all." This passage refers not only to the diversity of gifts dispensed among his people, but it refers also to the diversity of operations in converting sinners.

There is a difference in the times when the Spirit begins to work on the hearts of men. Some are moved upon when very young. I have no doubt some are born again at the age of three or four years. The sovereignty of God cannot be called in question. The Spirit goeth "where it listeth." But these early conversions are the result, to some extent, of early instructions, and in answer to the earnest prayers of parents. Some such persons often doubt the genuineness of their conversions, because they have not experienced such decided convictions as others speak of who have lived longer in sin. Perhaps, however, like Samuel, they have been called before they were old enough to recognize the voice of God. They have no remembrance of the time when they did not love God. They must be instructed accordingly; and it is a great mistake to attempt to judge of their experience by some other person's standard.

There is a difference to be observed in the kind of truth to be presented to different persons with a view to awakening them. Some can be moved by the constrainings of the love of Christ; others may be aroused by the terrors of the law. It is common for most persons to place a great estimate on the value of that particular class of truths that interested them, and to think the method which secured their attention preferable to any other.

There is a difference in the length of time in which the Spirit strives with men. Some persons he follows after for years; others may never have more than one distinct call. If that is rejected, they are forever lost.

These differences of operations are owing, in part, to the way in which the Spirit is treated. If it is rejected deliberately, he may leave the soul at once. But in other cases men sin ignorantly: seeking the truth, but unconsciously submitting to some unrecognized influences which hinder the Spirit's operations; and God forbears. All these cases are to be treated differently.

There is also a difference in the degree or depth of conviction in different persons. Some need only to know the will of God concerning them, and they yield at once. Others are more stubborn in the natural disposition, and will not yield unless God puts the screws to them and almost kills them. Our instructions to the anxious must make "a difference" according to the different conditions of the person with whom the Spirit is striving.

There is a difference in the manner in which relief comes to persons. Some find it gradually, hardly knowing how or when. Others find the relief at once, and never forget the time or place when the burden rolls off from their minds. The conversion may be as genuine in the one case as in the other. Two men may be going up a long, steep hill, each with a bag of sand on his back. In one of these bags there is a hole, and the sand gradually falls out, and the man hardly perceives the lessening of the load, but soon it is all gone; the other carries his load, and it seems to grow heavier and heavier. All at once the straps break, and the bag falls to the ground. He knows the moment when the burden fell. But in the one case the relief is as actual and real as in the other. Each has got rid of his burden.

So also there is a difference as to the way in which light comes into the soul. Some see but a very few rays at first. Conversion is to them like the dawning of day. They never see any great light; can hardly tell whether any change has come over them or not; and because they have not felt, as some say they have, they are tempted to doubt the reality of their hopes. Still they love God, and love his people, and love his service. Others experience a divine illumination. All at once light is poured into their souls. The change is so great that they never forget the time. These persons need to be taught that the genuineness of their conversion does not depend on the degree of light they have enjoyed, but on the state of their affections; whether they love God and keep his commandments; whether they are in sympathy with Christ, his service, and his people. There was a difference between the conversion of the eunuch and that of Paul. But Paul never bases the reality of his conversion on the mere miraculous circumstances which attended it.

But I am constrained to say that I have never depended as much as some have on instructions to the anxious. Rather I have insisted on immediate decision — on instantaneous repentance, and faith in the Lord Jesus. In the anxious-room I depend more on prayer, on prevailing supplication with God, than on all the instructions which can be given. Everything is dark to the sinner until enlightened by the Spirit; and no coaxing, no teaching, no driving will compel or induce the devil to leave his palace in the human soul, until the stronger than the strong man armed comes upon him and binds him. Then the work is done, and done effectually. Hence I get all on their knees, and set them to crying to God (both saints and sinners), till he sends down salvation. I have known fifty souls to be converted in one season of prayer, that is, before we have risen from our knees.

VII.

ADVICE TO YOUNG CONVERTS.

THE first duty required of a new-born soul is to be baptized into Christ. They are dead to sin, dead to the world, and dead to the penalty of the law. These great facts in their spiritual condition they are enjoined to symbolize, by being "buried with Christ in baptism."

They also believe in the death and resurrection of Christ, and are required to express that faith in baptism. When they go down into the liquid grave, they say they believe that Christ "died for their sins, and was buried;" and when they come up out of the water, they set forth their belief that he rose from the dead; that he liveth, liveth forever, and that all his believers will be raised from the grave, and exalted to a share in the glory of Christ forever and ever.

The New Testament makes no provision of a moment's delay between the exercise of faith and the act of baptism.

2. Be careful to maintain secret prayer. Jesus says, "Enter thou into thy closet, and when thou hast shut to thy door, pray to thy Father, which is in secret, and thy Father, which seeth in secret, shall reward thee openly." It is blessed, indeed, to retire from all the world, to be shut up with God, when no human eye sees, and no human ear hears. The thought that God will listen to our cries, will sympathize with our trials, and assist and deliver us in all our perplexities, is itself full of comfort.

In the matter of prayer, great care should be taken to establish regular seasons of prayer. Let nothing interrupt your engagements with God. If you only visit your closet when it is convenient, you will be tempted to neglect the privilege of prayer, from time to time, until it is dispensed with altogether. The man who does not take pains to wind up his watch at stated seasons, will seldom have correct time.

3. If it is in your power to do so, maintain family prayer. Joshua said, "As for me and my *house*, we will serve the Lord."

If the husband and father are absent, the wife and mother should lead in the service. It is desirable, in cases where the husband is not a Christian, that the pious wife maintain the appointment.

4. Study the word of God. "Search the Scriptures," said Jesus. And the Bereans were complimented as being more noble than those of Thessalonica, in that "they searched the Scriptures daily." The words which Jesus speaks are "spirit, and they are life."

Do not read the Scriptures in the spirit of controversy, but of candid and prayerful self-application.

Read the word of God frequently. It will bear reading over and over again. Let not a day pass without reading a portion of this precious message of God to your souls.

The perusal of this sacred book will improve the intellect and purify the heart. A person who has a good knowledge of the Scriptures has a good education. It is said that many of the children of the early Christians could repeat the entire Bible, from the beginning to the end. The Bible is the chart to direct us to heaven; a lamp to light us through this dark world to the better land.

5. Make the service of God your business for life. Let everything else bend to that. "Seek first the kingdom of God, and all these things shall be added unto you." Do all things "to the glory of God." Engage in nothing on which you cannot ask the blessing of God. Make all other claims secondary and subservient to religious duties. Thus you will fill your places in the church, in the prayer-meeting, and bear

your share in the support of the ministry and the spread of the gospel at home and abroad.

Never shrink from the performance of duty in social worship. Be ready to speak, to pray, and to engage in every good word and work. The Savior has given us the test and the standard: "If any man will come after me, let him deny himself, and take up his cross, and follow me."

In this connection, I may add, that it is of the first importance to aim at a symmetrical development of character. Some men will talk in meeting, but will give little or nothing to support the gospel; others will give freely as the Lord has prospered them, but will neither speak nor pray in public. Every grace and every talent must be cultivated, that we may grow up unto "the perfect man, unto the measure of the fulness of Christ." When only some graces and gifts are cultivated and others are neglected, the character grows out of shape, and becomes a deformity. Sometimes we meet with a man who prays and talks like a saint, and is as penurious as a miser; another man deals out his money freely for Christian purposes, but never has a word to say for Jesus, nor a prayer to offer for the conversion of a "world lying in wickedness." Some people tell us that they have no gift to pray or speak in the prayer and conference meeting, but you will generally find them ready to take part in the business meeting, especially if there is quarrelling going on; on such occasions they can speak with the vehemence of a Demosthenes and the fluency of a Cicero.

6. "Exercise yourselves unto godliness." Without exercise you will experience the evils of spiritual dyspepsia. A Christian cannot safely allow a single day to pass without seeking to do something specially with a view to doing good to others, or overcoming sin in himself. As every part of the body is strengthened by use and exercise, or weakened for the want of them, in like manner our spiritual natures grow in grace by reason of the active devotion of our powers to the service of Christ.

7. Guard yourselves against the liabilities of your own

weaknesses. Satan knows what they are, and will tempt you accordingly.

If in former times you have been accustomed to the use of strong drink, your safety requires that you "touch not, taste not." "Look not thou upon the wine when it is red, when it giveth his color in the cup."

Do as did a man in the State of Illinois, who had cultivated a thirst for strong drink. At the time of his conversion he was owing a bill at a rum-shop, but he did not dare to trust himself across the threshold; so he put the amount of his indebtedness in an envelope, and fastening it to the end of a pole, stuck the pole into the window, and ran off as if all the devils in hell were after him.

Have any of you been addicted to the use of tobacco? Wage a war of extermination with this wretched practice. Tobacco was made to kill insects, not human beings. There is none of the brute creation that will eat it, except the long-haired goat, that climbs the side of the mountains of the East.

Tobacco softens the brain, weakens the intellect, enfeebles the body, vitiates the appetite, and hurries its victims to the grave.

The use of tobacco is a filthy habit. A person who is a great smoker can be scented wherever he goes. He taints the very atmosphere with the poisonous odor that exhales from his breath and pervades his clothes; and he must either be accommodated with a spittoon wherever he goes, or be running to the door, or window, or fire-hearth, to keep himself from the disgusting alternative of spitting on the carpets of his friends.

Some of you, perhaps, have been novel readers. If so, I beg you to do as did the heathen who were converted in the days of the apostles. They brought their books together and burned them before all the people, and counted the price of them, and it amounted to fifty thousand pieces of silver. When I closed my meeting in the Baptist Tabernacle, New York city, I called upon the congregation to bring together all their novels and other pernicious books. A great heap of books was collected, which for once were made useful in furnishing material for a brilliant bonfire.

I warn you against all light reading, for the following reasons: —

a. It involves a waste of precious time.

b. It weakens the mental powers. A person can read novels from morning till night, without exercising his powers of thinking. It promotes intellectual indolence, and disqualifies a person for close application and original thinking.

c. It gives false views of life. Its scenes are unreal. They rarely find their counterpart in the actual world. The imagination becomes disordered, and the mind loses its relish for the matter-of-fact duties and realities of life.

It is rarely the case that a woman who has given herself up to the practice of reading novels makes a good housekeeper. The temptation to read "the last novel" is stronger than her sense of obligation to her husband and children. The novel must be devoured, even though her husband goes without his meals and her children are compelled to wear unmended garments.

d. I need hardly enter into an argument to prove that the practice of reading novels is a serious hinderance to growth in grace. It begets a distaste for the duties of prayer, reading the Bible, and seeking out opportunities of doing good to the many objects of Christian sympathy which abound in the walks of real life. A person who has tears to shed over scenes of fancied sorrow, rarely has any to spare when called to look on the scenes of actual woe.

e. Remember that Christianity is a radical principle. A Bible Christian cannot be a conservative. Christianity is progressive in its nature. It aims to overthrow the kingdom of the devil, and to oppose and remove everything which is opposed to God and holiness.

The world and the devil are evermore in favor of compromise. This truth relates alike to religion and politics. But "what fellowship hath light with darkness? or Christ with Belial?" In regard to all subjects, take your position on God's eternal truth, and stand there, though earth and hell oppose. Christ resisted unto blood, striving against sin.

Let your influence always be decided and open against slavery, intemperance, and oppression, and in favor of all reforms which tend to elevate the condition of the race; and be willing to suffer, and, if need be, die for your conscientious convictions. "He that seeketh his life, shall lose it, and he that loseth his life, for my sake and the gospel's, shall find it."

VIII.

ACTIVE BENEVOLENCE.

BENEVOLENCE is in the nature of all holy beings. Love to God and love to man are the legitimate expressions of this principle. Man, in his primeval estate, was possessed of a nature that did love God supremely, and could have loved his neighbor as himself. But when he fell, the governing principle of his soul was changed from this holy impulse to that of a supreme love of self. In conversion, however, this original outgoing of his nature reasserts itself, and in the supremacy of this restored principle he becomes a new creature.

All the Christian graces spring from love. And as this love towards sinful and suffering creatures takes the form of an earnest and practical sympathy, Christians find themselves having the same yearning mind after their fellows which was also in Christ Jesus.

Consequently we all lay all of our earthly possessions on God's altar, and consecrate our time, our talents, our money, and, if need be, our lives, to the work of doing good — of glorifying God in laboring for the salvation of the world. Self, which is the great law of our fallen natures, is now ignored; we are restored to our original condition of communion with God, and fellowship with angels, and sympathy with men.

We propose to show the duty of exercising the grace of Benevolence.

1. The duty of benevolence is taught by the voice of nature.

The sun does not shine for itself, but for others. The clouds do not pour down their refreshing showers for themselves, but for others. The earth does not yield its great variety of delicious and golden fruits for itself, but for others. God did not fill the earth with beautiful and fragrant flowers, and wrap the earth in its green carpet, for himself, but for man; nor did he make the various orders of the brute creation subordinate to man's authority, and subservient to him, for his own gratification or necessity, but for man's.

The selfish man has no sympathy with God in these regards; nor is he in sympathy with angels and good men. All nature is breathing forth the spirit of benevolence. We see it with our eyes; we hear it with our ears; we inhale it in every breath; we partake of it with every morsel of food we eat; and if we do not reciprocate it, but remain selfish, cold, dead, and senseless to all the obligations these exhibitions of his goodness impose, we are worse than blanks, or drones; we are fit for nothing but to be cast out and trodden under foot.

2. God enjoined the duty of active benevolence upon his covenant people, the Jews, and without it they could not be numbered among his people. Every man must pay one tenth of all for the support of the ministry, and one tenth for their sacrifices, or burnt-offerings, which made twenty per cent.; then they had to build and rebuild their temple, observe all of their feasts and fasts, attend all of their protracted meetings, which were frequent and sometimes long continued; in addition to all of these, once in seven years debtors were all released, servants all set free, and their lands were allowed to rest. Moreover, they were required, when gathering their harvest, to let fall some hands full for the poor, and to leave more or less of all kinds of fruits for those who had none.

Their zeal for the Lord of Hosts was so great, that on some occasions they mortgaged their lands and all they had to maintain their worship; yet this people rose rapidly in wealth, intelligence, refinement, and power among the nations of the earth; and when the honor of their divine Master required it, they brought forth their tithes and offerings so freely and so abundantly that they had to be restrained.

3. We have the example of holy angels to enforce the duty of active benevolence.

All of their visits to the children of men, for six thousand years, have been visits of mercy and benevolence. During all these thousands of years no angel ever came down to set up a kingdom for himself, or to gather up silver, gold, pearls, or precious stones, with which to enrich himself, but always for the sake of doing something for others; now confirming the wavering, now strengthening the feeble-minded, and ever attesting their profound interest in the several phases of Christ's ministry for the redemption of man.

4. The holy apostles taught and carried out this principle of benevolence.

They consecrated themselves, their all, to the work of Christian benevolence, the good of mankind, and the glory of God. They neither faltered nor turned aside from this work. They lost sight of all self-interests. They had but one object in living. "They counted not their lives dear unto them."

Paul said, "I am ready not only to be bound, but also to die at Jerusalem, for the name of the Lord Jesus." Again, "I am determined to know nothing among you, save Jesus Christ and him crucified." Their love to God and man was so great, their benevolence so unabating, that it led them to endure imprisonment oft, and stripes above measure. They were beaten with rods, stoned, in perils oft, perils by the heathen, in perils in the city, in perils among robbers, in perils among false brethren, in weariness and painfulness, in hunger and thirst, in fastings often, in cold and nakedness, homeless and houseless; yet, prompted by pure benevolence, they went on, until they sealed their testimony for the truth with their lives. O God, how ashamed I feel when I contrast my benevolence with theirs! If the apostles had pursued the course which some persons in modern times do, it would have overthrown the whole kingdom of Christ. But none could doubt their sincerity; none could question their motives; all must have been convinced that they were prompted by a disinterested spirit. Their benevolence was not an abstract principle, confined to creeds and books, but an active, controlling, propelling power, which made them omnipotent for good.

5. But the crowning example of benevolence is furnished in the mission of the Son of God. His errand to this world was purely an errand of love for us. He came not to be ministered unto, but to minister. "God commendeth his love toward us, in that while we were yet sinners Christ died for us." Paul calls the coming of Christ to save us, God's "unspeakable gift," and presents his spirit as the model and inspiration of true Christian benevolence. "Ye know the grace of our Lord Jesus Christ, who, though he was rich, for our sakes became poor, that we through his poverty might be rich." We are exhorted to "let the same mind be in us which was also in Christ Jesus," and are solemnly reminded, that "if any man have not the spirit of Christ, he is none of his."

6. The whole of God's word breathes and enforces the duty of benevolence. The book itself is a benevolent gift from God to man. The ends which it designs to accomplish are all benevolence, and the duty of benevolence is taught on almost every page. Let us listen to a few sentences.

"Whatsoever we would that men should do unto you, do ye even the same unto them."

"Freely ye have received, freely give."

"He that hath two coats, let him impart to him that hath none; and he that hath meat, let him do likewise."

"Sell that ye have and give alms. Provide yourselves bags which wax not old, a treasure in the heavens that faileth not."

"And I say unto you, Make unto yourselves friends of the mammon of unrighteousness, that when ye fail they may receive you into everlasting habitations."

"Therefore, as ye abound in everything, see that ye abound in this grace [benevolence] also."

"As we have therefore opportunity, let us do good unto all men; especially unto them who are of the household of faith."

"Charge them that are rich in this world that they be not

high-minded, nor trust in uncertain riches, but in the *living God*, who giveth us all things *richly* to enjoy; that they do good; that they be rich in good works, ready to distribute, willing to communicate; that they may lay hold on eternal life."

7. Benevolence does not improverish us. God delights to make happy the poor and the needy, and to have his gospel preached and his word extended to every creature; and wherever he sees an agent who will dispense to the poor, and give liberally to spread the gospel, he delights to furnish him with the means. He can bless all around him. Hence unto him that hath shall be given, and he shall have more abundantly.

"Cast thy bread upon the waters, and thou shalt find it after many days."

"He is ever merciful, and lendeth, and his seed shall be blessed."

"A good man showeth favor and lendeth; surely he shall not be moved forever. The righteous shall be held in everlasting remembrance."

"There is that scattereth and yet increaseth, and there is that withholdeth more than is meet, but it tendeth to poverty."

"The liberal soul shall be made fat," and "he that watereth shall himself be watered." "Honor the Lord with thy substance and with the first fruits of thy increase; so shall thy barns be filled with plenty, and thy presses burst out with new wine."

"There is that maketh rich, yet hath nothing; and there is that maketh himself poor, and yet hath great riches."

"But the liberal deviseth liberal things, and by liberal things shall he stand."

"Give and it shall be given unto you, good measure, pressed down, shaken together, and running over."

Now, if we believe these sentiments, expressed by men inspired by the Holy Spirit, we must admit that benevolence is not the road to poverty, but the way to prosperity.

8. Benevolence makes both the giver and the receiver happy, and the former more than the latter.

"It is more *blessed* to give than to receive."

"Blessed [or happy] are the merciful, for they shall obtain mercy."

"The blessing of him that was ready to perish came upon me, and I caused the widow's heart to sing for joy."

The more closely we conform to the laws of God's moral government, the more effectually we secure our own happiness, and every deviation from those laws must produce misery.

Man is so constituted, that he must practise benevolence to his fellow-man, or not only suffer in his moral character, but jeopardize his immortal soul.

The falling under the controlling power of self-love and its constant gratification, with no ventilation by benevolence, is like the constant increase of steam without ventilation, until the frightful explosion takes place. In these times of great worldly prosperity, we do well to keep our eye upon the safety-valve, and to ventilate by benevolence, or we may burst our boilers, and go to perdition.

9. Benevolence is pleasing to God. The apostle says, "I am full, having received of Epaphroditus the things which were sent from you, an odor of sweet smell, a sacrifice *acceptable, well-pleasing to God.*"

"God loveth a cheerful giver."

"To do good and to communicate forget not, for with such sacrifices *God is well pleased.*"

If, then, benevolence is well pleasing to God, the want of it must be very offensive to him. The selfish, penurious, hide-bound soul must be an offence to him, and a disgusting object to all benevolent, holy beings, in the universe. The good things of this life are designed for three distinct objects: 1. To feed and clothe the body; 2. To educate the intellect; and, 3. To cultivate the heart, or to educate men for heaven. When they are used for either of these objects they are a blessing; but when turned into another channel they become a curse. If hoarded up, they feed and strengthen the root of all evil. If laid out for display, for vain-glory, for sinful and foolish amusements, they strengthen all of the vile passions of our fallen nature, which must be crucified, or they will destroy our souls.

"If ye live after the flesh, ye shall die."

These passions are the thorns which choke the word and render it unfruitful. These riches and carnal indulgences rear the dam, and raise the pond which drowns men in destruction and perdition. What, then, can we do with the surplus avails of our industry better than to exercise the principle of benevolence, and give it full scope in pleasing God, making our fellow-men happy, and producing a God-like peace and bliss within our own souls?

But the great anxiety of many is to lay up for their children. They seem to think that, though Jesus has said, "Lay not up on earth treasures for yourselves," yet they may lay up treasures on earth for their children.

It is, undoubtedly, the duty of all parents to see that their children are comfortably fed and clad; that all of their corporal, intellectual, and moral necessities are met; that they are trained for the highest possible degree of usefulness and happiness: but to put them in a condition of ease and affluence, where neither their brain, their bones, nor their muscles will be taxed, is to do them the greatest possible injury. Piety never outlives the third generation in the midst of abounding wealth, and seldom the second. We who are parents can see that it is not easy to induce our children, even in the absence of the means of cultivating the carnal propensities of their fallen nature, to start in and persevere in the way to heaven; and how much more difficult when they abound in all the means to gratify their ambition, their pride, their vanity, their love of pleasure! The stream against which we all have to struggle to reach heaven is mighty; but, in their case, the influences by which they are surrounded set in like a flood, and become almost irresistible. The Savior, fully understanding all these things, exclaimed, "How hardly shall they that have riches enter into the kingdom of God!" "It is easier for a camel to go through the eye of a needle than for a rich man to enter into the kingdom of

God ' Borne along by this current, they may at times look heavenward, and think of their parents, who have gone before them, and make some feeble efforts to reach the promised land. But, alas! the current is too strong for them to resist, the temptations too great for them to overcome, and they go down, one after another, until they are all destroyed.

Many parents may look down from heaven, and see the obstacles which they have placed in the way of the salvation of their dear children, by not conforming to the divine rule in carrying out the principle of active benevolence. They now understand, as they never did before, "They that will be rich fall into temptation and a snare, and into many foolish and hurtful lusts, which drown men in destruction and perdition."

Even if we had no regard to the future, it is a bad policy to lay up riches for our children. It is well known that the most of our successful business men began with nothing. Our most able preachers of the gospel, our lawyers, physicians, and statesmen, are self-made men, who are indebted to the heavy tax upon their own efforts for success. Viewing the subject in this light, it is not strange that John said, "Love not the world, neither the things which are in the world;" "If any man love the world, the love of the Father is not in him."

Nor is it strange that Jesus pronounced the man a fool "who layeth up treasures on earth, and is not rich towards God." Well might the wise man say, "Give me neither poverty nor riches." The man who is not a benevolent man cannot be an honest man; because all we have and are belong to God, and not to ourselves.

God commands us to "do good unto all men as we have opportunity," to "love our neighbor as ourselves," to "deal our bread to the hungry," to "go into all the world, and preach the gospel unto every creature." Can we shut up the bowels of our compassion against the needy, hoard up God's money, withhold the gospel from the perishing, and be honest? It is impossible. We defraud the needy; we embezzle our Lord's goods, pervert the end of our being, and shut up the kingdom of God against men. In fact the faithful discharge of our duty, in the best use of everything committed to our care, can hardly be regarded as benevolence; it is but discharging a duty which we owe to God and man. When we have done all, we have done no more than that which it was our duty to do, and are unprofitable servants.

What will Jesus say, in the day of reckoning, to him who has wasted or withheld his Lord's money? Will he not be more likely to say, "Bind him hand and foot, and cast him into outer darkness," than to say, "Well done, good and faithful servant"? May God enable us so to live, and so to occupy, as that when he comes to call us to an account, he may say to us, one and all, "Ye have done what ye could." "Enter ye into the joy of your Lord."

IX.

RESTRICTED AND MIXED COMMUNION.

[It is believed that much of the unkind feeling, among all denominations, and uncharitable remarks about each other, proceed from a misconception of each other's sentiments; and there is no one thing more generally censured than restricted communion, as practised by the Baptist denomination, and that because it is so greatly misapprehended or so little understood. The design, then, of this little Tract, is not only to direct all candid inquirers after truth to the apostolic practice, but also to rectify mistakes, to remove prejudice, and to promote Christian union.]

BY *mixed communion*, I mean the custom of inviting members of all denominations to the communion table; and by *restricted communion*, I mean confining the invitation to the members of the same denomination.

Mixed Communion.

1. It has no tendency to increase brotherly love. The truth of this statement is obvious, from the well-known fact, that notwithstanding Pedobaptist churches have, to some extent, practised mixed communion ever since they have existed, and Baptist churches have never done it, yet there is no more union, no more brotherly love, between any two Pedobaptist churches than there is between the Baptist churches and any one of the Pedobaptist churches; and I think all observing men, who have travelled and mingled to some considerable extent with Christians of all denominations, will bear me out in saying, that there is more unanimity of feeling, more concert of action,

between Baptists and Presbyterians, than there is between Methodists and Presbyterians; or between Baptists and Methodists, than there is between Presbyterians and Methodists. Hence there can be nothing in partaking of the bread and wine by members of different and distinct bodies which tends to increase Christian affection or Christian fellowship.

2. It has no tendency to bring the different denominations together.

The ground of separation lies farther back — it is found in an honest (to speak with all charity) difference in sentiment, in different views of church building; and reason teaches there can be nothing in an occasional interchange of communion among some of the floating members of these different bodies which tends to do away their difference in sentiment, or to bring them all into one body. I would ask, Has it ever done it in one single instance since these bodies have existed as such? I challenge the world to produce one — nor is there a prospect that it ever will, for it has already been shown that there is no more union between Pedobaptist churches, which have practised mixed communion ever since they have existed as distinct bodies, than there is between Baptist and Pedobaptist churches.

3. Mixed communion, like the fifth wheel in a carriage, is uncalled for. Each church or denomination have their own regulations, and all may commune at home as often as they think proper; and if they are located, in the providence of God, where there is no church of their own denomination, and there is one of another, if they wish to commune with it, why not first become a member of it, and then walk with it, and act in keeping with their profession? And if there is a reason why they cannot in conscience become a member of such a church, the same reason must be in the way of their communing with it. It is but seldom that even the greatest sticklers for mixed communion ever commune with any other denomination. Scarcely a leading, stable, prominent member of an open communion church can be found who ever communes out of his own denomination. Ask a man, How long have you been a member

of an open communion church? Twenty years. How many times did you ever commune with any other denomination? Why, I do not *know* as I ever did. Well, how great a privilege can that be which you never wish to enjoy?

4. Mixed communion compels a church to commune with its excommunicated members. It is not an unfrequent occurrence for persons excluded from one denomination to become members of another; and if members in good standing in any Christian churches are invited to sit at the table, then these excommunicated members may come back without any reparation, and take their seat at the table of the church from which they have but just been expelled. Should it be said that they are answerable for such conduct, and not the church? I would ask if it is not an awkward position for a church to place themselves in, to put all power out of their own hands to exclude a man from their communion? A wicked, subtle, designing man may bid defiance to the church, the ruling elders, the presbytery, and the synod, or all combined, to prevent his claiming and occupying a seat at their communion table. The principle of mixed communion, then, annihilates the authority of the church, and gives Satan an opportunity of trampling it, with all of its officers, under foot. An occurrence of this kind is now fresh in my mind. It took place in the town of Henderson, Jefferson County, N. Y. A devoted and conscientious deacon of a Congregational church commenced a labor with a member of the same church for unchristian-like conduct, but could obtain no satisfaction. He then took one or two brethren with him, spread out all the circumstances before them; but he still justified himself, and abused his best friends, who were laboring for his good. The church was at length compelled to exclude him. He then went to a neighboring Methodist church, shed a few crocodile tears, and told them he had been persecuted because he had honestly changed his sentiments, and he was unanimously received. The next communion season which this Congregational church enjoyed (or would have enjoyed, but for mixed communion), he comes forward, and with great care takes his

seat at the table by the side of the deacon who took up the labor with him, for the express purpose of aggravating his feelings. The deacon says to a member of a Baptist church present (with whom he was very intimate), Brother Cole, what shall I do? I do not feel as though I could commune with that man. Brother Cole answered, I pity you, deacon, from the bottom of my heart, but I cannot relieve you; this is the effect of your wrong views of communion. The church was thrown into such a state of perturbation as to disqualify them to receive so holy an ordinance with pleasure or profit.

5. Mixed communion compels us to commune with those who are guilty of crimes for which we should feel ourselves bound to exclude our own members. For instance, suppose a Baptist church practised mixed communion, and one of its members should be guilty of attending balls, or a dancing-school, and the church should pursue a gospel course of labor, and could not reclaim her; she says she will go where she pleases, justifies *herself* and condemns *them;* they would now feel themselves solemnly bound to exclude her from the church, and no more admit her to the table of the Lord. But suppose, upon their invitation to all in good standing in other churches, a member of an Episcopal church, who had repeatedly attended balls and dancing-schools with this excluded member of the Baptist church, should take her seat at the table, the church would be compelled to commune with her, though guilty of the same crime for which they had just expelled one of their own members; the church has no power over her to call her to an account. She says, I belong to another body; my church tolerates me in choosing my own amusements, and pursuing them at my pleasure. In view of all these difficulties connected with mixed communion, I ask the candid and unbiased reader if it would not be best, all things considered, for each denomination to commune by itself, even if we were not bound by Bible rule and apostolic examples.

6. If the communion is extended out of the denomination, it is more difficult to find a stopping-place than to stop at the

boundary line of the denomination. There is almost an endless variety of Christian denominations in the world, and all embrace more or less truth in their creed, and the most of them may have some true Christians among them. Doubtless there are some true Christians in the Papal church, for God says, Come out of her, my people; and they could not come out, if not there. Some true Christians may be found among the Arians (called Christians); but to open the door to all these denominations, would be no better than to open it to all the world; and to open it to a part, and not to all, is to exclude some whom Christ loves, and that upon more uncharitable grounds than those taken by the Baptist denomination, because the Baptists make a distinction between church-fellowship and Christian-fellowship; and others unchristianize all whom they exclude from the table.

Restricted Communion.

It may be seen from the apostolic example that no person, however pious, has a right to participate of the Lord's supper until baptized. Baptism is everywhere required immediately after repentance or faith in Christ, and there is not a single instance recorded in the word of God where the communion was administered before baptism. See Acts ii. 38: "Then Peter said unto them, Repent, and be baptized every one of you." 41st verse: "Then they that gladly received his word were baptized; and the same day there were added unto them about three thousand souls." Here we see the order of the Christian church at its establishment; they, 1. repented; 2. they were baptized, and after that they were admitted to the communion; see the 46th verse. The same order is marked out in 1 John v. 8: "There are three that bear witness in earth, the Spirit, and the water, and the blood." Here it may be seen the Spirit (which indicates the new birth) comes first; the water (which is baptism) comes second; the blood (which is the communion) comes third; and we are charged, in 1 Cor. xi. 2, by the inspired apostle, to keep the ordinances as they delivered them to us. And who dare reverse this order? And to show still further that the apostles uniformly and invariably required all first to repent, and then to be baptized before they were admitted to the Lord's table, look at Acts viii. 12: "But when they believed Philip, preaching the things concerning the kingdom of God, and the name of Jesus Christ, they were baptized, both men and women." 13th verse: "Then Simon himself believed also: and when he was baptized he continued with Philip." It is equally clear that the eunuch did not commune until after being baptized. See Acts viii. 35, 36, 37. The jailer and his house likewise were baptized the same hour of the night in which they believed. Note Acts xvi. 31, 32, 33: "And they said, Believe on the Lord Jesus Christ, and thou shalt be saved and thy house; and they spake unto him the word of the Lord, and unto all that were in his house, and he took them the same hour of the night and washed their stripes, and was baptized, he and all his straightway." I also direct the candid inquirers after truth, to Acts x. 47 and 48: "Can any man forbid water, that these should not be baptized, who have received the Holy Ghost as well as we? And he commanded them to be baptized in the name of the Lord."

All, therefore, who take the Bible for their guide, follow the apostolic example, and keep the ordinances as they were delivered unto them, must insist upon every one's being baptized before he is invited to the Lord's table.

Now it may be seen that all who believe sprinkling, pouring, or plunging, is baptism, can commune, without violating conscience, with all Christian denominations, though, as has been shown, there is nothing gained by the practice, but much lost. And it is equally clear that those who believe sprinkling or pouring is not baptism; that none are baptized but such as have been immersed on the profession of their faith; cannot commune with any but those who have thus been baptized, without violating their conscience; yea, more, without a palpable violation of Bible rule, and the subversion of the apostolic example. Every candid and intelligent person then must see, that the

Baptist denomination act consistently with themselves: that is, if their views of baptism are correct, their action in relation to communion is right; and the moment they invite those to the communion table who have not been immersed, they are chargeable either with dishonesty or insincerity — dishonesty, in not acting in keeping with their sentiments; or insincerity, in what they profess to believe.*

That there is no gospel baptism short of the immersion of a believer in Christ, is quite certain from the following facts: —

1. The meaning of the word. The word *baptize* is a Greek

---

* See the candid testimony of a Presbyterian minister, taken from the American Presbyterian: —

"Open communion is an absurdity, when it means communion with the unbaptized. I would not, for a moment, consider a proposal to admit an unbaptized person to the communion; and can I ask a Baptist so to stultify himself and ignore his own doctrine as to invite me to commune with him while he believes I am unbaptized? I want no sham union and no sham unity; and if I held the Baptist notion about immersion, I would no more receive a Presbyterian to the communion than I would now receive a Quaker.

"Let us have unity, indeed, but not at the expense of principle; and let us not ask the Baptist to ignore or be inconsistent with his own doctrine. Let us not, either, make an outcry at his "close communion," which is but faithfulness to principle, until we are prepared to be 'open communists' ourselves; from which stupidity may we be forever preserved. Let us war not with his close communion, but with his doctrine that immersion is baptism.

"It has been quite the fashion of late years for commentators, who were ambitious to be thought candid and liberal, to concede to the Baptists that baptism is immersion. The volumes thus far issued of Lange's Commentary assume this, or assert it wherever the subject is presented. Dean Stanley, in his charming books, does the same; and so with others; and these men continue to practice both sprinkling and infant baptism. Such inconsistencies I am utterly unable to comprehend. If I believed what they teach I would be under the water before a week should pass by. My faith in such men is shaken — men who do not follow their beliefs.

"No, let us have no unity — and strive to have none — that cannot be in consistency with our doctrine. How *can* two walk together unless they are agreed? Let the unity stop where the agreement ends."

word; it cannot mean everything — to dip, pour, and sprinkle: the Greek word *rantize*, means to sprinkle, and *baptize*, to dip. This word is translated *dip* in the German tongue, and in some instances in our version, where it does not refer to the ordinance of baptism. "He to whom I shall give the sop, when I *dip* it;" the word rendered *dip* here, is baptize. "He whose vesture is *dipped* in blood." "That he may *dip* the tip of his finger in water." The word rendered *dip* in all of these cases is baptize.

That the word *baptize*, or *bapto*, its root, cannot fairly and honestly be translated so as to express anything short of immersion, is admitted by the most profound linguists in Germany; by all learned authors, both ancient and modern; by the Edinburgh Encyclopædia; and by the Greek church, who understand their own language, and never call sprinkling *baptism*, or who never call baptizing *rantizing*, or rantizing *baptizing*. What action, then, can be more plainly expressed, more clearly defined, than Christian baptism, if the word were translated? The following passages would read thus: "Repent and be *immersed*." "Go teach all nations, *immersing* them." "He that believeth and is *immersed* shall be saved."

2. That baptism is nothing short of immersion, is obvious, from its being called a burial. See Rom. vi. 4: "Buried with him by baptism into death." Col. ii. 12.: "Buried with him in baptism, wherein also ye are risen with him through the faith of the operation of God, who hath raised him from the dead." All can see that neither sprinkling nor pouring is a burial. How would it read, Buried with him by *sprinkling*? Buried with him by *pouring*?

3. That sprinkling it not baptism, is certain, because it does not represent the thing signified. Baptism is designed to show forth our death to sin and the world, and our faith in the death, burial, and resurrection of Christ; it also shows to the world that Christ, having been raised from the dead, has become the first fruits of them that slept, and that he will enable us to exclaim, O death, where is thy sting? O grave, where is thy victory? See 1 Cor. xv. 29: "Else what shall they do who

are baptized for the dead, if the dead rise not at all? Why are they then baptized for the dead?" Here the apostle is speaking upon the resurrection, and argues that the ordinance would be without meaning if there be no resurrection.

4. That Christ and the apostles required immersion, and not sprinkling, is obvious from the circumstances recorded in the New Testament. They came from Judea and Jerusalem, and from the region round about, to be baptized in Jordan. "John baptized in Enon, near to Salem, because there was much water there." They went down into and came up out of rivers, which never would have been done, never is done, to sprinkle persons.

Objections. — 1. It is said the Greek preposition *eis* means *unto*, and that there is no evidence that the baptized went "into" the water, or "came out" of it. I need not say a word on this subject to the Greek scholar; but let the English reader bear in mind that this rendering of *eis* in other passages where it occurs, would destroy all the miracles recorded in the Bible, and overthrow the whole system of Christianity. We are told the three Hebrew children were cast *into* the fiery furnace, and there was not the smell of fire on their garments. What miracle is there in this, if they only went *to* the furnace?

In like manner, we are informed that Daniel was thrown *into* the den of lions, and that they did not attack him; but if he was merely taken *to* the den, of course the lions could not get hold of him. And again, how easy to say that the swine merely went *to* the sea. Were we thus to resort to such a wicked and dangerous perversion of the several accounts contained in the Sacred Scriptures, we could easily explain away many of its recorded wonders.

The same mode of cavilling will overthrow the future punishment of the wicked. God says the wicked shall be cast *into* hell; but who knows, according to this wonderful invention, but that they will be carried only *to* hell? Then, worst of all, there is no evidence that any of us will ever enter *into* heaven.

We may go *to* heaven, but *into* what place or condition we shall enter God only can tell.

2. It is said that there were not water conveniences in Jerusalem sufficient for the immersion of the three thousand persons who were converted on the day of Pentecost. But all who are acquainted with the history of that city, and many who have visited it, know it contained five pools of water, in either one of which that number of persons could have been conveniently immersed.

3. It is said, also, that three thousand persons could not have been immersed in one day. I beg my dear readers to bear in mind that there were present on this occasion at least eleven apostles, and these alone could have immersed the whole of them in less than three hours. I have myself immersed in the Crooked Lake, N. Y., sixty persons in twenty-eight minutes, by the watch, and that too without undue haste. Besides, it is altogether probable that the seventy disciples were also there; and these, added to the number of the apostles, could have rendered the administration of the ordinance to so many a matter of perfect ease. Indeed, in the matter of time, we are of the opinion that it requires scarcely any more time to immerse a given number of candidates than it does to *sprinkle* water upon them. So that nothing important is gained in time by supposing the three thousand to have been sprinkled, unless we imagine that the rantism was performed on them *en masse;* and there is as much reason for imagining this latter method as for imagining that they were sprinkled at all.

4. It is thought by many that the jailer must have been *sprinkled.* This notion rests upon the supposition that he was rantized in the cell where Paul and Silas were confined. The record, as contained in Acts xvi. 33, is, that he took them the same hour of the night, and washed their stripes; and was baptized, he and all his straightway. The account itself implies more of service and preparation than could be conveniently performed within the narrow limits and unfurnished apartments of a prisoner's cell; besides, it is hardly to be supposed that the jailer

would have subjected his household to the inconvenience of passing from the house to the cell in order to be sprinkled. But when we remember that in the East the prison yards contained pools, or tanks, for the purposes of ablution, it is easy to see how readily they could have been immersed. Besides, the account further states, that after they had been baptized, he brought the apostles into his house, so that the family must have gone out of the house to be baptized; whereas, if sprinkling had been the mode, it is more reasonable to suppose that the apostles would have been taken into the house for the purpose of performing the ceremony.

From this view of the subject, it may be seen that the Baptist denomination, in the practice of restricted communion, are not bigoted nor uncharitable; that they are conscientiously keeping the ordinances as the apostles delivered them unto us, adhering strictly to Bible rule; making the word of God the rule of action, and not the consciences and traditions of men. It should be understood that those who practise restricted communion, do not say by it that they do not fellowship Pedobaptists as Christians, but that they do not fellowship Pedobaptism, or sprinkling; nor do they say that they do not love them as much as they love themselves. They could not commune with themselves had they been sprinkled, and not baptized; and we are not commanded to love our neighbor better than ourselves, but are strictly forbidden to love ourselves, or our neighbors, more than we love God. There may be in a community hundreds of young converts who have not been baptized, and are not yet members of any church; and however dear these converts might be to the church, and to the Savior too, no consistent church would feel themselves justifiable in inviting them to the communion table. Why not? Because they have not been baptized, nor have they been regularly inducted into the church; for the same reason a consistent Baptist church cannot invite a Pedobaptist to the table of the Lord, and yet they may love them as they love these young converts, and

Christ may love them too; yea, as they love themselves, and treat them just as they would be treated in like circumstances. When Christ took the twelve apostles into an upper room, and broke the bread to them, there were many other true Christians in Jerusalem, who were not invited to participate with them, because not yet regularly admitted into the church; because something more than faith in the Lord Jesus Christ was requisite to their being admitted to the Lord's supper.

From what has been said, it may be seen that the Christian world is divided upon the subject of baptism, and that this is the cause of their separation at the communion table. And two things are worthy of note in this matter: *one* is, should they commune together, the Baptist must violate his conscience, and nothing would be gained by it; they would still remain distinct bodies, and the whole ground of controversy would remain unsettled. The other is, however desirable it may be for all divisions to be done away, and all the members of Christ's family to be harmonized in one body, the Baptist cannot go over to the Pedobaptist churches without violating conscience, or going contrary to his honest views of Bible rule and apostolic example, because he *does not*, he *cannot* believe sprinkling is baptism, or that unconscious babes have any right to the ordinance. But the Pedobaptist can come over to the Baptist denomination without violating conscience, because he does believe immersion is baptism, and that true believers are proper subjects for that ordinance.

I would now ask the convert, who is not yet a member of any church, to consider, that if you remain where you are, you exclude yourself from communion with all Christian churches; and if you join a Baptist church, you are excluded by Bible rule from communion with Pedobaptist churches; and if you join a Pedobaptist church, you exclude yourself from communion with the whole Baptist denomination, and that too when the Baptist denomination are bound by conscience and by Bible rule to maintain the stand they have taken, and Pedobaptist churches can come over to them without violating their conscience, and all practise one way, and have "one Lord, one faith, and one baptism," and one communion table, one church, and all striving for one and the same things.

It may be asked, How can they commune together in heaven, if not on earth? We answer, there will be no bread and wine administered in heaven. Christian fellowship we all have on earth; all Christians will have it in heaven. Church fellowship is interrupted here by our different views of church building; but in heaven there will be no difference of opinion — all errors will be done away. Had infant baptism, and all other errors, been kept out of the church from the apostolic day down to the present period, there had been no schisms, no breach of communion on earth. The sin, then, of our separation at the Lord's table on earth lies at the door of those who introduced, and those who still practise, infant sprinkling. Let this corruption of the Papal church be done away, and all Protestant churches may come together.

I may be asked, Can Baptist churches commune with a person of good standing in a Pedobaptist church, who has been immersed upon the profession of his faith in Christ? I answer, in my opinion they can do it without violating any Bible rule, though it has been made to appear that mixed communion is attended with many difficulties and no advantages. I say it can be done without violating any Bible rule, and that, because, notwithstanding there is an inconsistency in a baptized believer remaining in and communing with an unbaptized church, yet we are not positively required by the word of God to exclude from our fellowship a brother for every inconsistency. But as God does require in his word that all persons should be baptized before they come to the communion table, and as the primitive church did comply with this requirement, we cannot extend the communion to an unbaptized person without violating this Bible rule, and going counter to the apostolic example. Lastly, I would ask, Is there anything more unfriendly or exclusive in restricting the communion of each denomination to itself, than there is in restricting any other church act to itself? such as the reception, discipline, and exclusion of members, the consecration, or setting apart of the officers of the church, or their deposition? It is not the practice of mixed communion churches to invite persons belonging to other denominations to participate with them in these things. And why? Because they belong to another body. Nor do we complain of them for it, by calling them bigoted and uncharitable; and yet I see no reason why we might not as well complain of bigotry in this thing, as they in our choosing to commune by ourselves. We think, inasmuch as there is a difference of opinion, and this difference of opinion has caused or produced different denominations, that the best course we can pursue is to go together as far as we think alike, then part in friendship, and let each denomination pursue its own course, without aspersions or abuse, until the errors which separate us are removed; and then these distinct organizations may be dissolved, and all enter one body, drink into one spirit, and rejoice in one Lord, one faith, and one baptism; and then all can sit down at one communion table. And that the Lord would hasten this glorious period, let all who love Zion most sincerely and devoutly pray. Amen, and Amen.

SERMONS.

I.*

LESSONS TAUGHT BY THE OX.

"*The ox knoweth his owner, and the ass his master's crib; but Israel doth not know, my people doth not consider.*" — ISAIAH i. 3.

IN this connection the Lord is urging a very just and grievous complaint against his own people for their stupidity and forgetfulness in matters of duty; and he carries this complaint first to the heavens, and says, "Hear, O heavens!" because the heavens are more faithful in answering the end of their being than man. The sun has never refused to shine, for one moment, since God separated the light from the darkness; the moon has always been faithful, and reflected her pale rays upon the pathway of the traveller; and the stars have never ceased to twinkle. They all answer the end of their creation. But man has become an opaque body. Man is as a wandering star. He has left his orbit, and he passes on and on, and withholds the light which God appointed him to reflect, and which he is capable of reflecting upon his fellow-men. And then he carries this complaint to the earth: "Give ear, O earth!" implying that the earth even is more faithful to answer the end of its

---

* Delivered Sunday morning, November 25, 1866, in the Bloomingdale Baptist church, New York city.

creation than is man; for the earth has never withheld its increase from the time God made it until now. The sun no sooner melts away the banks of snow, breaks up the frosty fetters of earth and warms its bosom, than vegetation springs forth, the fields are covered with green, and the trees with foliage; and in a little time we find the earth burdened with the precious fruits of abundant and varied vegetation. Even where there is no root or seed planted, we find the mushroom springing up in the walks of men. The earth will not be barren or unfruitful; it will answer the end of its creation. But, alas, how many barren souls there are in the human family! how many there are who utterly fail to bear the fruits of the spirit of love, meekness, faith, and joy in the Holy Ghost, humility, and all the graces of the Christian, which we ought to produce in abundance! In fact there are many who utterly fail to produce a single one of these fruits.

What extreme barrenness and unfruitfulness there is even on the part of many of the children of God! And I do not wonder that God says, "Hear, O heavens, and give ear, O earth;" and he adds, "I have nourished and brought up children, and they have rebelled against me." What a pathetic appeal is this! "I have nourished and brought up children, and they have rebelled against me." Perhaps some of us who are parents feel the force of this complaint. We have reared our children from their infancy, we have watched over them by night and by day, we have toiled early and late, and to the extent of our capacity, to provide for their necessities and their comfort, and to make them respectable in the world; and they turn their backs upon us, they trample our precepts under their feet, and some hard-hearted miscreant has more influence over them than the father who begat them, or the mother who brought them forth, and watched over them from tender infancy up to womanhood or manhood. So God says, "I have nourished and brought up children, and they have rebelled against me." He has brought us up from infancy, and fed us with the fulness of wheat, with milk, with butter, with oil, and with honey, and supplied all our wants; and we, his children, have turned our backs upon him, have trampled his precepts under our feet, and have followed in the way of darkness and death. And so God may well complain of the children of men, and cry out, "Ah, sinful nation, a people laden with iniquity, a seed of evil doers." And then he says, "The whole head is sick, and the whole heart is faint. From the sole of the foot even unto the head there is no soundness in it, but wounds, and bruises, and putrefying sores; they have not been closed, neither bound up, neither mollified with ointment."

The figure is this: The father is castigating the wayward son who sets up his will against his father's; and the father lays on the rod, again and again, until his whole person may be gored with blood, and show the marks of the rod; and the father pauses, and says to the son, "Why should ye be stricken any more? Why stand out against your father, and put him to the painful necessity of laying on the rod?" He would rather receive the stripes on his own back than lay them on his son, if it would answer the same purpose; but the son stands out in rebellion, and the father is compelled to chastise him. So God deals with the children of men. He deprives them of their earthly possessions; he lays those who are near and dear to them on the bed of death; one after another of their friends is borne to the grave, and God chastises them; and yet they stand out, and utterly fail to answer the end of their being. And then he says, "The ox knoweth his owner" (the stupid, lowly ox knoweth his owner), "and the ass his master's crib; but Israel doth not know, my people doth not consider."

Now the doctrine of the text is simply this: The ox, the stupid, lowly ox, and the stubborn, refractory ass, have more sagacity in their sphere, and more submission to the will of their owner, than man has in his sphere to the will of his Owner. This is the doctrine of the text.

1. Now notice in the first place, "the ox knoweth his owner." There is not an ox in all this world, which has long been owned,

fed, and driven by one man, but knoweth that man from every other man; and very often he becomes very much attached to him. He knows the sound of his voice, his coming in and going out, and understands what he wants him to do; but, alas! how many of the human family know not their rightful owner — God.

How many there are who are ignorant of the very being of God. The fool hath said in his heart, There is no God. He shuts his eyes, and can see no God; he closes his ears, and can hear no God; and he says, "I am determined to acknowledge no God;" and he goes blindly on, and never knows his Owner. Yet the evidences of God's existence are all around him, on every hand; and so plain as not to be gainsaid or resisted for a moment. God has displayed his existence in every blade of grass that grows, in every leaf that flutters in the wind, in every stream that softly murmurs through the landscape, and in the sunbeam, and in the sky. Around us, on every side, we see the work of Almighty God; and yet men shut their eyes against these evidences, and cry out, "There is no God." They do not know God.

Why do not acorns grow on pumpkin vines, and pumpkins on oak trees, if everything happens by chance? If things were left to chance, and pumpkins grew on oak trees, it would be dangerous to stand under them on a windy day, and have pumpkins, weighing one hundred pounds each, tumbling down and striking you on the head. And yet you say there is no God.

Would to God this infidelity were confined to those who openly profess infidelity; but, alas! there is too much of it to be found in the church among the professed children of God. When God is chastising us for our rebellious spirit, and for our waywardness, and is laying on the rod more or less severely, as the case may be, how many are all the time ascribing their afflictions to chance and luck! They say, "It so happened," "It was their luck," and act as though their owner was not chastising them, but all their misfortunes were the result of blind chance. They do not know God. They do not see or recognize the hand of God which is dealing with them, and laboring to bring them to terms of submission to his will. Hence we see that God may well complain, and say, "Israel doth not know; my people doth not consider. Ah, sinful nation." I knew, in my experience, a deacon of a Christian church who had a dairy of ninety-nine cows, and who wanted to have the round number of one hundred cows. He had a poor neighbor who had but one cow in the world with which to supply the wants of a large family of children with milk and butter, and this wealthy deacon, in order to secure a debt which the poor man owed him, took his only cow. Well, all through the summer he complained of having very bad luck. His butter would not come, skippers got into his cheese, and the murrain broke out amongst his cows. He did not know God; "it so happened" that he had very bad luck. He probably lost a hundred times more than the amount of the debt his poor neighbor owed him. God was chastising him in this way; he was laying his rod upon him, but he did not know God did it.

And so when God chastises us, and lays his rod upon us; when we find sickness and death entering our families, and we are compelled to sustain heavy losses in our fortunes; when he is thus dealing with us to make us wiser and better, how many of us fail to see God, to hear his voice, and to recognize him in all his dealings with us! And hence God says, "Israel doth not know; my people doth not consider." There never was an ox or ass so stupid as not to know when his master was chastising him. When Balaam arose and saddled his ass, and started off to curse Israel, and the angel of God came and stood in the way, and the ass saw the angel and turned aside, and Balaam smote him, the ass knew who smote him. He did not think that he had had very bad luck and a most unfortunate trip. No; poor stupid man, who does not know his Owner, would have reasoned thus; but the ass knew from whom he received every single stripe, and when God opened his mouth he rebuked the madness of the prophet.

There are many thousands who never understand that all their stripes come from God, their rightful owner. Very often God lays the rod of affliction upon a family who are irreligious, and will not come to Jesus. No sermons, no prayers, no tears, no tender expostulations can melt their hearts or subdue their wills, and bring them to the feet of their dear Redeemer, to know their owner, until God lays on the rod, works against their worldly interests, and brings them low down in the dust. Then they are moved to pray for grace from our Lord Jesus Christ. I have labored in some towns where certain families could not be reached; and after years had rolled round I have returned to find those very same families reduced from wealth to poverty; to find that they had suffered sickness, the loss of friends, and distresses of every kind; and that through the special providence of God they were now ready to come to Christ, and recognize him as their rightful owner. So God chastises the children of men, but they do not know him, and they stand out and revolt more and more. Squire S., a splendid man and able lawyer, in Athens, Cherry Valley, N. Y., said, "I would never submit my heart to God. I never knew my Creator until God entered my family and took my two little boys. He called them away; and when they were laid side by side in the grave, I was completely broken down and subdued. I went to my room and bowed down on my knees, and called on God for mercy; and God, for Christ's sake, forgave my sins." So God chastises the children of men in order to bring them to submission to his will, and to make them know their owner.

2. But we remark again, they do not know enough to come at the bidding of their owner, and yet the ox does. You go out to yoke a pair of oxen, and you find them lying down, chewing the cud. Go inside the yard, and speak to them, and they will rise up and bow their necks to receive the yoke. They know you are about to yoke them, but they do not lie still and refuse to rise, and say, "If you want to yoke us come here;" or, "We do not want to work to-day;" or, "We fear

that if we bow our necks to the yoke we may change our minds, and run off and break up the team." They do not stand out, and cavil and parley, like many sinners, but they obey the command of their owner, and bow their necks to the yoke in submission. But God comes and calls for sinners, and he says, "Come unto me, all ye that labor and are heavy-laden, and I will give you rest. Take my yoke upon you, and learn of me; for I am meek and lowly of heart, and ye shall find rest unto your souls." But sinners will not come. They say "We dare not promise; we dare not resolve; we fear we shall not hold out: if God wants to convert us, why cannot he convert us as we are? why must we go to him?" Thus they stand out, and cavil and parley; and God may well say, "Israel doth not know; my people doth not consider."

I remember that on one occasion in Jefferson County, in this State, a Universalist, named R., came six miles to hear me preach. He had not heard a sermon for ten years; but having received strange reports about the speaker, he was moved by curiosity to see what kind of a being I was. Before he came to the meeting — being a man of bad temper, and having no grace to control his temper — he had beaten one of his oxen most unmercifully; the ridges stood out over its whole body, and it was scarcely able to stand on its feet; and as God would have it, I preached from this very text that day. I spoke of God's goodness; what a kind owner he was; that he never gave an unnecessary blow, and yet men rebelled against him; while the ox very often had a bad master, who beat him unmercifully, yet the creature would obey his owner, and do just as he bid him. The man became very uneasy, and thought that some one had told me about his beating the ox. He said to himself, "If I could find him out, I would cowskin him." Soon after, he said, he resolved to cowskin me for dragging him out and exposing him before so many people. He thought of leaving the house, but said, "If I go they will all look at me, and know that Knapp means me;" so he kept his seat, and sweat it out. After the sermon he went home, and said, "Wife, I have not heard a sermon before for ten years, and I got preaching enough to-day to last me another ten years." He retired, but could not sleep; he could not help thinking what a kind owner God was, and that he had never served him, had never loved him, had never done a single thing to please him; while he had been cruel and unkind to his oxen, and yet they had served him and obeyed him in all respects. In the morning he went out to yoke his oxen, and it so happened that it was the near one which he had beaten so badly the day before; and as he approached them, holding the bow in one hand and the yoke in the other, and called to them, the near one rose up and came to him, and bowed its neck to the yoke. At this evidence of submission to his will, the man, remembering the sermon he had heard, dropped the yoke, started back, and cried, "O God! thou hast ever been a kind owner, and a merciful God to me, and I have never obeyed thee in the first thing; this ox has had a cruel and hard master in me, and yet he will do everything I tell him. God have pity upon me." He was so overcome by his feelings that he could do no work, and he went into the house, and said, "Wife, if you have a mind to go to church again, I will go down with you;" and they came and reached there at the commencement of the nine o'clock meeting. When he rose up to state these facts, and ask for our prayers, he fell his whole length on the carpet, and was converted to God before he left the house. Now see what a powerful preacher the ox is! The stupid, lowly ox evinces more sagacity and more submission to the will of his owner than man in his sphere, and hence God sends us to learn wisdom of the ox. A strange pass we have come to, when we must be sent to school to the ox and ass to learn wisdom; and yet God sends us to this school, and to this school we must go.

3. Then we observe again, that the ox knows that his owner has a yoke for his neck, and yet men do not know that God has a yoke for their necks, as well as a crown for their heads; and that if they will not wear the former, they never can the latter. If you ask me, "How do you know the ox has so much

discernment?" I answer, approach an ox with a yoke on your shoulder, and frequently he will rise up to receive it. He knows it is for his neck. How many of the human family there are who never seem to understand that God has a yoke for their necks, who are not willing to be bound, or to make any sacred and solemn vows to their owner, but who only care to study their own pleasure, and to have their own will and way, rather than be united with people who love God, and who have given a solemn pledge to serve him all the days of their life! And hence it is that God says, "The ox knoweth his owner, and the ass his master's crib: but Israel doth not know; my people doth not consider."

4. We may observe again, the ox knows for what the yoke is designed; that it is designed to capacitate him for hard service; and that he understands this, is certain from the fact that when you lay the yoke on his neck he will frequently begin to loll. This is the result of an association of ideas. An ox will loll when he is doing very hard service in the heat of the sun, and when the yoke touches his neck he associates it with hard service, and the sensation is for the moment produced; and yet how many are there in the church who, when they unite themselves with the church, do not understand that it is to qualify them for hard service in the cause of religion that God is putting his yoke upon them! They only come out and profess religion in order to secure peace of mind, to quiet conscience while they live in pleasure, knowing that they will have somebody to help them to the kingdom of Jesus. What would you think of an ox who reasoned thus: "I will bow my neck to the yoke, and if I get too lazy to do my share of the work, the other ox can draw me along too;" thus consulting his own indolence and interest, instead of the interests of his owner? The truth is, my beloved friends, God has called us away from the affairs of this world unto the kingdom of his dear Son, that we may work for him, that we may be workers together with him, not co-workers, for that implies partnership in the stock. God says, "Go thou into my vineyard, and work to-day." Suppose

an ox, after you had yoked him, in order to capacitate him for work, should lie down in the sun, or range around the green pasture and enjoy himself?—you would knock such an ox in the head; but the ox understands that the yoke is intended to capacitate him for hard service, and he bows to it, and obeys the commands of his owner. And we ought to understand, when we identify ourselves with the church of the living God, that it is to qualify us to work for the kingdom of the Lord Jesus Christ, that we may be laborers together with him, and go forth everywhere, doing good and striving to win souls to the dear Redeemer. It is good for a man that he wear the yoke, and that he wear it in his youth.

5. But, again, the ox seems to understand that the yoke is so constructed as to divide the burden according to the strength of the team. For instance, if the oxen be of equal strength, the point of draft comes in the centre of the yoke; but if one of the oxen be stronger than the other, the staple is removed nearer one end than the other, so that the strongest ox shall have more than half of the burden to bear. And when the yoke is laid upon their necks, and they are ready for work, they do not, when commanded to move forward, shrink back, and one or the other find fault because he has the heaviest share of the burden to bear, or complain that the load is unequally divided, or slip his neck out of the yoke; but he settles down to his work, and moves forward.

Now understand that Jesus Christ has constructed his yoke on the same principle. No one is required to do more than he or she is able to do. In reference to moral influence, every one is required to love the Lord his God with all his heart, and with all his mind, and with all his soul, and with all his strength. Now God never commanded that little boy there to love him with all the mind, the heart, the soul, and the strength of an experienced and disciplined Christian. He could not do it if God demanded it of him. He may be able to do it by and by, but he cannot do it now. So God requires every one to love him with all the heart he has.

And, in like manner, we are required to give, so far as our fortunes are concerned, according to our several ability. Each is required to give according to what he hath, not according to what he hath not; but every one should give something, and should do something, to sustain religious worship, and to extend the kingdom of our dear Redeemer throughout the world. Where God has given a great deal, he expects more than where he has given but little; but he requires something from us all; and we should settle in his yoke, which is lined with love, and galls no man's neck, and work with all our strength for the honor and glory of our divine Owner. We should not shrink back, and complain that the burden is greater than we can bear. O, think of the burdens Jesus bore for us! And is it not enough for the servant that he be as his master, and for the disciple that he be as his Lord?

6. It may be observed still further, that men do not seem to know that their owner will not overload them; yet the ox duly considers this. When a man drives a team of oxen up to a pile of stones, or boxes, or barrels, or anything which he wishes to remove from one place to another, he considers the strength of the oxen, and he puts the burden on according to their strength; he also takes into consideration the state of the road, and every advantage or disadvantage which they will have to encounter. When all things are in readiness, he gives the command, and they move on and on. They do not look back at the load, and say that is too great a load for any team to draw, and we are not going to draw such a burden as that, and lie down and try to get their necks out of the yoke, but they settle in the yoke, and strive again and again and again, until, if it be within their power, they move on.

But how unwilling His people are to draw! How unwilling they are to work for the conversion of the world! How often they shrink back, and fail to draw the burden that God lays upon them! The Spirit of God may move upon your mind to induce you to go to a certain family, and talk and pray with them on the subject of religion They have no light on the subject, and are groping their way in midnight darkness down to the pit, and the tender Spirit of God is urging you to visit that family, and talk, and pray with them; but you say, "Lord, I cannot do it. Lord, I am but a poor, weak brother; and what will they think if I go to them, and talk to them on the subject of religion? I pray thee have me excused. Let some one else go, who is more worthy and capable than thy servant." They refuse to go, and will not draw a single pound. Now I want you to understand that whenever God moves you to go and pray and plead with a sinner, that the Spirit is at the same time striving with that being. When the eunuch was riding along in his chariot, the Spirit of God was striving with him, and bringing the words of the prophet to bear upon his mind. The same Spirit told Philip to go that way. He went, not knowing why; and when he came within sight of the chariot, the Spirit told him to join himself to the chariot, and he did so; and Philip said, "Understandest thou what thou readest?" and he answered, "How can I, unless some one teach me?" and Philip got up into the chariot, and opened his mouth, and preached unto him Jesus. The Spirit that moved Philip was at the same time laboring with the eunuch, and striving to bring him into the kingdom of God's dear Son. I remember many striking incidents of the kind in modern times. While I was preaching in Boston, a brother felt himself impelled to visit one of his neighbors, and converse with him on the subject of religion; and his wife also desired to go and converse with that neighbor's wife, although they had not conferred together before. At length the brother went to see his neighbor, and he found this man, who had been very sceptical, under deep and pungent convictions. He greeted him cordially, and told him that he was grateful that he had come, for he had long desired to see him and converse with him about the state of his soul. This brother also found his wife there, conversing with his neighbor's wife, and the two were speedily converted to God.

When the Spirit comes, and moves on your mind to go and talk and pray with the sinner, go. Do not shrink back, and say, "It is a greater load than I am capable of bearing." I would have you understand, my beloved, that God has said, "My grace shall be sufficient for you," and "As thy days are, so shall thy strength be." We shall always find the truth of these passages if we try the experiment. I cannot tell what God would have done for me if I had always bowed my neck to his yoke, and had never shrunk back, in one single instance, from the time I was converted until now. Thirty-five or six years ago a brother said to me, "How long do you expect to live, brother Knapp?" "Well," said I, "I may live five or six years." At that time I was preaching two or three times a day; preaching and praying night and day, and delivering fifteen or sixteen sermons a week, and it was wearing upon me. I had not then learned to husband my strength as I have since. "Well," says he, "you will not live two years." Little did I think that God would sustain me to preach on for thirty-five or six years to come, day and night, and permit me to witness what I have as the effects of his truth, through all the United States of America. If any one had told me then what God was about to accomplish by such an unworthy worm, I might have said, "If the Lord should make windows in heaven, then these things might be."

In order to let you see, that as our days are, so shall our strength be, I will refer you to a striking incident, which came under my own observation when I was pastor of a church in Watertown, N. Y. Brother O. was one of my deacons,— a devout, conscientious, godly man, and his wife a pious woman. His father had consecrated him by prayer to the work of foreign missions. He was a printer by trade, and the Board of Foreign Missions, about the time to which I refer, were in want of some one to print the Bible in the Burmese language — some one who had faith, and who would labor to do good wherever the providence of God should direct him; and they called on Deacon O. He then had but one child, a sweet little daughter eighteen months old; and the question revolved itself in sister O.'s mind, over and over again, "Can I leave this dear child, and never see it again until we meet at the judgment seat?" for it was understood that you could not bring up children in Burmah, as the sin and corruption of the heathen might prove their ruin. Finally, she said, "Send by whom thou wilt, only excuse me: I cannot give up my babe;" and they declined the appointment. God came and took her child away by death speedily. A few years rolled around, and she embraced another daughter; and when this child had reached an age when it could be safely left by its mother, a second call came from the Board of Foreign Missions, and again the question arose, "Will you go and preach the word to the heathen?" Sister O. looked at her babe, whom she loved with all the love of a mother, but she answered this time, "Lord, I will go. Thou hast said, My grace shall be sufficient for thee. I will venture. Lord, I will go."

In the mean time I had removed my family to Oswego; and when they started for Boston, from which point they designed sailing, they came by way of Oswego, and called on my wife in my absence. Sister O. told my wife, that as she gave the child a last embrace, and imprinted on its lips a last kiss, she turned her face towards the heathen world, and towards Jesus for the fulfilment of his promise. God filled her soul with a joy unspeakable. "Why," said she, to my wife, "I have enjoyed more real happiness in sailing from Sackett's Harbor to Oswego, than I ever enjoyed in my life before. God has filled my soul, and I feel that I can rely upon his promise,—'As thy days are, so shall thy strength be.'"

Sister B., when the companion of her youth was buried in a foreign land, having toiled his life away, and when she was left a lone widow, far away from relatives and friends, wrote that she gathered consolation by repeating this passage: "No man hath left father or mother, house or land, for my sake and the gospel's, but he shall receive a hundred fold in this present time, and in the world to come life everlasting." She said, "Whether I have come up to that stipulation or not, I have realized the fulfilment of the promise a hundred fold. I have had more enjoyment in the heathen land, in the service of God, than I ever had in the world before." Yes, God means just what he says; and if you bow your neck to the yoke, he will reward you a hundred fold here, and in the world to come give you life everlasting. And "as thy days are, so shall thy strength be."

7. It may be observed again, that we do not consider how much we cost our Owner. The ox costs but little. He is fed upon straw and provender, and soon comes to maturity, and a very few dollars will purchase a good yoke of oxen; but God has raised us up as his children; his holy angels have watched over us; he has clothed us, and fed us, and supplied our wants; his guardian care has been round about us day and night. And then look at the price of our souls' redemption. Nothing less than the life-blood of God's dear Son could save the soul. Yet "Israel doth not know, my people doth not consider," how much they cost their owner.

8. Then, again, they do not seem to consider that the strength of every one is called for. No doubt many of you have seen a number of oxen yoked together to draw a building or an unusually heavy load, and have observed the order and the steadiness with which they have settled down to their work when the word of command was given, and how they have all pulled together until the burden moved. Now, when God requires us all to take hold and work for him, how few there are who settle with the yoke, or even straighten the chains. They want somebody else to draw. The ox does not reason in this way: "What little I can draw will make no difference; I will stand still and let the others, who are stronger and abler than I am, do the work;" but each ox knows, when the command is given, what he is expected to do, and he does it. Now, suppose that every member of this church, to say nothing about other Christians, had taken hold at the beginning of this meeting, and all had done what they could for Jesus: had gone to see their neighbors, and prayed with them; had visited them in their parlors, in their stores, and in their kitchens, and had made an effort to win their souls to Christ, who knows what might not

have been accomplished by this time? Converts might have been made by hundreds. How few there are who do anything to help move on the ark of God. And God says, "The ox knoweth his owner, and the ass his master's crib: but Israel doth not know; my people doth not consider."

9. And then they do not know when their strength is most needed; and yet the ox seems to know. Often, while travelling, I have noticed the husbandman with his team of oxen; and I have observed that when they came to the foot of a hill they would straighten themselves, and prepare to exert the additional strength that was necessary to draw the load up the hill. How many church-members there are who will draw down hill like a yoke of unbroken steers; who are always ready and willing when there are no burdens to bear and no hardships to be endured; but when the times are dark and lowering, when there are debts to pay, and it is evident there must be a great struggle or else the church will languish or die, they fall off; they absent themselves from church; they have nothing to give, no assistance to render: they will not draw a single pound.

Just so it is when there is any great reform to be accomplished, such as the temperance reform, or the abolition of slavery, or the removal of any other blighting and sweeping curse that may exist among the people. When all is dark, and public opinion is on the wrong side, there will only be now and then an individual who will come right out and face it, and play the man for God. The mass of the church are cowed, and quail before public opinion. They look only to their selfish interests and reputation among men, instead of looking at principle and working for God. I remember very well when we formed the first temperance society in America. We had the opposition of deacons and church-members, as well as the opposition of the masses of the wealthy, and those who were indifferent to religion. We had to preach, and pray, and toil on early and late, and struggle to get the load up the hill; but these same men were all ready to jump on when we had reached the top, and all wished to share in the honor and the spoils of the glorious victory we had achieved by divine assistance. They were all willing to ride down the hill, but they were not so willing to help us to draw up the hill. It was so with the cause of Abolition. I remember very well when even here in the Northern States the mass of the people were apologists for slavery. The minister could not lift up his voice against this great and crying sin of the nation without being met with scowls from scores, and sometimes hundreds, of the church-members. Their politics would be touched, and they would hold back, and would not draw a single pound. We had to struggle and toil on and on until we had got the load to the top of the hill, and then they jumped on. Then all were abolitionists, and had always been abolitionists, and if it had not been for us radicals, they would have succeeded in abolishing slavery long ago! Poor souls! the Lord pity you! The devil knows better than that. The fact is, if it had not been for those who were more earnest than these conservatives, the end would never have been reached. But come on; better late than never; and give all glory to God who has achieved the victory.

Elder Leland, who used to hunt foxes and deer over the mountains of Massachusetts, used to say, that on the start, when the hunter set out with his hounds, nothing could be heard but the sound of the hounds baying over the mountain top, or ringing through the valley; but when they caught sight of the game, every little whiffet set up a yell, and the voice of the hounds was drowned by their noise. This is true of reformers. A good brother in Pennsylvania, now in heaven, had been a faithful and thorough-going anti-slavery man for years, but when the war broke out, and converts to anti-slavery principles were multiplied, he seemed to grow silent, and have nothing to say. A friend asked him, "Why, brother Aaron, how is it you are so still now, when you have all along been such an ardent advocate of the abolition of slavery?" and he replied, "I cannot be heard for the noise of the converts!" Let them come.

It is well for us to understand where our strength is most

needed; and when we see any reform, which should be brought about for the good of the world, we should settle in the yoke, and help to pull at the foot of the hill. Well, we are now struggling at the foot of the hill with the word of God. We are laboring for the salvation of tens and hundreds of souls, and I would to God that before next spring hundreds of thousands might be converted in the city of New York; but only a small band is engaged in this struggle. There are very few who are willing to make the required sacrifices, and settle in the yoke, and exert all the strength which God has vouchsafed to them, in order to win souls to Christ, and carry the work to perfection.

10. But, again, it may be observed that the ox knows enough to draw in the dark; and yet many Christians will not draw a single pound in the dark. As long as they see their way clear, and feel like it, they go along very well; but as soon as a cloud comes over their minds, they stand as still as a stone. They will not draw in the dark, but the ox will; and if night overtakes him before his owner has reached his destination with the load he is drawing, the ox will draw as well as if it was day. So we, as Christians, ought to work for God, trusting in him, and moving right on in the performance of every Christian duty.

11. So, again, it may be remarked the ox knows were to find water. You turn an ox or an ass into a hundred-acre field, and if there be water in that field he will not suffer from thirst long. They are sure to find it. They will not perish under the heat of a summer's sun while there is water in the enclosure. But how many men there are who, though God has opened a great Fountain for Judea and Jerusalem, and hath said, "If any man thirst, let him come unto me and drink;" and though the water is as free as the air, yet wander about, and cannot find this living stream! There are sinners who are thirsting and inquiring for the water of salvation in this congregation to-day, who act as though they could not find it. They go around in the dark hours of the night, in their secret chamber; they come to the meetings, and converse with one and another; but after all that

is said and done, they fail to find this Fountain of living waters; they fail to slake their thirst, and cure the fever of the mind.

The ox, if you cut a hole in the ice, will almost tumble in, if it is necessary, to reach the water; and he will reach it and slake his thirst, if it is possible, before he leave the place. The difficulty with the sinner is, he is looking too high, and he stumbles over the simplicity of the gospel of Jesus Christ, and fails to be lowly enough to have his wants supplied.

The truth is, my friends, the difficulty lies in the want of disposition on your part—it is not a want of sagacity. You certainly know as much as the ox or the ass, but your heart is in opposition to God and to religion, and you are unwilling to come to God's terms, and receive the waters of life. Here, then, is the grand difficulty. You have seen swine break into a garden, and if you try to drive them out, and set the dog on them, they will run round and round, and by the place they came in, as though they could not see it; but get them out once, and the moment they want to come back they will make a bee-line for the place. I have many a time taken a sinner, and have shown him the way to God; have resolved all his doubts, and made the way as plain as the alphabet; but when I would bring him to the point, and, with God's help, try to drive him through, he would pass by as quick as thought. They do not wish to go to heaven. They do not wish to come down to the feet of Jesus, and slake the thirst of their souls in the waters of eternal life.

12. Then, again, we find that the ox knows enough to pray. When he is in want, when he has been fasting all night, and the manger or crib is empty,—when the owner walks into the yard in the morning all the live stock are up, and all begin to pray: the ox begins to loo, the horse to whinny, and the sheep to bleat; they all pray, and pray in their own native language. There is no restraint. The ass does not say, "If I only had as smooth a voice as some animals I would pray to my owner, and ask him for what I want; but I have such a hoarse, uncouth voice, that if I should pray I would frighten the sheep out of

the yard." Each one has his own way of expressing his wants, and cares not for the opinions of others. And their owner understands them, and supplies their wants. If the sinner would lift up his voice, and cry, "Lord save me, or I perish!" if the backslider would cry unto the Lord, and every human soul would cry aloud in sincerity, God would open the windows of heaven, and pour out his blessings upon them. It is pride which dooms millions of souls. They will not pray to God because they fear man more than they fear their Creator.

13. Then, again, it may be observed the ox and the ass know their respective and appropriate places. The term rendered "crib" here, means *stall*—the place where he is cribbed, or the stall where he belongs. Every good farmer will have a particular stall for each animal, and each animal soon comes to know its place, and always occupies it. I remember more than thirty years ago, when I was preaching in this city, that I was invited to go out to Long Island, and lecture one evening in the village of Newtown. I passed the night with a gentleman who kept one hundred cows, and brought milk to the city. In order to have the milk ready in season, the men brought the cows up to the stable in the afternoon. I noticed that each cow knew its particular stall, and went right along until it came to it, and then turned into it. I looked on with amazement, and thought, if I could find a church where all the members knew their places, and kept them like these cows, I would like to be its pastor. But, alas! "the ox knoweth his owner, and the ass his master's crib: *but* Israel doth not know; my people doth not consider." They get into the wrong stalls; one member gets into his neighbor's stall, and they commence hooking, goring, and crowding one another. Very often a long-horned deacon gets into the minister's stall, and commences goring him; others get into the deacons' stalls, and all is clashing and confusion; and God may well say, "The ox knoweth his owner, and the ass his master's crib: *but* Israel doth not know; my people doth not consider." Alas! some church-members seem to think that all the minister must do is simply to preach

to please the people. He must have no voice in the business of the church, no voice in its government, and no voice or control in its affairs; and that when he does not please the congregation they may set him adrift. Now this is subversive of the whole arrangement of the church of God. The minister is his overseer. He is placed, in the providence of God, at the head of the church, and he is to rule over its affairs with all the influence that God's grace shall secure to him. The congregation ought to honor him, and rejoice, and feel blessed if their leader is capable of leading them on from strength to strength, and building them up in the faith of our Lord and Savior Jesus Christ. But, alas, the confusion that follows their not knowing their places, and keeping their places! and this arises from the depravity of poor fallen human nature. God may well say, "The ox knoweth his owner, and the ass his master's crib: but Israel doth not know; my people doth not consider."

May God add his blessing, for his Son's sake. Amen.

II.

ENTHUSIASM.

"*Thou art beside thyself; much learning doth make thee mad.*"
ACTS xxvi. 24.

I PROPOSE, on this occasion, I. To prove that all consistent Bible Christians have, in all ages, been looked upon by unbelievers and formalists as "beside" themselves, enthusiasts, or possessed of the devil.

Paul was speaking forth "the words of truth and soberness," when Festus cried out, "Paul, thou art beside thyself; much learning doth make thee mad."

On the day of Pentecost a similar charge was preferred against the apostles. In fact they "were filled with the Spirit," but they were accused of being "filled with new wine."

The Pharisees said, concerning Christ, that "he hath a devil."

In like manner were the ancient prophets regarded; and from the days of the apostles to the present, men of earnest conviction, undoubting faith, and fearless courage, have been denounced, in their own generations, as madmen, fanatics, and fools.

The reasons are obvious. To true Christians religion is a living reality. Its truths are ever before them. They believe all that God has said about heaven and hell; all things else are as trifles, compared with the solemn realities of eternity. They regulate the affairs of time, its prospects and its pleasures, and personal gratifications, according to the demands of this profound conviction. With them time, talents, honors, pleasures, money, life itself, are nothing in comparison with the worth of the soul, or with the sufferings of Christ in dying to save it.

The dead formalist, the careless unbeliever, behold their enthusiasm with feelings of contempt. They see no occasion for it, and account for it on the theory of mental delusion, or, perchance, of hypocritical pretension. Alas! their vision is dim. The god of this world hath blinded their minds, so that "having eyes they see not." They do not realize any necessity for strong feelings, for zeal and energy in prosecuting the cause of salvation, and so they cry out, "*Animal excitement!*" "*Enthusiasm!*"

The different views which these two classes take of this subject may be illustrated by the following circumstance: A clergyman, riding along in the northern part of the State of New York, saw a woman coming out of her house in great haste, and screaming, with the air and tone of the wildest excitement, "Help, help!" Rushing on to the bank of a river, she leaped into the stream, and sank out of sight. The minister put spurs to his horse, and hastened to the spot, thinking that she was surely insane; but as he reached the bank, he beheld the woman rising to the surface, and grasping the form of her little boy, who had fallen into the water a few minutes before. At once the clergyman changed his mind. Instead of regarding her as mad, he looked upon her as very rational and heroic, and considered her excitement as a fitting expression of a just estimate of the importance of the occasion. Just so formalists, hypocrites, and worldlings. They do not appreciate the great motive-power by which the spiritually living Christian is prompted. "He that is spiritual judgeth all things, but he himself is judged of no man." Hence the "carnal" think of the "spiritual" that their zeal, their earnestness, their haste, their sacrifices for the salvation of souls, is a sort of madness, an uncalled-for excitement.

What could an unbelieving world have thought of Noah, who was spending a fortune, toiling night and day, in building an ark for the salvation of himself and his family, in the day when floods should overwhelm the earth? His neighbors had no faith in the testimony of God concerning the threatened visitation. Suppose a traveller coming along where the ark was being constructed, at a time when it was nearly completed; pulling up at the inn, he asks the keeper, "What is that great structure I saw up the road? It is so huge that no team can draw it, and no water can float it?"

Innkeeper. "Why, that is an ark."

Traveller. "An ark? What is that for?"

Innkeeper. "Well, an old man, by the name of Noah, in this neighborhood, has a notion in his head that the great God is going to drown the world, and he is building this ark for the preservation of his family and a pair of every kind of animal."

Traveller. "Is this man a fool, or is he crazy, or a hypocrite?"

Innkeeper. "Well, there are different opinions about him. Some think him crazy; others say he is a downright hypocrite, desirous of making a stir in the world. Others surmise that he has some great speculation in view; but most people give him the credit of being sincere, but laboring under a delusion. He certainly warns the people of the approaching flood, sometimes with tears; and I know that he has expended a fortune in the enterprise, and is up early and late."

The people in the day of Paul doubtless talked about him in the same way. We can imagine how some of his old associates spoke of him. One said, "I really thought that Paul would amount to something." Another remarked, "He might have been somebody if he had not got excited about these miserable followers of the Nazarene." "Yes," said another, "he might have occupied a high place among both the Jews and the Romans, and commanded a high salary, and been one of the first men of his age, but he has completely thrown himself away by joining this illiterate set of fishermen. He has made a fool of himself." But how little did they know of the weighty considerations and mighty power that were actuating him! How little they realized the unseen influences that were inspiring the apostle Paul to count all things as loss and dross for the excellency of the knowledge of Christ Jesus the Lord! And how little do they, who are enveloped in the atmosphere of worldly honors, ease, and emolument, know the motives by which those are actuated who lay their all on God's altar! "We are to look not on the things that are seen, but on the things which are not seen; for the things which are seen are temporal, but the things which are not seen are eternal."

Before we proceed further, it must be understood that souls are saved by a faithful use of the means which God has appointed to that end, and lost for the want of such a use of the means; just as our natural lives are maintained by a timely attention to the means of self-preservation, and are lost for the lack of that attention. Parents have no more reason to expect that their children will be saved, if the means which God has appointed to that end are neglected, than they have a right to suppose that they will be fed, and clothed, and educated, unless the means appropriate and necessary to these results are duly observed.

Now it is easy to see in which matter we ought to feel the greater concern, and by which consideration we ought to be the more excited. The necessities of the soul are as much greater than those of the body as eternity is longer than time, or as the soul itself is of more value than the body.

II. But let us define Enthusiasm. I use the term in its most popular acceptation. In this sense it stands opposed to the idea of consistency or propriety. An enthusiast is one who exhibits more interest in a subject than its importance demands; whereas a sober-minded man is supposed to display no greater interest in a subject than is in proportion to the value of the end in view. To illustrate: Suppose, as you are riding along on horseback, a woman comes rushing out of her house, and with the aspect of horror and agony, and in tones of piteous anxiety she calls on you for help, immediate help. Her boy has fallen into the well and will drown. You leap from your horse and hasten to the rescue. All right. You pass on, and before long another woman comes rushing out of her house in the same plight, crying, "Help! help!" You ask yourself, "What in the world is the matter now?" You put spurs and whip to the horse, and riding up to the gate, spring from your horse, and inquire the cause of this great alarm, and she explains, "Why, sir, I came to draw water, and dropped my pitcher, and broke it all to pieces!" You feel provoked enough to apply the whip to her. And why so? Because in this case the woman was an enthusiast, and in the other case the woman acted consistently; and yet they both, in deportment, acted alike. In the one case, however, the occasion demanded or justified the excitement; in the other, it did not.

Now let us contrast the interest which men feel in the sacrifices which they put forth to save souls, with the interest which they manifest, and the efforts which they make, to secure worldly ends.

1. Notice the efforts of men to accumulate wealth. They rise early, sit up late, toil hard, encounter all the perils of the deep, expose themselves to all the miasmas and epidemics of every clime. They will leave home and loved ones, and rush on to California, or into the wilderness of the oil regions; expend millions of money as an experiment, in the hope of obtaining more, and often sink all they have; and yet all these wonderful expressions of anxiety excite no complaints on their part, because they see an object in view.

But let ministers and Christians open their eyes upon the condition of millions of human souls ready to perish, liable every moment to come short of that "rest which remains for the people of God;" to fail of durable riches and righteousness; let them see them standing "on slippery places, while fiery billows roll below," and feel and act accordingly; let them "cry aloud and spare not;" lift up their voice like Paul, or Luther, or Whitefield; lay their money upon God's altar, and be in earnest to save souls, — and the cry is heard, "Thou art beside thyself: much learning, or much religion, doth make thee mad!" The cry of "Animal feeling," "Enthusiasm," resounds through the air.

2. Notice the interest manifested in politics. Our country is divided into two standing political parties, and sometimes a third party comes up. Each party has its regular sets of candidates for office, and each is over-anxious to succeed, and, as election draws near the anxiety increases; and yet, as a matter of fact, there may be little or no choice in the candidates. Both may be good men, or more likely neither of them fit for the station. But the whole country is moved: a mighty moral earthquake convulses the whole land. Men, women, and children are all excited, from the shores of the Atlantic to the shores of the Pacific. Millions of money are paid out to publish and disseminate partisan documents. Hundreds of thousands of dollars are staked on the results of the election. Log-cabins and liberty-poles are erected, and flags are flung to every breeze. Farmers, mechanics, merchants, doctors, lawyers, and sometimes ministers, all join in one universal chorus. And when the contest is ended, and one party has come out victorious, a mighty shout is heard throughout the whole United States of America; the telegraph wires are all electrified; balls and parties are multiplied, and the booming cannon roars along through the valleys, and comes thundering over all the mountains. Millions more of money are expended in parades and festivals; but all this is well in the eyes of the world. Formalists, hypocrites, and worldlings have nothing to say against excitement or animal feeling.

But let there be a contest between the friends and the enemies of Jesus about the coming of Jesus into every heart, and through all the world, and the dethroning of Satan; and let them manifest half the zeal, expend half the money, make half the sacrifices, to accomplish this end, and all these unbelievers will cry out, "*Enthusiasm!*" "*Wild-fire!*" "*Animal feeling!*" "Thou art beside thyself: much religion doth make thee mad."

3. Notice the interest excited on account of bodily sickness. Let any member of the family be taken sick. How soon the doctor is called! The messenger is sent in post haste, by day or by night, and at any or all hours. No one talks about late hours,

or of being disturbed of their rest. The wife or mother bends over the sick bed for days and weeks together; scarcely lays aside her garments for months; and if the loved one is taken away, all the family are bathed in tears; the neighbors all come in to weep with them, and on the funeral occasion all the congregation are proud to weep. But if we see the great mass of sinners on the brink of ruin, *dying the death that never dies*, and cast our eyes towards Calvary and see Jesus bleeding, extending his arms towards them, and hear him saying, "Look unto me, all ye ends of the earth, and be ye saved," and exclaim, with good old Jeremiah, "O, that my head were waters, and mine eyes a fountain of tears, that I might weep day and night, for the slain of the daughter of my people," the whole infidel world chimes in with those who "are at ease in Zion," crying out, "*Animal feeling!*" "*Excitement!*" "*Thou art beside thyself.*"

4. Look at the money expended, and the interest taken upon the subject of education. Think of all the schools of every kind, from the infant school up to the college: district, private, family schools, academies, seminaries, all in full blast the year round, and the mass of the rising generation spending from twelve to twenty years in attaining mental culture. Many study half of the night, and some all of it, and in many instances break down their healths, and come to a premature grave. But no Universalist, no Unitarian, no infidel, no formalist, complains of all this expense of time, money, health, and life. All think they see an end to justify it. But when a school is opened in which to educate men for heaven, and lectures, prayers, expostulations, and appeals are multiplied, and the servants of God become more and more earnest in the matter, the worldling, the formalist, the infidel, and the devil, all cry out, "Thou art beside thyself: much religion doth make thee mad."

5. Let a fire break out in a city. The bells are rung, the engines rattle and thunder along the streets, and the cry of Fire! Fire! Fire! is shouted from street to street. Men, women, and children turn out at a late hour of the night, and rush to

the scene. And what, after all, is the matter? An old blacksmith shop is on fire! And yet no one goes round picking up the evils of this general turn out, complaining of being out at a late hour in the night, and that such a one got run over and badly injured, and such a one got wet through and through by the carelessness of the firemen, and another lost his life in the burning building.

But when God's watchmen discover that the fire of God's wrath is kindled, and that it burns to the lowest hell, and call on all "to flee from the wrath to come," to turn to the stronghold until his indignation be over, they are charged with enthusiasm; with being unduly excited.

Suppose a man is sinking a well. After getting forty feet below the surface of the ground the sides cave in, and he is buried beneath the fallen earth; but, by means of some timbers, air enough reaches him to keep the breath of life in him for a time, and by putting your ear at the mouth of the cave you can just faintly hear him cry, "Help! Save! For God's sake, save!" But while some hasten on with spades and shovels, some throwing the dirt one way and some another, all working on without regard to rules of propriety in the handling of their shovels, suppose a set of lookers-on should gather around, stand aloof, and find fault, saying, "This man throws his dirt very carelessly; that man ought not to take off his coat, he will get cold; it is now after nine o'clock, and they ought to go home; 'too much excitement;'" what would you think of these cool-blooded croakers? If the man buried alive was your son, brother, or husband, you would denounce them as heartless, inhuman, murderous wretches.

6. Let our country be invaded, our liberties threatened, and our government in danger of being overthrown. See, then, what an excitement! As in the case of the Revolutionary struggle, or as during the recent Rebellion. In such events, our husbands, brothers, and sons turn out by the million. Our treasures are poured out like water, and our blood flows like rivers. No sacrifices are too great to make, no suffering too

intolerable to be endured. All this is patriotism! But when we proclaim to the world that Satan has rebelled against the government of God, and has involved this world in the conflict, and that the struggle is now going on, and that infinite consequences depend on the issue, even the eternal destiny of millions for weal or for woe, and we bestir ourselves accordingly, calling for men, for treasures, on all to pray, to labor, and to come up to the "help of the Lord, the help of the Lord against the mighty," the world thinks we are distracted, and cries out, "Thou art beside thyself!"

III. We proceed to show that the deepest interest we can feel, the greatest sacrifices we can make, and the most mighty efforts we can put forth to glorify Christ, and to save souls, are consistent and proper.

1. There is no caution in the word of God against feeling too much, or giving too much, or doing too much. But, on the other hand, God is, and always has been, urging his people to bring "their tithes into the store-house;" to "pray without ceasing;" to "seek first the kingdom of God, and his righteousness;" to go into his vineyard and work. Jesus says, "No man hath left father or mother, brother or sister, husband or wife, houses or lands, for my sake and the gospel's, but he shall receive an hundred fold in this present time, and in the world to come life everlasting."

2. Jesus always defends those who do and feel the most for his causé, and rebukes those who complain of them. When the woman came to anoint him against his burial, and broke the box of precious ointment and poured it on his head, a heartless Judas charged her of waste, of undue excitement. But the Savior replied, "Let her alone. The poor ye have always with you, and ye may do them good when ye will, but me ye have not always;" and adds, "Wherever this gospel is preached, this shall be told as a memorial of her." A monument has thus been erected to her memory more durable than any of the monuments of Greece or Rome. The formalist, the unbeliever, thinks all that is done to honor Christ, and to save souls, is a perfect waste.

When Jesus was riding on his way to Jerusalem, a holy enthusiasm came over his d.sciples, and the whole multitude of them broke out, crying with loud voices, and began to rejoice and praise God for all the mighty works which they had seen, saying, "Blessed is he that cometh in the name of the Lord." But some in the multitude said, "Master, rebuke thy disciples" (those formalists thought them unduly excited); but Jesus replied, "I tell you, if these should hold their peace, the stones would cry out."

When the poor widow cast her two mites, even all her living, into the treasury of the Lord, the formalist and the unbeliever thought her enthusiastic and extravagant; that it was her duty to save it for sickness and old age. But Jesus defends and applauds her, and declares that she had cast in more than all the rich, who of their abundance had cast into the treasury of the Lord, for she had of her penury cast in all of her living. Here is a monument erected to her memory. And whilst the formalist, the hypocrite, and the worldling complain of excitement, and of undue anxiety on the subject of religion, Jesus stands and weeps over Jerusalem, exclaiming, "O Jerusalem, Jerusalem, how often would I have gathered your children together as a hen doth gather her chickens under her wings, and ye would not." The big tears rolled down the manly cheeks of the Son of God. His great soul was stirred to its depths by the madness and folly of that city in turning their backs upon, and rejecting their best friend, and their only Savior.

Paul felt his spirit stirred within him when he saw a city "wholly given to idolatry."

Jeremiah cried out, "O, that my head were waters, and mine eyes a fountain of tears, that I might weep day and night for the slain of the daughter of my people." And again: "Rivers of waters run down mine eyes because they keep not thy law."

God complains of these hypocrites in Zion because they 'eat the calves from the stall, and the lambs from the flock, and drink wine from golden bowls, and stretch themselves upon beds of ivory, and are not grieved fo the afflictions of Joseph."

3. No one regrets, at the hour of death, that he had felt too much, given too much, or done too much for Christ, or to save souls. Such a regret was never felt by a sane man. It never fell from human lips. It was never written in a book: moreover it never will be. All the regrets are on the other side. How many, on their death-bed, have expressed the deepest regret that they had done no more for the honor of Christ, and to benefit their race; to reclaim this fallen world, and to bring rebellious man back to God! How many have been burdened with the one desire to live their lives over again, in order that they might correct their mistakes in these respects; devote themselves to the service of God with the zeal that fired the hearts of prophets and apostles, and of the hosts of good men who counted not their lives dear unto them!

4. The consciences of wicked men justify the exercise of the most intense interest on the subject of religion. During Whitefield's absence in this country, a graceless bishop called on Lady Huntington for the purpose of remonstrating with her because of her enthusiasm. She had expressed her dissatisfaction with his cool, heartless, and perfunctory performances, and he hoped to dispel her prejudices, and reconcile her to the proprieties of the service of the Church of England. Finding his efforts to be vain, he began to upbraid himself for having lain ordaining hands on the head of Whitefield. Lady Huntington replied, "Reverend and dear sir, permit me to say, that when you come to your death-bed, the remembrance of your part in the ordination of Mr. Whitefield will be the occasion of your least regrets." The prediction was fulfilled; for when brought to the bed of death he sent his servant to Whitefield to ask his prayers for the dying bishop.

While I was in Boston, in the year 1842, laboring day and night, and exerting every energy of body and mind to save souls, a Universalist came from Salem to hear me preach, and remained for a few days in attendance on the meetings. He went home and told his friends that "Knapp was the only consistent 'hell-and-damnation' preacher he knew of."

A Universalist minister in Auburn, N. Y., when I was laboring there, said he "did not blame Mr. Knapp for his course; that if he believed as Mr. Knapp does, he would leave his family, and go forth preaching day and night, from place to place, until his voice faltered in death."

Thousands of unconverted persons are amazed at the stoical indifference of professed Christians. They know that if religion is anything it is everything.

5. Who can doubt but that the millions of the departed dead look down with astonishment at the comparative indifference of the Christian world concerning the subject of religion? The waves of worldly cares, business, and pleasures of every kind, are sweeping the teeming millions of earth into eternity. Soon they are forgotten. Some look back from heaven, some from hell; and the latter mingle, with the wails of despair, the reproachful lamentation, "No man cared for our souls!" and the former are utterly amazed that they should have cared so little about themselves or their fellow-men. From their point of view the things of time and sense dwindle into utter insignificance, and the great things of eternity become all and in all.

O, ye slumbering saints! ye formalists! Rouse ye from your lethargy. Brave the ridicule of the world. Be it your glory that you bear this reproach: "Ye are beside yourselves in your zeal for the glory of God and salvation of men."

III.*

THE CALLS OF THE GOSPEL.

"*O Jerusalem, Jerusalem, thou that killest the prophets, and stonest them which are sent unto thee, how often would I have gathered thy children together, even as a hen gathereth her chickens under her wings, and ye would not!*" — MATT. xxiii. 37.

WE should all bear in mind that Jesus Christ, so far as his human nature is concerned, was the son of Abraham, and was especially identified with the Hebrews. "He came unto his own, but his own received him not; but as many as received him, to them gave he power to become the sons of God." Beyond all question he felt a very warm attachment to that people; and who, I ask, that is at all familiar with the Scriptures of the Old Testament, and with the history of the Jews as a people, does not feel an overwhelming interest in their condition and final destiny?

Jesus, on this occasion, was nearing Jerusalem, and from Mount Olivet looked down upon the city, over which he had often wept and prayed, and upon the ears of whose inhabitants he had often poured forth volumes of burning and affectionate truth. He saw their destiny. They were turning their backs upon the Savior, their best friend; they would have none of him; they were about to reject the gospel of Jesus Christ, the true Redeemer. His omniscient eye ran along the track of the future, and viewed their whole history, not only down the stream of time, but their prospects beyond the narrow limits of time. As he looked, the tears rolled down his cheeks, and he broke

* Preached in New York, November 26, 1866.

out, in the language of our text, and said, "O Jerusalem, Jerusalem, thou that killest the prophets, and stonest them which are sent unto thee, how often would I have gathered thy children together, as a hen gathereth her chickens under her wings, and ye would not." Now here we see that Jesus loved the people. He bewailed their folly. He looked back upon their former history, and he saw that they had been killing the prophets, and stoning those who were sent unto them; for it had been death to any man, in all ages, to receive a commission from the great God, and carry that commission out with fidelity and in the fear of God, regardless of what men might say or think of them. Hence he says, "Thou that killest the prophets, and stonest them which are sent unto thee, how often would I have gathered thy children together, as a hen gathereth her chickens under her wings, and ye would not. Behold, your house is left unto you desolate."

We propose, this evening, to take up the care and kindness of Jesus Christ for the souls of men, under the beautiful and significant figure of the care and kindness of a hen for her chickens. A more striking and forcible figure could not be found in all the works of creation. It far surpasses and utterly casts into the shade all the figures drawn from the stars or from history, or from the arts and sciences. It is a living portrait, or figure, to all who understand it, through all succeeding ages, down to the end of time.

I. We remark, in the first place, that the hen hath a call that we denominate a *common call.* By this she calls to her brood, and clucks them along in her pathway, and by it she prevents them from rambling away among the corn and standing grass, and from being lost. Hence she repeats this call over and over again, from morning until evening. Scarcely an hour or a moment passes but that she repeats this common call — calling after her brood. Hence we denominate it the common call, because it is repeated over and over and over, again and again. And so Jesus has a call to the children of men, which may be denominated the *common call.* "Unto you, O man, I call, and my voice is unto the sons of men."

This common call may embrace the *voice of nature.* The stars are all calling upon the children of men. The sun, in all its splendor and glory, answering the end of its creation, is calling upon the human family to reflect that love which they are capable of reflecting, with as much fidelity to God and man as it reflects its natural light.

God speaks to the children of men by all these, the workmanship of his hand, and continues to call, not only day after day, but night after night. How beautifully the Psalmist speaks of the voice of nature, when he says, "The heavens declare the glory of God, and the firmament showeth his handy work. Day unto day uttereth speech, and night unto night showeth knowledge. There is no speech nor language where their voice is not heard." Mark that. There is no people or tribe under the whole heavens who cannot hear of the goodness of God as uttered by the voice of nature. So that the heathen themselves are without excuse. But for their blindness and depravity, their love of sin and waywardness, and opposition to God and holiness, they would hear the voice of God through all the works of creation, and be constrained to bow down and worship him.

This common call is heard in everything which God has presented to our consideration as the workmanship of his hands. His voice is heard in the roaring of the distant winds, and in the stillness of the calm; in the rumbling of the thunder, and in the forked lightning; in the rolling of the distant ocean, and in the gentle murmur of the little rill that flows on down the landscape; — All call upon the children of men to love and serve God, the Author of their being, and to receive Jesus Christ as their Savior.

This common call likewise embraces the *word of God* in this Christian land. For God has given us his word to enlighten our understanding, and direct our footsteps through this vale of tears to the promised land. This may be included in the common call, because it is a common privilege to the entire human family, so far as the gospel has yet been extended. Whether you give heed to the voice of God, as it may be heard from his word or not, that word is continually speaking. Awake or or asleep, at home or abroad, the voice of the Lord is uttered and reiterated again and again. God is calling — calling unto the children of men by his precious words, that they may live, and not rush on down, and perish in eternal death.

But observe still further, that this common call likewise embraces *the common means of grace;* such as the stated ministry of God's holy word, and such as the usual social meetings in which we worship the living and the true God, and by which the children of men are invited to embrace Jesus Christ and live. In fact, God has thrown open the doors of the sanctuary, through all our cities and through all our country towns and places; and wherever human beings live, there the voice of God — this common call — may be heard. This is true, not only upon the Lord's day, but in many places on every single day and night in the week. As if it were not enough that he should call all day long upon the Sabbath, but Jesus, by his care and kindness, would follow them up, and beckon or call after them, and cluck them along, as it were, and keep them under his wings, that they may not ramble away, and lose sight of their only Friend and Protector, and perish forever, for want of the grace and mercy he is willing to impart. He gives the children of men repeated and continued opportunities of salvation. Just think of the faithfulness of God in this respect! I have thought of it many a time. In ranging the world round and round, I have never found a place where a faithful messenger has not gone before me. Some man of God, some messenger of Jesus Christ, has gone before me, and has lifted up his voice in Christ's stead to the people, beseeching them to be reconciled to God. Missionaries of the cross have climbed the mountains, threaded the valleys, and gone among the highest and the lowest, among the rich and among the poor. Thus God is calling after the children of men day after day, year in and year out. But, after all, Jesus may say to you, "How often would I have gathered thy children together, even as a hen gathereth her chickens under her wings, and *ye would not!*"

II. But the hen has another call, which we denominate the the *special call.* It is only given when she has found some food or drink which her brood needs, and invites them to participate in the provision she has made for their wants. She then changes her dialect, and speaks in another language. They all understand the language, every one of them, before they are twenty-four hours old, and they come running in from every direction, in obedience to this special call, and receive the food to which they are invited. They do not stand back and parley, as sinners do, and say, "If you intend to feed me, old hen, why don't you come here and feed me?" and "Isn't one place as good as another?" and "I went two or three times, and did not get anything. Some other one stepped in before me, and took it all. You picked out all the speckled chickens and gave to them, and won't give anything to me." But, satisfied with these cavils, sinners starve to death or perish, as the result of their rashness and imprudence; chickens, however, come again and again, and keep on coming until by and by they get something.

Now mark, that Jesus Christ has a special call, and this special call may be regarded as embracing *the special means of grace;* for there are common means, and there are special means of grace. Look at the parable of the marriage supper. The king sent out his servants at supper-time to tell all that were bidden to come, for all things were ready; but they all, with one consent, began to make excuse. And the servants reported accordingly, and the question was asked, "What shall we do?" Shall we keep on uttering the old common call, the old appeal, cling to the old course, persevering in the use of old measures? No. Let us change our measures. "Go out into the highways and byways and compel them to come in, that my house may be filled."

Some people tell us, in modern times, that they are opposed to special means of grace; opposed to protracted meetings, to special efforts, to earnest, long-continued, persistent efforts to rescue sinners from threatening danger, and bring them into the liberty of the sons of God. But not so was Jesus. Not so were any of his apostles. When one course of measures failed, they introduced another, and another still. When all common or ordinary means failed to bring them into the marriage supper of the Lamb, they went out into the highways and hedges, — that is, where a great many roads cross each other, where there are masses of human beings gathered together. They were to go into these places, and compel them to come in.

But you will understand that compulsion was not exercised by the ruler of the feast, only by his agents whom he sent out. It does not mean to compel them by physical force, but it means to compel them by the strongest possible power of persuasion. We are to compel, or constrain them, by all the motives drawn from heaven, and by all the motives drawn from hell; by all the motives of our obligation to God and to his Son Jesus Christ; by all the motives drawn from the enduring compassion of the blessed Son of God, who wept over Jerusalem, and said, "O, Jerusalem, Jerusalem, thou that killest the prophets, and stonest them which are sent unto thee, how often would I have gathered thy children together, even as a hen gathereth her chickens under her wings, and ye would not." We are to bring all these motives to bear upon the human family, and, if possible, compel them, or constrain them, to come in.

You are to understand that these special means of grace were all gotten up by Jesus Christ. You need not give this church or its pastor the credit of getting up these meetings. It was God that moved upon them to get up these meetings. It was God, my dear hearers, that influenced your unworthy speaker to come some fifteen hundred miles in answer to your request, to aid you in constraining sinners here in this city to come and feast their souls upon hidden manna. The Lord Jesus Christ is employing these means for the express purpose of inducing you to come and feed upon his love, and receive the waters of eternal life freely, without money and without price. We are told to "seek the Lord while he may be found, and to call upon him while he is near." When the hen utters this special call, she always has something right at hand for her brood; and when God utters his special call, and stirs up his saints to pray, and inspires his ministers to preach with more point, with more power, with more affection, with more cogency than usual, he is uttering the special call, and that special call implies that the bread of heaven is right here, at the door; you have only to come and partake, to eat that which is good, and let your soul delight itself in fatness.

I want you to remember that ministers cannot always preach as they do in times of revival. It would not be possible. Perhaps they could not live and preach so all the time. If Christians felt as they do in revivals, continuously, as some argue that they should feel, they could not live. It would be utterly impossible. I have known many a wife, under the special influence of the Holy Spirit, to feel a special anxiety for her husband, and many a mother to feel a special anxiety for her children, that would keep her awake nights and days together; and had she lived in that state of mind for six months, she would probably have sunk into an untimely grave. This anxiety is a special solicitude, aroused by the Holy Spirit, for the express purpose of reaching your souls, and bringing you into the kingdom of God and of his Son. Look at the sainted sister Colgate — Deacon William Colgate's wife. When I was in Brooklyn, laboring night after night, she was there, lingering until a late hour; she came again and again, weeping, and laying her interesting group of children on the altar, and soliciting the prayers of the saints, until God came and brought salvation to her house. She could not have lived very long in that state of feeling. God was stirring up that mother to utter the special call. And when, at the request of the father, I went to see his eldest son, Robert, one morning, I had not said three words to him before the tears started, and he said, "I can endure anything else but the tears of my father, and the prayers of my mother."

I tell you, my beloved hearers, it is Jesus Christ that calls to you, uttering his special call through father, or mother, or brother, or sister, or child. Thus God stirs them up to utter this special call, which is directly from God. While others may deride their tears, and make light of their emotions, and talk against excitement and animal feeling, they are but the agents of the devil to shut the kingdom of heaven against men; and Jesus, inspired by all of these things, urges his people on and on, by uttering the special call, and manifests the strength and purity of his love for the souls of the children of men.

III. But then we pass to speak of another call, which we denominate the *call of alarm.* The hen is all the time on the lookout for-danger. She is ever watching for the safety of her brood. When a boy, I used to wonder why a hen could discover a hawk, an eagle, a weasel, or a fox, so much quicker than I could, and I solved the matter by coming to the conclusion that she was all the time looking out for birds of prey, or for some danger. When danger threatened, she changed her dialect, and spoke in another language altogether, and sent out a call of alarm, until every chicken had found a hiding-place somewhere. And how amazed I have been in riding over the Western prairies, when the cry of alarm was given by the prairie hen, to notice that as quick as you could think, every single one was hidden, and so hidden that it would be difficult to find them. They understood the call of alarm, and availed themselves of it, for the purpose of preserving themselves from danger and death.

Ever since the fall of man, not only have every species of animal in all God's world had their enemies, but the human family have also had their enemies. God has furnished the whole of them with some means of self-defence. Some depend upon the suppleness of their limbs to bear them away beyond the reach of their pursuers. Others use their wings to fly from their enemies, and thus escape the ravages of their pursuers, who are hard upon their track. Others betake themselves to the rocks and dens of the earth: I learn from old hunters that the deer never takes more than one or two bites of grass without raising his head to see if there is any danger or enemy near. They are all the time on the look out. I have noticed that the canary bird that dwells in the house, and is reared in a cage, and watered and fed from the hand of an attendant, never picks up more than two or three seeds without lifting up its head to see if there is any danger near. God has given us to understand that we have our enemies, and he says, "Watch and pray, lest ye enter into temptation." Your adversary, the devil, is going up and down the earth, like a roaring lion, seeking whom he may devour. God hath put us on guard against him, and told us to watch and pray, lest we enter into temptation.

But, alas! how much more careless are a great many human beings than the brute creation! When the hen utters the cry of alarm, the brood betake themselves quickly to the coop; but when God sends out the call of alarm to the wicked, they seem to give it no heed. They talk against being frightened into religion; they doubt whether there really is any devil, because they have not seen him, and do not know that the devil is at their heels. They fancy they are perfectly secure, and avail themselves of no refuge, no hiding-place from the wind, no covert from the storm, no resting-place in that Rock which was cleft for thee and for me; but they rush right on, down into the very clutches of their enemy, and are taken down into eternal night, as the result of their stupidity and folly.

But what is this call of alarm? I answer, the *word of God* contains some very startling passages, which are designed by God as a call of alarm, to startle sinners back from the rocks upon which they are liable to split. I will quote two or three: "He that, being often reproved, hardeneth his neck, shall suddenly be destroyed, and that without remedy." One would think that such a passage as that, coming from God himself, would be enough to startle every human being, and induce all to fly to Jesus Christ, the Rock of Ages. Another: "Now consider this, ye that forget God, lest I tear you in pieces, and there be none to deliver." An awful text!

Luther Merritt, with whom I have labored in protracted meetings, once told me that a friend of his preached on that text one night to a crowded audience, in which were infidels, and scoffers, and Universalists. At the close of the sermon, he said, "If there is any man in this congregation who is willing to meet his God to-night, and to measure arms with the Almighty; who doubts Christianity, let him rise up." A young man rose in the gallery, and said, "I am prepared to meet the Christian's God to-night. I fear him not. I am ready to measure arms with your God before the dawning of another day." That young man came down from that gallery on that bright, cold, moonshiny night, mounted a young and furious steed, and started for home. On the way the horse became frightened, and threw him upon a stick, that ran through his body, and tore his vitals out of him. When his friends found the horse in the yard in the morning, they went in search of the rider, and found him dead and ghastly — his disfigured body proclaiming the violence of the judgment that God had visited upon him. I will quote it again. "Consider this, yet that forget God, lest I tear you in pieces, and there be none to deliver." God tore his vitals out of him in the silence of the night, when there was none to deliver, and he went to meet his Judge, whom he had challenged to combat, and found that no man could contend with his Maker and prosper.

There are a great many passages of Scripture that God has given us as calls of alarm; but they are the expressions of his love. There is just as much love and kindness in the heart of the hen when she utters this alarm as when she utters the special call, though it may not be so pleasant to the chickens. It is all done from the best and highest regard for their good. In fact, if there be any difference, there is a stronger expression of love in the call of alarm than in the special call. She utters this call as if their very lives were in danger, as they really are. There is just as much love in the heart of Jesus Christ when he says, "He that believeth not shall be damned," as when he says, "He that believeth and is baptized shall be saved." It is only another way of expressing the same love, the same regard for the interests of the children of men. He would apprise you of your approaching danger, that you may find a refuge in his bleeding side, and be safe in the promised land, where no danger can approach.

But, alas! you will not heed the call of alarm. You say, "I do not like to hear so much about hell and damnation; the ministers are trying to frighten us into religion." Why doesn't a chicken reason thus, and say to its mother, "I do not like to hear such warnings and such alarming preaching as this. Why don't you tell us smooth and beautiful things, and dwell upon some pleasing themes; and what harm have we little chickens done, that there should be anything to tear us limb from limb? We don't believe in such themes as this, by which you are striving to frighten us."

What would you think if you were to hear a hen calling her brood of chickens along after her, seeking to hide them in a great ledge of rocks, and near the base of which there was a cavity running twenty or thirty feet into the rock; an eagle is sailing along, and turns his piercing eye down on the hen, and she spies him and sends out a cry of alarm. What would you think, I say, if the chickens did not run, but stood still, and complained of being frightened? We have a better opinion, say they, of our Creator than to think that he has made us to be torn to pieces and devoured when we have done no harm. And thus they remain cavilling, until the eagle fastens upon them and carries them away. You would think that the chickens had no common sense; no instinct at all. But the fact is, that on the cry of alarm, almost as quick as you can think, every single one of them will have fled into the cleft of that rock. Here is Jesus, the Rock of Ages, cleft for thee and me. He sends out the call of alarm — "Flee ye into the mountains!" and "Turn ye, turn ye, for why will ye die?" but instead of fleeing to Christ, until his indignation be passed by, ye go right on in sin, and perish, as ye fall into the hands of your enemy, the devil, who goeth about, like a roaring lion, seeking whom he may devour.

Hence we find this call of alarm uttered over and over again;

but many there are who will not avail themselves of this expression of kindness. Then Jesus says, "O Jerusalem, Jerusalem, thou that killest the prophets, and stonest them which are sent unto thee, how often would I have gathered thy children together, even as a hen gathereth her chickens under her wings, and ye would not!"

This call of alarm embraces also alarm in *preaching*. God calls some ministers to dwell upon terror more than others. We have gifts differing one from another. Some men have a peculiar gift to dwell upon the terrors of God's law. The apostle Paul said, "Knowing the terrors of the law, we persuade men." And those men whom God calls to excel in that kind of preaching, — to startle people, to alarm their fears, to excite their interest, and thus secure the salvation of their souls, — must do it, or God would smite them. They are bound to do it by the love they bear to the Savior, to the truth, and to the souls of men. Now, I say, that when you are resisting all these things, and complaining, you are resisting the Spirit of the living God, and complaining of those who would do you good.

Observe further, that this call of alarm embraces also *striking and alarming providences*. I will give you a few. Deacon Colgate, more than twenty years ago, told me a fair instance. As a vessel was about to sail from this port, the officers made a farewell supper. As the canvas was being spread to the breeze, the captain arose, and passing the brandy round the board, called on the company to drink to the following utterance: "Now, boys, in twenty days, Liverpool or hell." They sailed on and on over the Atlantic for nineteen days. On the twentieth day they struck a rock and the vessel filled, and on that twentieth day they were — not in Liverpool!

Sometimes God steps aside from his ordinary course and smites presumptuous sinners dead, that they may stand as beacon-lights to warn others to shun the rocks on which they struck. During the Black Hawk war, in Illinois, at the time when God sent the cholera among the people, an officer cursed God for sending the cholera into their midst. With an awfully blasphemous oath he opened his mouth, and God smote him down even as the oath trembled on his lips. Sydney Dyer, whom I baptized nearly forty years ago, who was a drummer-boy in that army, told me that the statement was correct. He saw the very man whom God smote down while uttering that blasphemous oath against the King, Immortal and Invisible. So God sometimes smites the wicked by these special providences, which are calls of alarm.

When I was preaching in Watertown, in this State, a company of lads, on starting to skate, called at a hotel and took each a dram, and one lad said, as he started, "I will skate to hell in five minutes." He sprang off, struck an air-hole, and went out of sight within five minutes, and never has been seen from that day to this. God utters the call of alarm when he says, "Consider this, ye that forget God, lest I tear you in pieces, and there be none to deliver."

IV. We remark again, that there is another call, which we denominate the *brooding call.* You who live in the city have noticed, I presume, when you have been visiting the country, that when the hen comes off with a brood, how artfully she manages, and how diligently she toils along from place to place, during the day, uttering her "cluck, cluck," all day long; and by and by, when the evening shades begin to gather, and the dark night is coming on, and the chilling damps of the evening dew begin to settle, she hastens away to the coop, or to some place where she may rest quietly with her flock until the dawning of another day; then it is that she changes her dialect, and speaks in another language altogether. As she spreads her wings, the brood all understand her language, and huddle around her, and cover themselves with her feathers as she spreads her wings over them. I suppose that the Savior had the words of the Psalmist in his mind — "He covereth them with his feathers" — when he uttered the words of my text. How cheerful and bright the little brood are when they come out in the morning, after having been kept all night long by the heat of the body, and protected from all harm!

So, sinner, let me tell you that there is a dark night coming on — the dark night of eternity, when the cold, clammy sweat of death will fall upon your brow; when your eyeballs shall no more turn in their sockets; when your pulse shall beat fainter and fainter, and your spirit will take its flight through the dark valley of the shadow of death. Who can be with you, and cover you there? Jesus! Yes, Jesus would give you to understand, as he utters the brooding call, "Come unto me, all ye that labor and are heavy laden, and I will give you rest." Yes, "Jesus can make a dying bed feel soft as downy pillows are." Jesus can warm and comfort your soul when the king of terrors is doing his strange work; and none but Jesus can do the helpless sinner good when he is urged on through this dark and dreary valley; and if he has no hope in God, his condition is terrible beyond conception. But how happy and cheerful is the soul that has taken refuge in Jesus?

I remember a lady, whom I baptized in Watertown, in this State, whose husband was an infidel, who sickened and died. On the last night of her stay on earth my wife watched with her. She lived in a large stone house. She revived just before her death, and was able to talk sufficiently loud to be heard through all the apartments of that building. After taking her leave of her mother and sisters, she turned her attention to her husband, and took him by the hand, and begged of him to prepare to meet her in heaven, and told him how the love of God was filling her soul; and then she began to sing, and sweetly sung until her soul took its upward flight. On the next day, that husband said to me, "Mr. Knapp, I would give everything in the world if all my infidel and Universalist associates had been here to see my wife die! It was enough to confound any man, and compel him to throw his scepticism overboard. Nothing but the love of God could support a person, and make him happy when dying, and enable him to triumph over the king of terrors, as my wife was happy and triumphed when her soul passed away in peace."

Yes, none but Jesus can warm, and cheer, and protect, and make happy your soul when you are passing through this valley of death, through which we must all, sooner or later, pass!

You have noticed, sometimes, the hen with her brood, late in autumn, when the chilling winds are beginning to whistle about on every side, and a dark cloud is rising in the west, that when the rain or hail begins to fall, if she cannot find some shelter or refuge where her brood can be protected in peace and safety, she will stand out in the storm, and spread her wings to protect them, and save them from the storm and danger. This makes me think again of Jesus. O, when the scalding drops of Jehovah's wrath shall fall upon the wicked, who but Jesus can protect their souls? Who but Jesus can spread out his wings to protect them from the rattling hail from heaven that shall fall upon the ungodly, who call not upon his name?

Yes, Jesus seems to utter the brooding call, as if he would not only be up to, but go beyond, every figure that can be employed to represent the compassion of a covenant-keeping God. "O Jerusalem, Jerusalem, thou that killest the prophets, and stonest them which are sent unto thee, how often would I have gathered thy children together, even as a hen gethereth her chickens under her wings, and ye would not." The Savior would have saved your souls from the wrath to come, from the avenger of blood that is on your track, from the eternal condemnation that awaits the ungodly, but you would not. Yes, the compassion of God is without a parallel.

Then, I observe again, after the hen has reduced herself to a mere skeleton in order to bring her brood into existence, and moves through the field, digging and toiling on, to provide food for herself and family, her love for her chickens is such that she takes food out of her own mouth for them, even when her own nature craves that food. This makes me think of Jesus again. Though he was rich, yet for our sakes he became poor, that we through his poverty might be rich. Jesus has bared his bosom to the spear. He has tasted death for every man. He sacrificed all the riches and glory of heaven, and became a man of sorrows and acquainted with grief. He became poor, that we might be rich. O, the compassion of Jesus is beyond a parallel in the universe of God. He loves us with an everlasting love. He thirsted, and hungered, and had no certain dwelling-place while going about and doing good, and whispering the accents of peace and mercy upon the ear of the poor sinner as he was moving on towards the eternal world. Yet sinners harden their hearts, and stiffen their necks, and stand out against the mercy and goodness of God.

Again, I have noticed that when the eagle or hawk approached near the hen, if she has not time to provide a place of refuge for herself and brood, she will stand out in the open field, and pitch battle with that which is too mighty for her to save her brood, and thrusts herself into the talons of the eagle or hawk, and the eagle bears her away, and upon the limb of a distant oak tears her flesh from her bones, and limb from limb, and thus she lays down her own life to save her brood. And this makes me think of Jesus. When Justice — iron-hearted and stern Justice — came and demanded the death of every human being, Jesus said to Justice, "What are your demands? I will meet them." And he laid down his life as a ransom in due season. He is taken by Justice and borne away to the cross — nailed to the tree, and crucified; and when his Father hides his face, he cries out in agony of soul, "My God, my God, why hast thou forsaken me?" and drops his head upon his bosom, and yields himself up to the claims of justice, that he might become the end of the law for righteousness to every one that believeth.

Here we see the compassion of the Lord Jesus, the King of Glory. And yet sinners harden their hearts and stiffen their necks against him.

My dying hearers, let me implore you to yield to the call of God. Be induced to yield to these calls of your loving Savior, before you have gone beyond the reach of hope forever. Will you stand out in rebellion, and perish, — perish eternally, —

because you scorn the message; because you stop your ears against the voice of the charmer, though he charm never so wisely?

May God constrain you by his Spirit, and by the power of his truth, and the love of Jesus Christ, to end the controversy, and come and be reconciled to God by the death of his Son, that your souls perish not.

IV.*

WHY THE WICKED LIVE.

"*Their foot shall slide in due time.*" — DEUT. xxxii. 35.

WE propose, this evening, to show you why the wicked live, and why the devil lives. God being good, and opposed to sin and misery, and to everything that produces misery among the world of mankind, and foreseeing the end of the wicked, the query may start in our minds, Why does he suffer the wicked to live? Why does he allow one man to enslave another, and require him to perform unrequited and hard service? Why does he allow another man to convert a good and nutritious substance, provided for man and beast, into a deadly poison, to waste away a man's constitution, to ruin his family, to beggar his children, to break the heart of the wife of his youth, to send the delirium tremens to so many families, and hurry so many to premature graves?

If God is good, why does he not cut these wicked men down, and send them to their long homes, and prevent all the misery which they will produce by living here upon his footstool? There are reasons why.

Many also wonder why God permits the devil to live, and why he does not either kill him outright, or chain him down in the pit, rather than permit him to go up and down the earth like a roaring lion, seeking whom he may devour. Yet the devil has just as good a right to live as you have; and if age is any recommendation, he has a stronger claim, for he is a great deal older; and if knowledge is any claim, he has a stronger claim

* Preached in New York, November 27, 1866.

than you, for he knows more than a million of you. He is a subject of God's moral government, and there are reasons why God suffers the devil to live, and there are reasons why he suffers wicked men to live. We are told in the text, "Their foot shall slide in due time."

Look at the real position of the human family. The figure of the text represents the whole surface of this earth as a vastly extended inclined plane, and at the base of this inclined plane there is a great gulf, or lake, burning with fire and brimstone, rolling and tumbling in awful grandeur. On this inclined plane there are some twelve millions of human beings, some dancing, some gambling, some drinking, and some carousing, and some praying, and some serving God, and some serving their lusts and their master the devil. Away up at the head of this inclined plane there is a beautiful landscape stretching on and on, farther than the human eye can reach. Those who are so happy as to reach the head of this inclined plane, and enter through the gates into the New Jerusalem, take up their harps and sing as they pass on and on over the green and flowery plains into the world of eternal day. Others are now and then sliding down and making a fatal plunge into the gulf beneath.

Why does God let the wicked live? The text says, "Their foot shall slide in due time." That is, when the due time comes their foot shall slide. And you will understand that the "due time" is when God has accomplished all the good that can be wrought by letting the wicked live. When God sees that by letting a wicked man live any longer there would be more evil than good resulting in the universe from the prolongation of that man's life, then his time comes, his foot slides, and he is dashed into the burning lake beneath.

1. We observe that God lets the wicked live because he is good and merciful, and loves his creatures, and does not delight in misery, but in the happiness of the human family; and he cannot bear to see a man sliding and sliding, and making that fatal plunge, just so long as he can, consistently with the greatest good of all, keep him out. He watches over him by night and

by day, and keeps his heart beating and his lungs heaving, and his guardian angel round about him. God is waiting and waiting to be gracious, and lets that man live on, inhaling the atmosphere, and drinking the water, and eating the fruits of the earth, and listening to the gospel's cheerful sound, and in the midst of all the means of grace. God lets him live on just so long as he possibly can and not have the prolongation of that man's life produce more evil than good.

Now, to illustrate this point, I will give you a fact. Deacon Sage, late of Rochester, but now in heaven, told me that there was an infidel living in Brockport, in this state, who was a gambler, a hard drinker, and, of course, a very rough, wicked man. One night, in the midst of a revelry, while shuffling cards around the board, he spoke of his wife, and said that he had the best wife in the State of New York. "Anything and everything that she can do to promote my happiness, she will do; and," said he, "she is a Christian, and she will serve her God and love her religion. Any sacrifice that she can make, on her part, to promote my happiness, she will make with cheerfulness. She never murmurs nor complains." Said he, "There is not her equal in this state; and I will bet five dollars now, that if you will go home with me to-night, and I order her to arise and prepare a supper, she will do it without one single complaint."

"Well," said one of the company, "I will take the bet;" and the money was put into the hands of another man of the company, and he took them home with him between twelve and one o'clock at night. His wife was in bed and asleep. He seated his company, awoke her, and ordered her to arise forthwith and prepare a supper for himself and his company. "Well, husband," said she, "leave the light in the room, and your wishes shall be complied with." She arose immediately, and dressed herself for the kitchen, and prepared them as good a supper as the house could afford. She sat down at the table, and waited upon the company with as much care, and attention, and kindness as if they had been the President and his Cabinet.

And when they got through with the meal, she retired to her room, and the company looked one upon the other in amazement. The man who had the money at stake handed it over, and said that he never saw the like before. The husband himself was affected by it, hard-hearted and wicked as he was. After the company had all retired, he sat down, and said he, "Wife, now I want you to tell me why it is that you treat me as you do, when I treat you as I do. I receive nothing but kindness in return for unkindness. Anything and everything in your power, that you can do to contribute to my happiness, you are willing to do. I cannot understand it." "Well, husband," said she, "I will tell you. I made up my mind, years ago, that all the happiness you will ever have will be in your lifetime, during the short space between the cradle and the grave, and then you will be tormented. But I expect to have my good things in the world to come. And all that I can do, all that I can suffer, and thus add to your scanty pittance of enjoyment, I will do with all the cheerfulness in the world." It went through and through him like electricity. He was bathed in tears. He bowed down and begged her prayers; and that man was converted to God.

Now, there was the principle of Christianity carried out in that woman. She understood, she had made up her mind, that, so far as she could judge from the evidence that she had, her husband would never repent; that he would live on in sin, and die in his sins; and in the world to come would have an ocean of misery. And all that she could do to increase the scanty pittance of his enjoyment she was willing to do; to make any sacrifice for him, no matter what, as she looked at the ocean of happiness, beyond the narrow limits of time, that was in store for herself.

In like manner God sees that all the happiness you will ever have will be while you are passing over this narrow isthmus 'twixt two unbounded seas. He sees this of you who will not turn and believe in and love and serve the Lord Jesus Christ. He sees that your foot will slide in due time, and all that he can do to lengthen out the brittle thread of your life, and extend the time of your enjoyment, he delights to do; and hence he watches over you awake and asleep. All the time, while Justice is crying, "Cut him down; why cumbereth he the ground?" Jesus wards off the execution, and you are spared until the due time comes.

But there is a point beyond which the forbearance of Jesus, though long continued, ceases to be a virtue; and when that time comes, and God sees that by letting that man live any longer, his existence will be productive of more misery than happiness, and be destructive of the greatest good of the whole human family, then the due time has come, and he must strike the fatal blow; and his foot slides, and he is dashed into a burning hell. He has then put God under the necessity of cutting him down, and sending him to his long home.

I have often thought of a certain judge, who, after a criminal had been tried before him and been found guilty, would rise up, address the criminal, and expatiate very eloquently upon the willingness of the jury, and of his own desire, to show him favor, and let him go free, if they could. "But, sir," he would say, "you must understand that there is a point beyond which forbearance ceases to be a virtue, and when you have reached that point, it is necessary that the terrible blow should fall;" and then he would proceed to pronounce the sentence of the law. As an officer of the government, from which he received his commission, he could do no otherwise. So, if a sinner will not repent; if he will live in sin; if he loves sin, and rolls it as a sweet morsel under his tongue, and tramples God's laws under his feet, and crucifies the Lord afresh, and puts him to an open shame; if he dashes the cup of salvation from his lips, and pushes his way downward to the chambers of eternal night, —then a time comes in which God must execute wrath upon him; then that due time comes, and his foot slides, and he is gone.

2. God lets the wicked live, lest by pulling up the tares he should also root up the wheat. You remember the parable

given by our blessed Savior. It seems that a certain man had sown good seed in his field; but his servants, going out upon the field, found tares springing up here and there in the field. They returned, and said to their master, "Did you not sow good seed in the field? Whence, then, are all these tares?' He said, "An enemy hath done this; while we slept he has sown these tares." You will remember that always, when Christians sleep, the enemy is sowing tares. Atheism, Deism, Universalism, Mormonism, and all other "*isms*" that are conjured up by the devil, are then being sown broadcast over the community. "Well," asked the servants, "shall we go and pull up the tares?" "No," said the master; "let them both grow until the harvest comes, lest by pulling up the tares you root out the wheat also."

To make this perfectly plain, we will suppose that you are looking on a surface of ten acres. You sow the whole surface to wheat. An enemy comes and sows tares all over this ten-acre lot. They come up all through the wheat. If you undertake to pull them out, with every tare you pull one, two, or three roots of wheat. Their roots are all entwined together, and so, by the time that you have gone over the surface of the wheat and pulled up the tares, you have completely destroyed the whole crop of wheat. Let both grow until the harvest, which is explained to be the end of the world, and then he says that he will gather together the tares, and bind them in bundles, and they shall be cast into the fire which is unquenchable, but the wheat he will gather into his garner; he will separate the wheat from the tares, the righteous from the wicked; the righteous will be received into heaven, the wicked will depart to hell — to that fire which is unquenchable. You see at once the force and beauty of this parable. I once knew a man who was an infidel, but whose wife was a member of the church of which I was pastor. They had sixteen children; but all of those sixteen children were converted before I left the town. One of the number entered the gospel ministry, and became a minister of the gospel of the New Testament. The family moved on in a sphere of usefulness and activity in the kingdom, and I have reason to hope that all, in due time, will reach the promised land, with many more souls won to Christ, and saved through their agency; how many eternity alone can determine. If God had cut that infidel down in his youth, he would have destroyed and rooted up all that wheat; not only the sixteen children, whose souls will reach the paradise of God, but hundreds and thousands who, through their agency, may be brought to Christ, and enter heaven to go out no more forever. Hence God lets the infidel live, and gathers all the good that he can from that man's existence, and overrules everything for the accomplishment of the greatest amount of good, until the due time comes; when God sees that more harm than good will result from the prolongation of his life, then his foot slides, and he is dashed into the roaring gulf beneath. "The wrath of man shall praise him, and the remainder will he restrain."

3. God lets the wicked live for the purpose of showing forth his long suffering. If God cut every sinner down for the very first offence, and executed wrath upon him that doeth evil, and showed no mercy, nor forbearance, nor long suffering, who would ever know the character of God? Who would ever understand the mercy, forbearance, and long suffering of our covenant-keeping God? This perfection in Deity must be developed to the admiration of all heaven, and earth, and hell. We read much of the long suffering of God in the Holy Scriptures. We witness the long suffering of God in the days of Noah, when the ark was preparing. God had pronounced judgment upon the whole world, and yet his mercy extended over them; he gave them time and space for repentance. He called after them, and warned them by his servant Noah; but by and by his long suffering could continue no longer. By and by justice, as a principle of God's moral government, must have its demands answered; and the flood came and swept them all away.

The long suffering of God is exhibited very strikingly in the history of his ancient people, the Jews. He appealed to that hard-hearted, stiff-necked, and rebellious people for year after year. Yet century after century rolled on, and they rebelled against him more and more. Their heart was fully set in them to do evil. But when the time was come, when he could no longer forbear, he cried out, "O, Ephraim, how shall I give thee up?"

The long suffering of God waited while they killed the prophets, and stoned them that were sent unto them, and beheaded John the Baptist, and crucified the Son of God. When the long suffering of God had been protracted as long as all the circumstances in the case would permit, he was compelled to say, "Ephraim is joined to his idols; let him alone." And Jesus may be compelled to say of you, O sinner, "He is joined to his idols; let him alone." "She is joined to her idols; let her alone." "Plead no longer; waste no more tears; waste no more prayers; spend no more breath in tender expostulation. The long suffering of God is sufficiently developed; now the due time has come; cut her down; for why should she cumber the ground?" It is on this principle that God says, "My word shall not return unto me void; it shall accomplish the end whereunto I sent it." What is that? A *sweet savor of God in Christ.* And a sweet savor of God in Christ of life unto life to them who embrace the gospel, and of death unto death to them who reject it. In either case it is a *sweet savor of God in Christ* both unto those who are saved and rise, and sing and shout, and magnify the riches of God's grace forever; and to those who sink down into dark despair, weeping and wailing, and gnashing their teeth, and gnawing their tongues for pain.

God's long suffering will be magnified in the condemnation of the wicked. All the heavenly hosts will look on and see how long God waited to be gracious; how long suffering he was to those who finally went down to hell; how his mercies extended from childhood to old age, or until the due time came when their foot slid, and they made the fatal plunge.

Ministers may stand up and preach the truth of God from day to day, from night to night, from year to year, and rejoice over every soul that repents and turns to God; and if they repent not, but sink to hell, they know that their preaching will not be in vain. God will be honored; Jesus Christ will be glorified; the gospel of the dear Redeemer, in all its beauty, and forbearance, and love, will be understood by all the assembled hosts when God shall judge the quick and the dead. But when the long suffering of God has been protracted as long as the case will permit, then the due time comes, your foot slides, and you are gone. Then there is no more hope.

4. In the next place, the wicked live in order that God may give sinners time and space for repentance. God is sincere in calling upon all men, everywhere, to repent. God is waiting and waiting to be gracious. He is unwilling, as the Bible says, that any should perish, but would that all should be saved, and come to the knowledge of the truth. God delighteth not in the death of him that dieth, but would that he should live. Do you suppose that, because the wicked will be cut down and perish in hell, and through all eternity, such is the choice of the great God? If so, you might suppose that God chose that every drunkard should be a drunkard; and every cruel, wicked man should whip his wife; and every knave should overreach his neighbor in trade; and that all the wicked and abominable things that are done under the penalty of eternal damnation should be committed. You must understand that God delighteth not in the death of him that dieth. It would be agreeable to the heart of Deity, to the heart of the Father, Son, and Holy Spirit, to see every sinner repent to-night; to see the entire world fall down and worship the Lamb; to see in every human body a broken heart and a contrite spirit; and to witness the pure, earnest devotions of the millions of the human race ascending to God like holy incense. But they will not do it.

So God gives men time and space for repentance. He gave the old world one hundred and twenty years in which to repent.

He gave the Ninevites time and space for repentance. They repented, and were saved. By crying mightily unto the God of heaven, God heard their cries, and waived his judgment, and prolonged the lives of the people of that wicked city. He gave the Jews time for repentance, even after he had foretold their doom. John the Baptist, who was a faithful and truthful preacher, went everywhere, preaching and crying, "Behold the Lamb of God, that taketh away the sin of the world." God gave them time and space for repentance, and all that did repent were pardoned and saved; and if all had repented, they all would have been pardoned, and sanctified, and saved. What else did Jesus mean in the text from which I preached to you last night? "O Jerusalem, Jerusalem, thou that killest the prophets, and stonest them which are sent unto thee, how often would I have gathered thy children together, even as a hen gathereth her chickens under her wings, and ye would not!" Does he not tell us here, that he was willing to gather that very people, those incorrigible Jews, who betrayed and crucified the Son of God, and cried out, "Away with him"? He was as willing to gather them together, and to save their souls, as a hen was to gather her chickens under her wings. And the reason why they were not gathered, and not saved, was because they "would not." O, that *damning "would not"!* "Ye will not come unto me, that ye might have life." "Turn ye, turn ye, for why will ye die?" "O that they were wise," saith God; "that they knew this; that they would consider their latter end; that it might be well with them and with their children forever."

God lets you live on, sinner, in order to give you time and space for repentance; and you will see, if you keep on, and wake up at last in hell, that you might just as well have been in heaven as anybody else. Somebody else has taken up your harp, and received your crown. You, like Esau, have sold your birthright. God spares your life from year to year; the Spirit strives; ministers preach; the church pleads; all the agencies that God possesses are moving around in your midst, and beckoning you on towards the celestial regions; but you will not go. Suddenly the due time comes; your foot slides; you are gone; you are irrevocably lost!

5. But, again, the wicked live in order that God may spread the gospel through their agency. He prolongs their lives even for the good of the righteous. We often look upon our persecutors as a great evil. We often look upon worldly, sensual members of the church, who are not satisfied with a faithful gospel ministry, who want a man-pleasing preacher, one who shall give them smooth words and fair speeches, and who, instead of preaching against their pride, and vanity, and worldly-mindedness, shall minister to their passions, and pamper their pride, and flatter their vanity, and help them on in the consummation of their carnal and selfish purposes. We look upon this class as a great calamity; but yet God overrules the existence of such persons for very wise and important ends. God maketh the wrath of man to praise him, and the remainder he restrains. We are enabled, when we see these classes, to distinguish between him that serveth God and him that serveth Mammon; to distinguish between the sons of Levi and those who are such in word and not in deed and truth. It draws the faithful to the mercy-seat, and they pray the more earnestly; they call upon God out of a pure heart, and all the persecution they endure only makes the gold shine the brighter. It is just so in reference to the wicked. We hear of the opposition of infidels, of the sneering of Universalists, of the persecution of wicked, ungodly men in every day and in every age of the world, and we think they are very serious evils; but after all they may be of very great service to the children of God; but I tell you that we never find a true, earnest, apostolic religion, except in times of persecution.

When Christianity appears in silver slippers, and glides along upon the soft carpet, — when everything goes on smoothly, and we have smooth and beautiful preaching, and no opposition from the wicked, — we have a sickly piety. Real piety then dies out. There is then no real soul in religion. There is nothing but mere form when we deny the power. But when we have anmies to oppose us, we are driven near the mercy-seat; we then know in whom we trust. We are constrained to take the word of God as a lamp to our feet and a light to our path, and to make straight paths for our feet as we lead the way on to heaven. So it is necessary for the wicked to live for the benefit of the righteous. We have not half enough persecution in the church. If you could only start the devil once, we would have something done. I was thinking of this as I came on the cars from Albany here — looking at the river, as I sat on the river-side, and watching the vessels. There was a little, gentle wind, and as the sails of the vessels filled, they moved on; a good wind in the direction in which they are moving carries them on in good speed; a side wind answers a very good purpose; and even a head wind is of more service than no wind at all, for they make some headway then; but in a dead calm, when the sails do not flutter, but hang down limber, there is no progress at all to be made. The object of the devil is to take all the wind out of our sails; to allay all public and open opposition, and produce a dead and still calm; to lull the church to sleep, and then to send out his emissaries and sow tares broadcast over the land, until the wheat is choked with tares, and there is no fruit produced as the result. I have always found, so far as my experience goes, that the greatest exhibitions of divine power have been where there was the greatest persecution. Amidst mobs, and threats of my life, and every conceivable effort on the part of the wicked to break up meetings and stop the work of God, I have always found that God then comes down and works like himself. When the enemy comes in like a flood, then it is that God works. During the mob in New Haven, I was waylaid, night after night, by those who thirsted for my blood; but God carried me right through, and I never lost a hair of my head. Had you been there then, you would have seen the workings of God Almighty's power. If you had been in Boston when I was preaching there, and witnessed the mobs that filled the square, and the infidels sitting up all night, making clubs to knock my brains out with, — but God knocked on their hearts, broke them, and saved their souls, — you would then have seen an exhibition of the power of the Great Eternal that you never will see in times when there is no opposition.

God through the devil, and the devil through wicked men, scattered the disciples of Christ who huddled up in Jerusalem, and they went everywhere preaching the gospel. More than half of our churches in cities originate in the agency of the devil. When churches will not branch off, start out, begin new interests, go up and possess the city, God always has a schismatic devil on hand to let out upon them, and compel them to do that which they ought to have done from better motives. A few years since, every church, of all denominations, from the Episcopalians up to the Baptists, in Elmira, N. Y., was divided into two churches, each one building a new house of worship, and thus doubling the amount of labor and their power for good. God says, "The wicked are my sword," and through this sword God has opened the way for the spread of the gospel among all nations. If there is any quarrelling to be done, or fighting, the devil is always on hand.

We must have wicked men, and we must have devils. We need them both. They drive us nearer to God. They make us pray more earnestly. They make us feel our dependence upon God more intently. They nerve up our souls to the work of serving God, and thus render very essential service in helping on the work of the Holy Ghost. Yes, we may well say, when the question is asked, "Why do the wicked live?" they live to serve God; or, rather, that God may serve himself by them, and make the wrath of man to praise him, while he restrains the remainder. God overrules all that the wicked do for some good purpose. Every good thing that can be reached by the infinite wisdom and power of God will be reached, and thus God will make the wrath of man to praise him, and he will restrain the remainder. I have been in meetings where men could not swear without converting somebody. I have known men, and Universalists, to get up in the midst of a congregation, and curse the minister to his face, and throw stones at him;

but God Almighty converted sinners just by those oaths. Sinners began to ask themselves, "Is this the company I am to have in hell? Have such outrageous miscreants in human form got to be endured through all eternity in hell? Then I won't go there;" and they fell right down and began to beg for mercy, and were converted to God. I have often thought that my enemies did me more good than my friends. No thanks to them, though, for it. There was a Judas Iscariot for the betrayal of our Lord and Master. I do not know where I should have landed ere this, if I had had no enemies, if all had been friends, and all been smooth sailing. I might have been exalted above measure, and fallen into condemnation. But my enemies are always watching for me. If there is a stain anywhere, they are sure to see it. If there is a spot upon anything in my course of operation, they are sure to detect it. They are all the time watching for us: hence we must be on our guard; we must set a double guard upon our lips in the presence of the wicked, lest the uncircumcised should triumph. God overrules all these things for our good and for his own glory.

6. Again: we need the devil and wicked men in order to test character. When God made this world, and placed Adam in it, you know that he placed him under the law, and laid a prohibition upon one single thing. He prohibited him from eating the fruit of one tree in the garden; but Adam, under the temptation of the enemy, and under the influence of his wife, plucked the fruit and ate thereof. The crown fell from his head, and he was driven out of the garden, and the flaming sword guarded the way to the tree of life. So God does not mean to let anybody into heaven until their characters are tested. It is not as easy a thing as many men think for God to keep a race of moral agents in obedience and subjection to his moral law. We have knowledge of but two kinds of moral agencies — angels and men. We know that many angels have fallen; they have risen up in rebellion against God, and been cast down into hell, and reserved in chains of darkness until the judgment of the great day shall come.

We know that the entire family of man have fallen. It seems as if it was not a very easy thing for even God himself to preserve a race of moral agents in a state of sinless perfection. Do you suppose that our first parents knew anything about the connection between sin and misery before the experiment had been tried? Not at all. Do you suppose that Adam and Eve had a conception of the tremendous results that would follow a violation of God's law? Do you suppose that they imagined that their son Abel would fall a victim to the rage and envy of another son, Cain? that they would look upon the manly form of their own son, with all the pangs of sorrow that racked their frame and continued to chafe them through life? They had no such conception. Do you suppose that they had any idea that millions and millions of their posterity would become demons, weeping, and wailing, and gnashing their teeth, and gnawing their tongues in pain, while the smoke of their torment should roll up from the depths of hell? They had no such thought. They knew nothing about the connection between sin and misery. It was not possible that they could know.

God does not mean to have any human soul or rebel in heaven until he is fully reformed, and his character fully tested. He knows the wickedness of man. You know that we are forbidden to lay hands suddenly upon any man; that we are not to ordain a novice, lest he should be lifted up in pride and fall into condemnation. It is not safe to introduce men into the ministry until they are tested; and if it is inexpedient to introduce men into the ministry until their characters have been tested, do you think that any one will ever be introduced into the paradise of God without having his character tested? Never! Never! This world, my friends, is a world of trial, and we need the devil to tempt and try the children of men, that their characters may be fully and thoroughly tested. We need the devil; we must have the devil to work with all deceitfulness and unrighteousness to tempt every character; and you find sometimes a great hoard of these miserable, filthy, impure spirits sweeping along through the community, bearing numbers away to the bottomless pit. They could not stand the test, and away they went. One will falter here, and another there. One is tempted away to the theatre, another to the gaming table, another to the accumulation of wealth, hoarding it up to gratify his pride, instead of doing good with it. Their characters are all tested, and such as stand the test, and resist temptation, and cling to Jesus, will finally be fitted and prepared for heaven, and will reach the promised land in due time, and never rebel against God again.

They have been led through much tribulation, for such is the way to glory. They can say, " I have fought the good fight, I have kept the faith, and there is henceforth laid up for me a crown which a righteous Judge shall give." All the temptations of hell can never draw them into rebellion again. It is a great thing to have escaped the pollutions of the world, and been washed in the blood of the Lamb, and entered heaven, where there is no more sighing, and no more temptation, and be permitted to dwell in the sunshine of God's glory forever. We must be tempted. The trial of our faith is more precious than gold. You remember that the barren fig-tree must be tried, and dug about until all hope of its bearing fruit becomes extinct, and then it shall be cut down as a cumberer of the ground. So the due time comes at length when the sinner has accomplished all the ends that God can reach by letting him live, and then he cuts him down.

7. Then, again, God lets the wicked live to spread the gospel negatively. I will give you a few instances. I will refer you to one in ancient days. You know that there was a time when the apostles of Jesus Christ were all poor, illiterate men. Luke, it is true, was a physician, and Paul was brought up at the feet of Gamaliel; but most of the disciples were poor. They had but little money. There were no missionary societies in those days. When God wanted to send missionaries away down to Rome, so as to spread the gospel as rapidly as possible, there were no missionary societies nor missionary vessels ready to send or take them. The devil had a terrible inkling after

Paul; he wanted to get hold of him. Paul was then making inroads upon the devil's kingdom wherever he went, and the devil laid hold upon him and put him in irons. When Paul appealed unto Cæsar, said the king, "Thou shalt go." The devil took him down to the port, and bore his expenses all the way. Here God made the wrath of man to praise him, and restrained the remainder. God wanted the gospel preached in Rome, and would have it preached there. God owned all the money that was in the devil's pocket, and made the devil hand it over. He took this missionary down to Rome, and kept him there for three years and six months preaching the unsearchable riches of Christ.

Look at the case in more modern times. In 1839, as I told the friends in a temperance meeting the other night, God sent me to Baltimore to preach. God began the work, in the first place, among drunkards. The rum-sellers became very much out of patience because they were losing their customers. They became very much filled with wrath and malice towards the unworthy Baptist preacher whom God employed in leading on the sacramental host from conquest to conquest, and they swore vengeance upon him. The young men constituted a temperance society, and invited me one night to preach a sermon on temperance. I agreed to do so. The rum-sellers had a meeting, and appointed a delegation to go and hear my sermon, and report. They came in and sat down behind the door, and as the service went on, and solemn, pointed, and pungent truths were preached, they began to feel the power of God's truth. After the service, they went back to make a report, and the old rum-seller, standing behind the counter, said, "What report have you to make?" "Well," said one, "we heard a great deal more truth than poetry." "But what did the elder say?" asked another. "I wish that you had been there and heard for yourselves," said one of the delegation. "But what did he say?" "Well," replied one, "he said, if you will mark, you will find the rum-seller dressed in fine broadcloth, and a fine shirt, and silk hat, and beautiful boots, carrying his head high, and living in ease and affluence; but you will see that you have on an old coat out at the elbows, old pants in strings; and you see," said he, "that it is just as Mr. Knapp says. There you sit with your broadcloth and fine shirt, while here I stand in all my rags. I begin to get my eyes opened. Moreover, he said that the rum-seller's wife will be dressed like a lady: she wears her silks and satins, and her beautiful hat; while your wife has on an old calico dress, rent and patched, and old shoes on her feet, and without a bonnet decent enough to appear in any congregation under heaven. And these things are all true," said the delegation.

The rum-seller began to feel indignant and vindictive, and poured out his anathemas on Knapp. "I won't hear that man abused," said Mitchel, one of the men; "I believe that he is a good man, and that he is doing good in the city. If you abuse him any more, I will leave your house; and you are afraid of losing your custom." He began to see through these landsharks. But the rum-seller felt so badly, that he kept all the time heaving up, heaving up, and pouring forth his invectives upon the preacher. Mitchel was as good as his word. He rose up, put on his hat, and said, "I will never drink another drop in your house so long as my name is Mitchel," and left. On the way home, said he, "Why can I not resolve never to drink another drop anywhere? *I will do it*," said he; and that night they got up a pledge of total abstinence from intoxicating drinks; and there began the Washingtonian reform that rolled over the Eastern States, and converted hundreds and thousands of inebriates.

Thus you see how God made the wrath of man to praise him. If it had not been for that old rum-seller damning Knapp, and cursing the Baptists, that great Washingtonian reformation would never have commenced, so far as we can see; and if so much good could be brought about by their heaping their anathemas upon your unworthy servant, I say, let them curse.

The God whom we serve, who can turn the hearts of the children of men as the rivers of water are turned, can overrule everything that occurs, for his own glory, and for the best interests of the human family.

Take an illustration in your own city. When I was preaching in the Baptist Tabernacle, in 1840, we felt very desirous, as the house was very capacious (the gallery would seat more than twelve hundred), that all should come and hear the gospel of Jesus Christ preached. We were conscious that circulating handbills, and putting notices in the paper, would avail but little, as men seldom notice these things, or pass them by, and they are soon forgotten. But at length God instigated the devil to go and move on Bennett, and get him to publish a notice of the meeting; and Bennett sent a reporter into our meetings, and he reported the speeches, and turned them "every which way," and mixed the sentences pell-mell, and made them appear very ludicrous, and some of them very ridiculous; and Bennett's paper circulated all through the city among all the infidels, and among all the Tammany Hall folks, who took that paper (and they were almost the only ones who did take it). We thus had an advertisement of our meetings. The devil advertised them at his own expense. And when we went over into Jersey City to baptize, we chartered a ferry-boat, and went over by thousands; and Bennett sent over his reporter, and there he got brother Everts pictured out like a clown, and myself like some old chuckle-headed drunkard, and between us two we took the candidates for baptism down into the water, and dipped them in horizontally. The newsboys sold the papers from street to street, and the infidels kept pouring in and pouring in to the meetings to gratify their curiosity. They read such very strange things that they thought that they must come and hear the preacher, and see whether he was an elk or a moose, and how long his horns were. And on they came.

Among the number was an infidel, who had not been to a meeting in ten years, and who had sworn with an oath that he never would enter the house of God again; and connected with the oath a wish that, if he did, the roof might fall in and kill him on the spot. He read in the paper what was said about God saving the people by scores and hundreds, and bringing them into the glorious liberty of the sons of God. He thought to himself, "I must go once; I must hear the man once;" and he came and took a seat in the body slips. Very soon the house was filled to a jam, above and below. Every standing-place was filled, and they were as thick as they could squeeze in. The porch was full — full even out into the streets. He sat there, and when the speaker arose and announced his text the house was very still and solemn. He looked upon the right, and saw all around him weeping; then upon the left, and they were all weeping; and he began to feel a strange sensation coming over him. He looked towards the door, as if he would like to escape, but there was no getting through that crowd. He then looked up to see if the roof was coming down, but the roof moved not. There he sat, as we spoke God's truth from the fulness of our soul. He was melted down and subdued, and induced to come to the seats at the close of the sermon, and was converted to God before he left that house.

We could not have done that but for the devil and wicked men. Though all the rest of the papers in the city had published our meetings, these infidels would not have come; but when their old master, the devil, began to advertise them, they thought that it was time to see what was going on. They kept pouring in and pouring in, until there were hundreds and thousands converted throughout the entire city, and the city was convulsed from centre to circumference. Hence God makes the wrath of man to praise him, and restrains the remainder. We see why God lets the wicked live, and why he lets the devil live.

I can look back upon the time when we, as Christians, really felt grieved when we read about slavery. I had never seen a slave, or a slaveholder, up to the time that I left the Institution at Hamilton. When I read the account, my heart was stirred within me. We prayed and preached, and lectured and wrote, and circulated tracts. We did everything that we could to break their bonds, and let the oppressed go free. We did all that we could to establish the broad principle that all men are free and equal; that all men had a right to life, liberty, and the pursuit of happiness, according to the laws that God had made for the benefit of the human race. But by all that was said and done we could not reach the slave; we could not break his bonds. The church and the abolitionists went to the extent of their power, but, in spite of all said and done, slavery was striking its roots down deeper and deeper into the soil, and its dark branches were stretching over all the United States. The government could not stir. We were bound by the constitution, and by the clamors of the Southern people. Between the two, the people of the North were completely hampered. Were it not for the devil and wicked men it would not have been abolished, perhaps, at all. But when Jefferson Davis, Mason and Slidell, and all those leading rebels, stirred up by the devil, sought to extend slavery all through the United States of America, and make all the territories slave territory,—when they sought to hold the reins of this republic until they could establish a vast aristocracy, and keep all the power in themselves,—then it was that these leading men accomplished what all the saints in Christendom could not do. God, of course, was standing behind the curtain and pulling the wires, and seeing them dance; and they danced until they trampled off the chains of the slave. God let them work; but he overruled this mighty, gigantic rebellion for the accomplishment of a vast amount of good. Eternity alone can tell how much. I rejoice, and I will rejoice, over the terrible conflict, although one of my dear sons fell on the field of battle.

O God, how majestic are thy ways! They are a great deep. Who by searching can find out God to perfection? It is a fearful thing to fall into the hands of the living God. Sinner, when you have served your master, the devil, and gone your length, and God has accomplished all the good that he can reach by letting you live, and you fail to repent, the due time comes; then your foot slides, and you are gone down to the depths of dark condemnation. Then there is no hope.

But mark our position. Here we are upon this vastly extended inclined plane; and at the base of this inclined plane there is a lake burning with fire and brimstone, rolling high and thundering loud. Every now and then one slips in and is dashed into eternity. Away along at the head of this inclined plane the landscape stretches on. Angels look down upon us. Our friends, who have gone before, look down upon us. "I have a father in the promised land." There is a mother in the promised land; here, a tender-hearted wife, who watered her couch with tears in intercessions to God for her husband; there are little babes that fell asleep in Jesus, all looking back wistfully, and beckoning us to come up to the promised land. But, alas! one refuses, and another refuses; they go on down to the termination of this inclined plane, and are there hurled into perdition. But while standing on the verge of eternal ruin, Jesus condescends to come down from heaven. He passes around on this inclined plane, and says to one and to another, "Will you come to the promised land? Will you come to the land radiant with glory, beaming with light?" He offers you his hand to conduct you up to the promised land. One goes; another refuses, and perishes. O, my friends, how quickly we shall all be in heaven or in hell! May God in heaven lead you to see how long his goodness and mercy have endured for you; but if you despise or neglect, your foot will slide in due time. We call upon you to make haste to turn and be saved.

We now invite all who wish the prayers of Christians to take these seats. Let all who profess religion, who feel that they need prayer, and wish the prayers of their brethren, come up. Let backsliders come, too. I tell you we are in a dying world; we are passing away rapidly; our destiny may hang upon the decision of a single night. I pray you all to come right up and fill these seats.

V.

THE NEW BIRTH.

"*Make you a new heart and a new spirit.*" — EZEKIEL xviii. 31.

"*Create in me a clean heart, O God, and renew a right spirit within me.*" — PSALM li. 10.

THERE is no discrepancy between these two passages. God creates within us a clean heart, and we make to ourselves a new heart. There is both a divine and human agency in every case of conversion. Sometimes greater prominence is given to the divine element in the account of the change; sometimes greater prominence is given to the human element.

I. Our first inquiry relates to the import of the phrase "new heart," or "clean heart." What is to be understood by it?

The term "heart" describes the moral activities of the soul, including the affections and the will. The command of God to us is, "Thou shalt love the Lord thy God with all thy heart, mind, might, and strength." And herein he requires us to give to him the supreme and unreserved exercise of our affections and wills.

Now every unconverted man loves self supremely, and wills to serve, and does serve, self entirely. Whether he gives for religious purposes or withholds, whether he prays or swears, God is left out of his reckoning: self is the supreme object of his affections. If he does a good act, it is not because he loves

God, but because he desires to be seen of men, or to merit reward from God; if he refrains from performing a good deed, it is because he is under the control of a selfish impulse; if he swears, it is to gratify a depraved passion; if he prays, it is from fear of personal suffering. He would, if he could, make himself the moral centre, around whom God, men, and devils should revolve, as planets around the sun. His precious, beloved self is the centre of moral gravity. The glory of God, the interests of his kingdom, the greatest good of the universe, are all overlooked or set aside; self reigns supreme.

If unregenerated sinners were to be admitted into heaven, there would be as many petty kingdoms, and as many little sovereignties, as there were unconverted hearts; and heaven would be worse than Mexico or South America, where faction is rising up against faction, and demagogues are plotting against and destroying each other. Every man would set up for himself, and all would unite only in one purpose of assailing and overthrowing the absolute, but righteous "throne and majesty of God."

Hence we see, then, before God and man can be reconciled, man must have "a new heart." He "must be born again."

II. In what does the change contemplated consist?

It does not consist in the creation of any new faculty of the soul. The original properties or elements of the moral nature remain unchanged in those things that are essential to their entity or being. Before regeneration man has the power of understanding, judging, loving, and choosing; and he has them after regeneration. But the new creature finds that these faculties of the soul have new objects, and take new directions. "Old things have passed away, and, behold, all things have become new." The things he once loved he now hates, and the things he once hated he now loves.

The word "create," when used to describe regeneration or the new birth, simply means the production of a new character. Thus God says, "Behold, I create Jerusalem a rejoicing, and her people a joy." He has given her people to understand that he would bring about such a change in their character and condition as would make them another people — a joy and a rejoicing, instead of a scandal and reproach.

I defy any man to tell what creation there is, in regeneration, other than the constitution of a new character. A regenerate man is, in his moral identity, the same conscious moral agent; but in his character, in the drift of his affections, pursuits, and pleasures, he is a "new creature." He loves new objects, is influenced by new motives, is enlightened by new views, delights in new associations, is subject to new laws, rejoices in new joys, and is inspired by new hopes. To all these he was once dead, but now he is alive. His heart was once a heart of stone, now it is a heart of flesh.

The governing purpose of the soul is changed from supreme love of self, to supreme love of God. It is now in harmony with the laws of God's moral government. It can unite in sympathy and accord with all holy beings in heaven and in earth in expressing holy impulses, obeying the will of God, doing good to his fellows, and praising God and the Lamb. Once self reigned supreme, but now self is lost in God, and God in the soul is "all in all."

We may enumerate the elements that enter into and constitute this change which is called "*regeneration*," or "*new birth*." First, a change of affections; second, of purpose; third, of sentiments; fourth, of views and feelings; fifth, of all our relations to God, to man, to the world, and to the devil.

III. Our third inquiry relates to the manner in which this change is brought about. How is it produced?

1. I remark, negatively, this change is not brought about, as some suppose, by the *irresistible* power of the Holy Spirit. I know of no passage in the Bible whose phraseology requires to be construed so as to teach the doctrine that the influences of the Spirit *cannot* be resisted; but I know of several which teach very clearly the doctrine that they can be resisted. The Savior said to the Jews, "Ye do always resist the Holy Spirit; as did your fathers, so do ye." What need is there of the cautions

against *quenching* and *grieving* the Spirit, if the Spirit cannot be resisted?

One writer (Toplady, I think) remarks that the sinner can "no more resist the Holy Spirit than he can resist a stroke of lightning." He, like all those who have taken this extreme view, seems to have overlooked entirely the great fact of the combination of the divine and the human agency in the act of regeneration. Those who hold the view of this writer suppose that God regenerates men by the use of arbitary power.

It is true that God might apply hydraulic or steam power to man, but it would not convert him. Nor would the lightnings of heaven, nor its thunders, convert him. Physical exertion itself is no more adapted to move mind, than moral power is to move matter. But who would think of making a powerful speech, eloquent in arguments, illustrations, and pathos, in order to knock down a stone wall, or to start the sturdy oak from its fastenings. Yet this would be no more unreasonable or absurd than to think of turning mind by physical force.

Mind can only be moved by motive—by moral considerations. Consequently God has filled the Bible with motives to induce men to repent and serve him. Yea, the whole world is teeming with motives, and God has appointed agencies, in all periods, to keep these motives before the people to induce them to break off from their sins and turn to him. Now is it reasonable to suppose that all these motives are to be dispensed with when a soul is to be converted, and the soul is to be wrenched around by merely physical power? by an irresistible force that makes no appeal to the moral faculties of our nature?

Why are not souls converted where no Bibles are circulated, no gospel preached, or where no motives are urged? One error always leads to others. Hence those who believe that men are converted by physical force, think that if the sinner can resist the Holy Spirit, it makes him stronger than the Almighty. But it must be understood that in a moral government the weaker can resist the stronger. Let us suppose that we wish to turn an inebriate from his cups. We send for

John B. Gough to try all the powers of his mirthful eloquence upon him, but he cannot move him. We try the skill and moral power of a Spurgeon, or any other distinguished speaker, in order to bring to bear upon him all the motives drawn from heaven, earth, and hell, to induce him to abandon his cups; but none of all these appeals can move him. But does this fact prove that this inebriate is stronger than any of these men, or all of them together? No. What, then, does it prove? It proves that the subject upon whom they have plied their power was so debased, so much under the power of his cups, that he could resist all arguments, from all sources, however powerful. In like manner the sinner is so depraved, so much under the control of the love and power of sin, that he can resist the Holy Spirit; a straw will carry him on in the current of his own debased inclinations, but neither the pleadings of his wife, the eloquence of his children, the arguments of the minister, the influence of the Spirit, the hope of heaven, or the fear of hell, will induce him to turn; "he loves darkness rather than light, because his deeds are evil." "Ye will not come unto me that ye might have life."

2. This change is not wrought by the Spirit's tucking something into the sinner, back of his will, to give direction to it. This would take all obligation to repent from the sinner, until this certain something was put within him.

But it is said, though the sinner has lost his ability to obey God, that God has not lost his right or power to command. I reply, that if the sinner has lost his ability to repent, and cannot repent until God restores that ability, then the sinner is under no obligation to repent without a capacity to do so; and God, as a reasonable being, would not require it. It would not be possible to make an intelligent being feel guilty for not doing that which was out of his power to do.

Suppose a man sent his servant for a pitcher of water, and that the servant, from mere ugliness, breaks the pitcher, and thereby incapacitates himself to bring the water; would the master be justifiable in demanding the water unless he supply some vessel in which to bring it? Surely not. He might be justifiable in punishing the servant for breaking the pitcher, but not for refusing to bring the water when it was out of his power to do so. So God might punish the sinner for all violations of law; but if he has lost his capacity to repent or believe, or to come to Christ, or submit to God, then neither God nor any reasonable moral agent would blame him for not doing so.

But this capacity is not lost. Hence God commands all men everywhere to repent; and their guilt in not believing in Christ, and not coming to God through him, is so great, that it is the damning sin of the world. It casts all other sins into the shade; — "of sin, because ye believe not in me." God comes out in his word and addresses all men as moral agents capable of obeying him, and pleads, commands, and threatens them in case they do not obey.

When I came out of the Institution at Hamilton, N. Y., in which I studied theology under the instruction of the lamented Dr. Nathaniel Kendrick (a better man than whom seldom lived), I went to work with the old theory of physical regeneration, and would often come in contact with an intelligent man who had been religiously educated, who would take ground like this: "I want to be a Christian; I desire it above all things; but the prayers of the wicked are an abomination in the sight of the Lord; and as no good thing can come out of a bad heart, I cannot repent nor believe until God changes my heart." There he was, waiting for God to come and convert or regenerate him. I could not meet this honest and intelligent inquirer with my erroneous views of the new birth. Hence I was compelled to investigate, analyze, and search the Scriptures more critically, until the subject became as clear as a sunbeam.

3. Nor is there any miracle in making a new heart. It is mysterious, and to us incomprehensible; but there is no suspension or counteraction of any of the laws of nature. God moves upon the human soul in accordance with the laws of mind, and in accordance with the distinctive laws of each

individual mind, and makes the sinner willing — not able — in the day of his *power*. The will surrenders, the heart yields, the conflict ends, sin is pardoned, and the soul is saved.

IV. By what agencies is this work accomplished?

We answer, "The Spirit and the bride say, Come." Nor is the agency of the soul itself dispensed with in a single instance. The bride embraces the whole sacramental host of God's elect.

The ministers of the gospel are commissioned to go and teach, i. e., disciple, or convert, *all nations*. Nor are they sent out alone. This one agency of itself would not be sufficient to convert a single soul; hence Christ says, "Lo, I am with you alway, even unto the end of the world."

The sinner is so dead to all spiritual things that man cannot quicken him into action; so blind that man cannot lead him to see; hence Christ Jesus, by the Holy Spirit, accompanies the faithful ambassador, and both agencies are combined; and then the sinner is required to use his agency to repent, to believe, to come to Christ, to submit to God; and without this repentance, this receiving of Christ by faith, this exercising of his own agency, he cannot make a new heart, cannot be converted. All these agencies are employed in the conversion of the soul. It is proper, therefore, for God to say, in the language of my text, "Make unto you a new heart;" and it is right for us to pray, "Create in me a clean heart, and renew a right spirit within me." Inasmuch as all these agencies are employed in the conversion of the soul, the change is sometimes ascribed to one of them and sometimes to another.

How often the new birth is ascribed to human agency! "Whom I have begotten in Christ Jesus." "I have begotten you through the gospel." 1 Cor. iv. 15. Paul speaks of Timothy and Onesimus as his own sons, whom he had begotten; that is, God had used his agency in begetting and giving birth to these souls, and that, too, through, or by, the gospel, as the instrumentality.

Conversion is sometimes ascribed to the agency of the sinner himself. "Seeing ye have purified your souls in obeying the truth." 1 Pet. i. 22. In the text the wicked are commanded to make unto themselves a new heart; and all the directions to repent, to turn, to believe, to submit, to come to Christ, are proofs positive that the sinner's agency is not suspended in conversion — that his eternal destiny turns upon his will. "Whosoever *will*, let him come unto me and take of the water of life." "Ye will not come unto me that ye might have life." "How often would I have gathered your children together, but ye would not!" This damning *will not* keeps millions out of heaven, and is all the time populating hell.

Then this change is still more frequently ascribed to the Spirit, because the agency of the Spirit is more prominent, more efficacious, than all the other agencies put together. It is not possible for man so to illumine the mind, so to soften the heart, and convince of sin, as to bring the sinner into subjection to the divine will. It is not possible, without the influences of the Holy Spirit, to bring all the motives presented in the word of God to bear with sufficient clearness and cogency upon the heart of the sinner to induce a full surrender.

Hence the Spirit is given to convince "of sin, of righteousness, and of judgment to come." Consequently we are told of the "washing of regeneration, and the renewing of the *Holy Spirit*." "Born of the Spirit." "You hath he quickened who were dead in trespasses and sins."

Now, to harmonize all these agencies, and make the subject perfectly plain to all, we will suppose a man walking along, in a dark night, upon the brink of a precipice, unconscious of his whereabouts or his danger. He nears the verge; it is five hundred feet to the bottom: just as he raises his foot to step off, a voice rings along the abyss and breaks upon his ear — "STOP!" At the same moment a man opens a lantern, and pours a stream of light upon his path, by which he discovers his danger: he springs back, and is saved.

The next day he steps into a store, and relates his marvellous escape, and says, "Just as I was taking the fatal step, a light shone upon my footsteps, by means of which I discovered my danger, and I was saved. Blessed be God for that light." Here he ascribes his deliverance to the light. In relating the circumstance to another person, he says, "Just as I had raised my foot, and was about taking the fatal step, a voice broke upon my ear — 'STOP, STOP!' Thank God for that word. O, how it rings in my ears now! But for that word I should have been a dead man." Here he ascribes his deliverance to the word *stop*. The neighborhood is excited, and keep coming in, and want to hear all the circumstances over again. He proceeds to repeat them; when he comes to his approach to the very verge of the precipice, he says, "My left foot stood on the edge of the rock, and as I had raised my right foot, and was about to take the fatal step, a light shone on my path, a voice cried 'Stop!' and I *sprang back in an instant.* I had well nigh lost my balance; but if I did not use the muscles and springs in my body once, why then I never did; and I am safe."

Now, that sinners all stand on a dangerous precipice is certain; and it is equally certain that they are not conscious of their danger. "They stand on slippery rocks, and fiery billows roll below."

The man of God lifts his warning voice, and cries, "Stop!" The Holy Spirit sheds the light of truth upon his benighted mind, and shows him his condition; but all this will not save him if he fails to put forth his own exertion; but if he employs his own agency and turns, he is saved. Now it is obvious that he saved himself; it is equally true that the minister saved him, and that the truth saved him, and his salvation is all of the Lord. God furnished the truth, commissioned all the agencies, and made them successful by the illuminating and constraining influences of the Holy Spirit. God says, "Make you a new heart, and be conscious of your weakness and dependence." Cry out, "Create in me a clean heart, and renew a right spirit within me."

It may be asked, How can an enemy of God, a hater of holiness, a lover of sin, on this principle become a lover of holiness, a hater of sin, and the fast friend of God? I answer,

God, by all the agencies and instrumentalities referred to above, leads the sinner to see his guilt and apprehend his danger; to discover that in all this conflict God is right, and that he is wrong; that God is too mighty for him to contend with and prosper. He may stand out and perish, or he may lay down his weapons, and surrender all into God's hands, and abide his pleasure.

When sinners make this surrender, God pardons. They now see that God has been their best Friend; has only opposed them in a course of sin, which was likely, yea, certain, to prove their ruin; that he has so loved them as to give his only-begotten Son to die for them, that they might not perish, but have everlasting life. They love him. They adore him. All the graces of the Christian spring up in the soul. They are new creatures. This is conversion. They have a new heart. Take an illustration in the late rebellion. The mass of the Southern people vindicated slavery; almost made themselves believe that it was right. They hated the Northern people, because they opposed them in this thing. Their opposition and enmity to the North continued to increase until it culminated in open rebellion. They took up arms, and went into the terrible conflict, for which they were not equal. At length they found that they must surrender or do worse: they laid down their arms; they gave themselves up to the government which they had opposed, and some of them became truly penitent. Many of this latter class were led to see that slavery was a system of iniquity which God meant to overthrow, and that the North were right, and that they were wrong. Now, where this conversion was thorough, their penitence was genuine, and they became truly loyal. Every man at the North or South, or the world over, who is worthy to be called a man, could forgive with all his heart, and receive them to his bosom. It would be perfectly safe to pardon all such persons, and restore them to confidence and to office; and the more these once haters of the government and its policy see and know of its clemency and uprightness, the willingness, nay, the desire, of our lamented President, as well as the government as a whole, to show them all the mercy and favor in their power, with safety to the country at large, the more will they love and admire the character and conduct of the government. But we must bear in mind that God's character and government are perfect; all others human, and consequently imperfect; and that God has done infinitely more for us than any earthly government has done or can do, and, as a matter of course, our love to him is supreme.

Reflections.

1. This view of conversion makes God the author of salvation, and man the author of damnation.

God gave his Son to die as an atonement for sin, and has furnished all the motives to induce men to repent, and called and commissioned all the agencies of men and angels to keep these motives before the people, and has given the Holy Spirit to make these motives effectual. And if they turn and live, God has turned them; and if saved, God has saved them; and because the sinner turns voluntarily, and accepts the gospel, he merits nothing, any more than a starving man merits something because he eats voluntarily when his benefactor sets food before him, and invites him to eat without money and without price; or than does the condemned prisoner merit his freedom because he accepts the pardon when offered to him.

On the other hand, man is responsible for his destruction. He is not lost because he was brought into the world with a sinful nature, nor because God did not take him by physical force and wrench him around, but because he wilfully rejected the offer of pardon; because he neglected the great salvation; because he stood up against all the motives and all the agencies employed by God to save him. After God had provided the feast, and given out the invitation, he made light of it, and is lost; not, I say, because he is a sinner, but because he rejected the Friend and Savior of sinners.

2. This theory of conversion is as much more beautiful than the old theory, and reflects as much more glory upon Deity, as

a moral government is superior to that government which controls the material world, or as mind is superior to matter. If mind were controlled by force, there would be no more happiness or worth in serving God, than the water-wheel experiences or possesses when it yields to the hydraulic power, or the grindstone when turning under the pressure of the crank. Nor would the praises of the millions on earth and in heaven reflect any more glory upon God than the millions of worlds by which he is surrounded.

3. This view of the subject strikes sceptics dumb, and knocks out the underpinning of Universalism.

The old theory represents God as an arbitrary being, saving one because it is his pleasure to do so, and damning another for the same reason, without any regard to their character or conduct. This view of the subject represents him as a kind and merciful Father, delighting not in the death of him that dieth, but doing all that can be done, upon the principles of a moral government, to save all, and as sending the wicked into hell because they cannot be reformed, because they will not come to Christ, that they might have life.

It seems as if almost any person of ordinary capacities could not help seeïng the absurdity of the distinction between the saved and the lost, if this distinction arises not from their character, but from the arbitrary pleasure of Deity. And when this sentiment is taught, the Universalist concludes that if the salvation of any turns upon the arbitrary pleasure of God, without any regard to character or conduct, it will be the pleasure of God to save all, and that all will be saved. But when they are led to see that man is a moral agent, accountable for every action, capable of obeying or of disobeying God, and that he cannot be forced into subjection, but must turn voluntarily, and that the only reason why they are not saved is because they will not be saved, because they will not submit to the only terms upon which it is possible for them to be saved, they are speechless. Their underpinning gives way, and they must settle down upon the Rock of Ages, or go down amid the sinking sands, and confess that their damnation is just.

APPENDIX.

STATISTICAL RESULTS OF ELDER KNAPP'S LABORS IN MASSACHUSETTS.*

THE following examination and calculations on the results of the labors of Elder JACOB KNAPP, in the State of Massachusetts, were made in the autumn of 1846; at which time there seemed to prevail a general impression, at least in the Baptist denomination, that the effects of his labors with the churches were anything but salutary. The pulpit and the press proclaimed the "disastrous results,"— such as "spurious converts," "excommunications," "unsettling ministers," "dividing churches," and the like. The spirit so prevailed with the clergy, that it was rare to hear an occasional sermon or an address, or even a Sabbath school essay, but it would contain a direct or indirect missile at "the revival," or its "measures." We conscientiously believe ministers and writers were not aware to what extent their minds were led by the spirit of the times.

While these things were thus passing, it occurred to us, "Is it so?" Are these statements and representations facts, or are they spectres of the imagination? Instead, therefore, of following the multitude, and crying, "Away with such a fellow from the earth," we quietly retired to our domicile, and examined our documents carefully, "whether these things were so." And we are compelled to say, we were surprised at the results. We found our own mind had been borne away by the tide of public influence to an extent we could hardly have believed.

Our examinations then extended to four years inclusive; commencing with the Associational year of the Evangelist's labors in each church;

* An Examination of the Comparative Statistical Results of the Labors of Elder Jacob Knapp in the State of Massachusetts. By A. WILBUR. Boston. 1855.

including that and the three successive years. The following was the result: —

Mr. Knapp commenced his labors in Massachusetts with the Baptist church in New Bedford, in the Taunton Association, in the summer of 1841. That church, during the four consecutive years, baptized 262, and excommunicated in the same time 28, or about 10½ per cent. on her baptisms. All the other churches in that Association, taken together, in the same four years, baptized 488, and excommunicated 105, or nearly 22 per cent. on their baptisms.

At the end of the four years, the church in New Bedford had gained in numerical strength 205, or 80¼ per cent. on her former number. All the other churches in the Association had gained in the same time 284, or 18½ per cent. on their former number.

The church in New Bedford, separately, and the other churches, collectively, have excluded *annually* about an equal proportion, compared with their numbers, viz., averaging about 1½ per cent. on their whole number.

His next labors in the state were in the Boston Association. Here they were mostly confined to five churches in the city of Boston. Two of the city churches did not invite him into their pulpits. One of these, with its pastor, was decidedly unfriendly to the whole movement, from beginning to end.

Those five churches where Mr. Knapp labored, baptized, during the four years, 1054 persons, and excommunicated 158, or 15 per cent. on their baptisms.

All the other churches in the Boston Association, taken together, baptized in the same time 1775, and excluded 336, or nearly 19 per cent. on their baptisms.

The two churches in the city where Mr. Knapp did not labor, baptized 122, and excluded 36, or 29 per cent. on their baptisms.

The church that was unfavorable, and took no interest in the movement, baptized 22, excluded 12, or 54½ per cent. on her baptisms. All these churches, thus separately classed, have excommunicated, on an average, *annually*, within a fraction of 1½ per cent. on their whole numbers.

The five churches where the Evangelist labored have gained in numerical strength in the four years 904 members, or 51 per cent. All the others in the Association, together, have gained 670, or a little over 13½ per cent.

The two churches in the city, above named, taken separate, in the same time have lost in number 72, or 8¾ per cent. on their former numbers.

The next labors of this Evangelist in the state were in the Salem

Association. Here also they were mostly had with five churches, viz., three in Lowell, the Second Church in Salem, and the church in Marblehead; although his labors in Marblehead were small compared with those of the other four churches. These five churches, during four years, commencing with the year of his labors, baptized 817, and excluded 143, or a little over 17 per cent. on their baptisms.

All the other churches in that Association in the same time baptized 669, and excommunicated 207, or 31 per cent. on their baptisms. These five churches also have excluded annually, on an average, about 1½ per cent. on their whole numbers. The other churches a mere fraction over.

The five churches have gained in the four years 508 members, or 26 per cent. The other churches gained in the same time 198, or a fraction less than 6 per cent.

These examinations, as before said, were made after the close of the four years; and they show to every candid mind, that the constantly reiterated complaints of "spurious converts," "numerous exclusions," &c., having reference to the Evangelist's labors, were without a shadow of foundation. But, on the contrary, the churches where he did not labor excluded many more, in comparison with their receptions, than those with whom he did, and each class about an equal proportion to their whole numbers.

We stated these facts, at the time, to several brethren, who said the public ought to have them; and at one time we fully concluded to publish them, but were deterred for reasons that will be given hereafter.

A few months since, a friend, who learned we had some facts relating to Mr. Knapp's labors, asked the loan of them. Our attention being thus again called to the subject, we concluded to extend the comparison throughout the state; and although the examination absorbed more time than we knew how to spare, yet we pursued it, and arrived at the following results: —

It will be remembered Mr. Knapp labored with eleven churches in this state; one in the Taunton Association, five in the Boston, and five in the Salem Associations. The results of these labors were reported in three Associational years, viz., 1841, '42, and '43. In making up the aggregate of baptisms, &c., of the other churches in the state, the intermediate year of 1842 is taken as the year of commencement.

The eleven churches, then, where he labored, commencing in these churches with the year of his labors, — as will be seen above, — baptized in four years 2133, and excluded 329, or a little over 15 per cent. on their baptisms. All the other churches in the state, taken together, baptized in the same time 6746, and excommunicated 1578, or 23⅓ per cent. on their baptisms.

Having recently showed the above to a brother, he suggested the idea of extending the comparison still farther. Wishing to make our examinations as satisfactory and conclusive as possible, we concluded to continue them for four years more, so as to include eight years; supposing any further calculations would be needless, as all influences for good or for evil would not extend beyond this.

In the eight years there had been added to the Associations in the state 42 churches, containing 3394 members. These are mostly new churches; some few are churches of some years' existence, but have recently united with the Associations. These 42 churches are not included in the following calculations, — only the churches which existed at the commencement of 1842. The propriety of this will be seen when it is remembered these new churches are made up from all the churches in the state, assisted in some instances by members from other states; and if their statistics were included, their whole influence would be thrown on the side of the churches in the state in 1842. Leaving out the new churches, and deducting the eleven in which the Evangelist labored, there remained in the state, at the commencement of 1842, 193 churches. Between these and the eleven the comparison is made.

We find then, in eight years inclusive, the eleven churches baptized 2625, and excommunicated 613, or 23 per cent. on their baptisms. The 193 other churches in the state, in the same time, baptized 8673, and excommunicated 2456, or 28⅓ per cent. on their baptisms. The original number in the eleven churches was 3984. They had gained in the eight years 1266, or nearly 31 per cent.

The original number in the 193 churches was 21,432. They had gained in eight years 254, or a little more than 1 per cent.

This discrepancy of gain being so great, it occurred to us, perhaps the 193 churches had been more largely drawn upon to form new churches. So, again, we betook ourselves to the task of examining the dismissions, and found the following result: —

The eleven churches, in the eight years, have dismissed to other churches, and to form new ones, 1543 members, or nearly 33½ per cent. on their average numbers.

The other churches in the same time have dismissed 6403, or nearly 30 per cent. on their average numbers.

So we found the eleven churches had done their full share, according to their numbers, in contributing in membership to build new churches.

We have given the facts; let them speak for themselves. They have been gathered from official documents, examined and compared with much care and labor, and, we think, may be relied on.

Any way one may look at the eleven churches, compared with the others, either of their Associations or of the whole state, they show themselves on the advantage ground.

Now, suppose the result to have proved just the reverse, — as has been represented, and is to this day supposed to be the fact by the community. We say, suppose these eleven churches had appeared comparatively to as great disadvantage as they do to advantage; what might, with propriety, — nay, what would be said? We offer no comments.

But, it will be asked by some, why bring these things out at this late period? — (and we shall look for censure from a certain class) — why were they not given to the public while the subject was before the people's mind? To this we answer, first, as before said, when the examination of the first four years was finished, we showed the results to several brethren, who strongly advised to publish them. We concluded to do so, but took occasion to show them to two brethren who were unfriendly to the revival movement, and spared not to speak against it. We chose to see what effect it would have.

After carefully reading our document through, they handed it back, saying, "Well, what of all that? IT PROVES NOTHING. If they (the converts) are not excluded, there are hundreds who ought to be."

It appeared to have no effect to suggest to their minds the possibility that they might be in an error. We were convinced that the public mind generally, at least in our denomination, was so fixed, that evidence on this subject, however conclusive, had lost its power.

Second, our attention has recently been called to the subject, as we said. It was again suggested that "these facts ought to be given to the public." We concluded also that the public mind, *generally* (not in all cases), is now so unbiassed that men can look at facts impartially, and give them their due weight.

Another incentive to publish was, that probably these lines would fall into the hands of many desponding disciples, who, for some years past, have been exercised somewhat as probably most of Christ's numerous disciples were, when the news spread over Palestine that "Jesus of Nazareth was crucified." Their meditations have been, "What did all this mean?" "We verily thought we were exercised by true religion." "If this is spurious, is not all religion spurious?" "If these converts are mostly spurious converts, am not I such? and are not all such?" — or "Where is the evidence of the true?" and the like. We met with many such, and endeavored to comfort them, by assuring them that the generally received reports concerning those revivals *were not true*, and that, so far as our knowledge extended, the converts of those revivals were, considering their numbers, as true and lasting as any converts of any revival we ever witnessed. We have sometimes thought, perhaps, for the sake of such disciples, it was a mistake not to have published before.

We will now propose a question to the reader of this pamphlet in Massachusetts.

Admitting that the revivals in 1841 and 1842 were as really the genuine operations of the Holy Spirit as have been any revivals since the apostles' days, and let the same course be pursued as was pursued by the ministry, the press, and the laity, towards the means, the measures, and the converts; might we not reasonably suppose it would legitimately produce precisely the state of things in the churches as was found in 1844, '45, and '46?

There is something unaccountable in men, good men, pious men, with reference to evidence of the operations of the Holy Spirit. No matter how judicious, candid, or pious (or all of these combined) a man may be, and no matter how the Spirit may be operating, — if from any cause his mind happen to take a turn against those operations, there seems to come over him a moral mist or darkness that wholly disables him to receive evidence in favor of the Spirit's power. Evidence that would be abundant and conclusive in any other case, is no evidence in this; or it is sometimes perverted, and becomes evidence against instead of in favor. We think we have observed this in many instances in the course of our pilgrimage, and in several have detected it in ourself. Never have we seen this indefinable, — what shall we call it? — delusive mysticism! no, that does not convey our idea; and we know no words in our circumscribed vocabulary that will. It is an indescribable something that comes over the mind and perverts the judgment on this particular subject, and affects no other. We say, we never saw it prevail in our denomination as it did in 1844, '45, and '46, in regard to the revivals of 1842. Inferences were drawn from false premises, and given forth to the public as true. Statements were made, and sent out, directly contrary to facts. Reports, almost innumerable, were circulated, which had no shadow of foundation; and some of the above were from good, well-meaning men, who intended no misrepresentation, but verily thought they spoke and wrote truth. Our charity for the Jewish Council which sat in Jerusalem in the year 29, with Caiaphas in the chair, was enlarged fifty per cent.; and never before did we so fully understand the spirit of that prayer, "Father, forgive them; they know not what they do." It would be endless and useless to revert to these statements and rumors, and then show their unreliableness; but for the sake of showing how easily a good man may slide into an error, and unintentionally misstate things, perhaps we may be permitted to name one fact.

In 1844 (it might have been in '45), a pastor in this city wrote to a distant body, that the people of his charge "had so lost their confidence in him (Mr. Knapp), that not twenty of his church would hear him preach unless he was a reformed man." We heard that such had been written. It so happened, a short time after this, Mr. Knapp was to preach on a Sabbath evening in the Tremont Temple; we attended the lecture, and sat on the side of the hall, where we could see to recognize about half of the congregation; and seeing quite a number present from that church, we had the curiosity to count them, and we saw fifty-two from that church whom we knew. As the congregation was passing out, a prominent member of that church came by, whom we asked if there were not more than twenty members of his church present. "Yes," said he, "more than a hundred." And we verily believe he spoke the truth.

We have named this circumstance only to show facts. We well know that pastor, and will say no one holds a higher place in our Christian affection than he. Further, we are ready to bear testimony that he will not intentionally misrepresent. But such was the general impression, and he imbibed it so strongly that he felt assured he stated the truth.

May we venture an opinion? — and whether correct or not, we are confident it would be supported by a large proportion of that church. Our opinion is, that there has not been a time since he labored in Boston, that any other man in the United States could call together a greater number of that church, to hear a sermon, than Mr. KNAPP.

Waiting for the Verdict. By Mrs. REBECCA HARDING DAVIS, author of "Margaret Howth," "Life Among the Iron Mills," &c., &c. One vol., octavo, illustrated, bound in cloth. Price, $2.00.

This is a story of unusual power and thrilling interest.

"It is not only the most elaborate work of its author, but it is one of the most powerful works of fiction by any American writer."—*New York Times.*

The Life and Letters of Rev. Geo. W. Bethune, D.D. By Rev. ABRAHAM R. VAN NEST, D.D. One vol., large 12mo., illustrated by an elegant steel-plate Likeness of Dr. Bethune. Price, $2.00.

This is one of the most charming biographies ever written. As a genial and jovial friend, as an enthusiastic sportsman, as a thorough theologian, as one of the most eloquent and gifted divines of his day, Dr. Bethune took a firm hold of the hearts of all with whom he came in contact.

Dr. Bethune's Theology, or EXPOSITORY LECTURES ON THE HEIDELBERG CATECHISM. By GEO. W. BETHUNE, D.D. Two vols., crown octavo (Riverside edition), on tinted paper. Price, cloth, $4.50; half calf, or morocco, extra, $8.50.

This was the great life work of the late Dr. Bethune, and will remain a monument of his thorough scholarship, the classical purity and beauty of his style, and above all, his deep and abiding piety.

"When the Rev. Dr. Bethune, whose memory is yet green and fragrant in the Church, was about to leave this country, he committed his manuscripts to a few friends, giving them discretionary power with regard to their publication. Among them was the great work of his life; in his opinion *the* work, and that from which he hoped the most usefulness while he lived, and after he was dead, if it should then be given to the press. This work was his course of lectures on the Catechism of the Church in which he was a burning and shining light.—*New York Observer.*

The Life and Labors of Francis Wayland, D.D., L.L.D. Late President of Brown University; by his sons, Hon. Francis Wayland, and Rev. H. L. Wayland. Two vols., 12mo., illustrated by two steel-plate Likenesses of Dr. Wayland. Price, $4.00.

This is a most interesting memoir of one of those noble specimens of a man, who now and then appear and direct, and give tone to the thoughts of their generation. The volumes are enriched by Dr. Wayland's correspondence with most of the leading men of his day.

DR. WAYLAND'S WORKS.

Principles and Practices of Baptists. By Francis Wayland, D.D. 1 vol., 12mo., cloth. Price, $1.50.

"We hope the book will find its way into every family in every Baptist church in the land, and should be glad to know it was generally circulated in the families of other churches."
Christian Chronicle.

A Memoir of the Life and Labors of the Rev. Adoniram Judson, D.D. By Francis Wayland, D.D. Illustrated with a fine Portrait of Dr. Judson. Two vols. in one, 12mo. Price, $2.50.

The Elements of Intellectual Philosophy. By Francis Wayland, D.D. One vol., 12mo. Price, $1.75.

Sermons to the Churches. By Francis Wayland, D.D. One vol., 12mo. Price, $1.00.

"Dr. Wayland is a clear thinker, and a strong and elegant writer. His Sermons are models worthy of study."—*Christian Intelligencer.*

The Life and Letters of Mrs. Emily C. Judson (Fanny Forrester), third wife of the Rev. Adoniram Judson, D.D., Missionary to Burmah. By A. C. Kendrick, Professor of Greek in the University of Rochester. With a steel-plate Portrait of Mrs. Judson. One vol., 12mo. Price, $1.75.

The Sexton's Tale, and other Poems. By Theodore Tilton, Editor of the New York Independent. Illustrated by an ornamental title-page and elegant tail-pieces for each Poem, printed on tinted paper, and bound with beveled boards and fancy cloth. One vol., 16mo. Price, $1.50.

This is the first collected edition of Mr. Tilton's poems, many of them as sweet as any thing in our language.

The Autobiography of Elder Jacob Knapp, the great Revivalist. One vol., large 12mo., with steel-plate Likeness of the Author. Price, $2.00

In this book the author gives an account of the many won derful scenes through which he has passed, more interesting and remarkable than any tales of fiction.

A new Enlarged Edition of Mrs. Putnam's Receipt Book, and Young Housekeeper's Assistant. A chapter on Carving has been added, and a very large number of new receipts, with special reference to economy in cooking. One vol., 12mo. Price, $1.50.

A Complete Manual of English Literature. By Thomas B. Shaw, Author of "Shaw's Outlines of English Literature." Edited, with Notes and Illustrations, by William Smith, LL.D., author of "Smith's Bible and Classical Dictionaries," with a Sketch of American Literature, by Henry T. Tuckerman. One vol., large 12mo. Price, $2.00.

Life of George Washington. By EDWARD EVERETT, LL.D. With a steel-plate Likeness of Mr. Everett, from the celebrated bust by Hiram Powers. One vol., 12mo., pp. 348. Price, cloth, $1.50.

"The biography is a model of condensation, and, by its rapid narrative and attractive style, must commend itself to the mass of readers as the standard popular Life of Washington."—*Correspondence of the Boston Post.*

The Science of Government, in connection with American Institutions. By JOSEPH ALDEN, D.D., LL.D., President of State Normal School, Albany. One vol., 12mo. Price, $1.50. Adapted to the wants of High Schools and Colleges.

Alden's Citizen's Manual. A Text-Book on Government in connection with American Institutions, adapted to the wants of Common Schools. It is in the form of questions and answers. By JOSEPH ALDEN, D.D., LL.D., President of State Normal School, Albany. In one vol., 16mo. Price, 50 cts.

"There is no more important secular study than the study of the institutions of our own country; and there is no book on the subject so clear, comprehensive, and complete in itself as the volume before us."—*New York Independent.*

Macaulay's Essays. The Critical, Historical, and Miscellaneous Essays of the Right Hon. THOMAS BABINGTON MACAULAY, with an Introduction and Biographical Sketch of the Author, by E. P. WHIPPLE, and containing a new steel-plate Likeness of Macaulay, and a complete index. Six vols., crown octavo. Price, on tinted paper, extra cloth, $13.50; on tinted paper, half calf or morocco, $27.00.

Sherman's March through the South. With Sketches and Incidents of the Campaign. By Capt. DAVID P. CONYNGHAM. 12mo., cloth. Price, $1.75.

"It is the only one that is entitled to credit for real ability, truth, and fairness."—*J. W. Geary, Maj.-Gen. U. S. A.*

Lieutenant-General Winfield Scott's Autobiography. Two vols., 12mo., illustrated with two steel-plate Likenesses of the General. Price, per set, in cloth, $4.00; half calf, $8.00. An elegant "large paper" edition of this valuable book, on tinted paper, price $10.00; half calf, or morocco, $12.50.

Milman's Latin Christianity. History of Latin Christianity, including that of the Popes to the pontificate of Nicolas V. By HENRY HART MILMAN, D.D., Dean of St. Paul's. Eight vols., crown octavo. Price, extra cloth, $20.00.

"In beauty and brilliancy of style he excels Hallam, approaches Gibbon, and is only surpassed by the unrivaled Macaulay."—*Mercersburg Review.*

Fleming's Vocabulary of Philosophy. With Additions by CHARLES P. KRAUTH, D.D. Small 8vo. Price, $2.50.

"To students of mental science this book is invaluable Dr. K. has done good service by the additions to the work of Dr. Fleming, and the whole volume is one which will be eagerly sought and cordially appreciated."—*Evangelical Quarterly.*

Long's Classical Atlas. Constructed by WM. HUGHES and edited by GEORGE LONG, with a Sketch of Classical Geography. With fifty-two Maps, and an Index of Places.

This Atlas will be an invaluable aid to the student of Ancient History, as well as the Bible student. One vol., quarto. Price, $4.50.

"Now that we are so well supplied with classical dictionaries, it is highly desirable that we should have an atlas worthy to accompany them. In the volume before us is to be found all that can be desired."—*London Athenæun.*

Key to Stoddard & Henkle's Element. Algebra, $1 25

Stoddard & Henkle's University Algebra.
For High Schools, Academies, and Colleges. By JOHN F. STODDARD, A.M., and Prof. W. D HENKLE. 528 pp.,. 2 00

Key to Stoddard & Henkle's University Algebra. 2 00

"I have examined Stoddard & Henkle's University Algebra. It is a thorough and elaborate work. It combines clearness and simplicity in its method and illustrations, and constitutes a valuable addition to the mathematical works of the day."—CYRUS NUTT, A.M., *Professor of Mathematics in the Indiana Ashbury Univ'y.*

"I have examined Stoddard's American Intellectual Arithmetic, and cheerfully recommend it to teachers and parents as a valuable elementary work, and one well adapted to the wants of pupils in the first stages of arithmetic. It is constructed upon sound and practical principles, and will be found an important addition to the text-books now in use in our Common Schools."—*Hon.* SAMUEL S. RANDALL, *Supt. of New York City Schools.*

"Stoddard's Arithmetical Series is now in general use in the schools of this county. They have stood the test for four years as the text-books in Arithmetic in our schools, and are considered by our teachers superior to any others now before the public."—*Mr.* S. A. TORRILL, *late Supt. of Public Schools of Wayne County, Pa.*

HOOKER'S PHYSIOLOGIES.

Hooker's First Book in Physiology.
For Public Schools, ... $0 90

Hooker's Human Physiology and Hygiene.
For Academies and general reading. By WORTHINGTON HOOKER, M.D., Yale College, ... 1 75

These books are text-books almost wherever they are known. The "First Book" is a text-book in the Public Schools of Boston, New York, Buffalo, and San Francisco.

"Professor Hooker's work on Physiology has been in use for the last year in the Normal School in this city, and it gives me great pleasure to express my convictions of its excellence as a text-book. In the course of my experience as a teacher, I have used the books of various authors on the subject of Physiology, but the work of Professor Hooker satisfies me much more fully than any other that I have used. It has the double advantage of being accurately scientific in its matter and arrangement, and of being expressed in correct and elegant English, a combination of the highest importance, and yet seldom attained to the extent exhibited in this book. I know of no book for which I would be willing to exchange it."—RICHARD EDWARDS, *Esq., Pres. Ill. Normal University, Bloomington, Ill.*

www.ingramcontent.com/pod-product-compliance
Lightning Source LLC
LaVergne TN
LVHW010134110826
845151LV00002B/352
* 9 7 8 1 4 2 5 5 3 9 7 6 4 *